NORWICH

in the nineteenth century

Edited by

Christopher Barringer

GLIDDON BOOKS
NORWICH NORFOLK

Published 1984
Copyright © 1984 with contributors

Gliddon Books, 19, Bedford Street, Norwich, Norfolk.

ISBN 0 947 893 008

Printed in Great Britain by
The Lavenham Press Ltd., Lavenham, Suffolk.

EDITOR

Christopher Barringer, M.A.
Resident Tutor in Norfolk, University of Cambridge Board of Extra-Mural Studies.
Publications: *History of the Lake District.* 1984.
  Yorkshire Dales. 1982.
  Editor of several local Histories produced by Adult Education Classes in Norfolk.
  Editor—Reprint of Faden's Map of Norfolk. Norfolk Record Society.

CONTRIBUTORS

Marjorie Allthorpe-Guyton, B.A., A.M.A.
Formerly Assistant Keeper of Art, Norfolk Museums Service.
Currently researching at the Courtauld Institute.
Publications: Four permanent collection catalogues for the Norfolk Museums Service:
  Henry Bright 1810-1873, 1973.
  John Sell Cotman 1782-1842, Normandy, 1975 (with Miklós Rajnai)
  John Thirtle 1777-1839, 1977
  John Sell Cotman 1782-1842, Early Drawings, 1979 (with Miklós Rajnai)
  A Happy Eye: A School of Art in Norwich 1845-1982.

J. K. Edwards, Ph.D.
Formerly Senior Lecturer, Norwich City College
Publications Various articles on the Economic History of Norwich in the Eighteenth and Nineteenth Centuries and many contributions to the Eastern Daily Press.

Rev. Richard Hale, M.A.
Sometime Scholar Jesus College, Cambridge.
Formerly Lecturer in Church History at Ely Theological College and Vicar of Gt. Shelford, Cambs.

Stefan Muthesius D.Phil.
Lecturer in the History of Art in the University of East Anglia.
Publications *The High Victorian Movement in Architecture 1972.*
  Victorian Architecture (with Roger Dixon). 1978.
  The English Terraced House. 1982.

John Pound, BA., MA., Ph.D.
Lecturer in History in the School of Education, University of East Anglia.
Publications *Poverty and Vagrancy in Tudor England.* Longman 1973.
The Norwich Census of the Poor 1570. Norfolk Record Society 1971.
Various articles on the social and political history of Norwich in Tudor and Victorian times.

W. David Smith, B.A., M. Phil., Ph.D.
Senior Lecturer in Education in the University of East Anglia.
Publications *Stretching their Bodies.* David & Charles 1974.
Various articles on the History and Administration of Education.

Martin Creasey.
Drawings.

Phillip Judge, B.A.
Maps.

The Editor and Contributors
dedicate this book to
RACHEL YOUNG

In acknowledgement of her many years of research into
and teaching about the history of Norwich. We and her
many hundreds of students have all admired her scholarship and benefited from her capacity to communicate both
her enthusiasm and her discoveries to others.

Preface

This is a collection of essays each of which is concerned with an important theme relating to nineteenth century Norwich. They have all been specially written for this volume and they all draw on a great deal of earlier work carried out by the authors over numbers of years. There are inevitably gaps, detailed stories of many of the major firms in the city still remain to be written. The Norwich Union is barely mentioned. There are still histories of the health provisions, of the treatment of the poor and many other aspects of social provision in the city to be written but this is a start.

The Editor's thanks go primarily to all the Contributors who so willingly and speedily provided their studies. Martin Creasy's drawings and Phillip Judge's maps do much for the appearance of the volume. Mrs Evelyn Smith has carried almost all the burden of the typing. Gerald Gliddon has kept the Editor up to the mark with overall guidance and advice. Finally Rachel Young has, as ever, provided many invaluable comments on much of the text, but the Editor takes responsibility for any errors which may exist.

Contents

Illustrations

(Ph) = Photograph

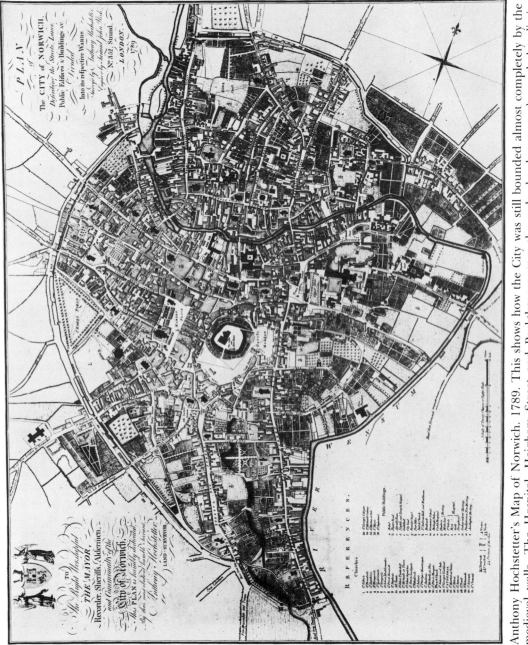

Anthony Hochstetter's Map of Norwich. 1789. This shows how the City was still bounded almost completely by the medieval walls. The Hospital, Heigham Street and Pockthorpe were the only developments beyond that limit. (Reproduced with permission from the copy in Norfolk Local Studies Library—hereafter N.L.S.L.)

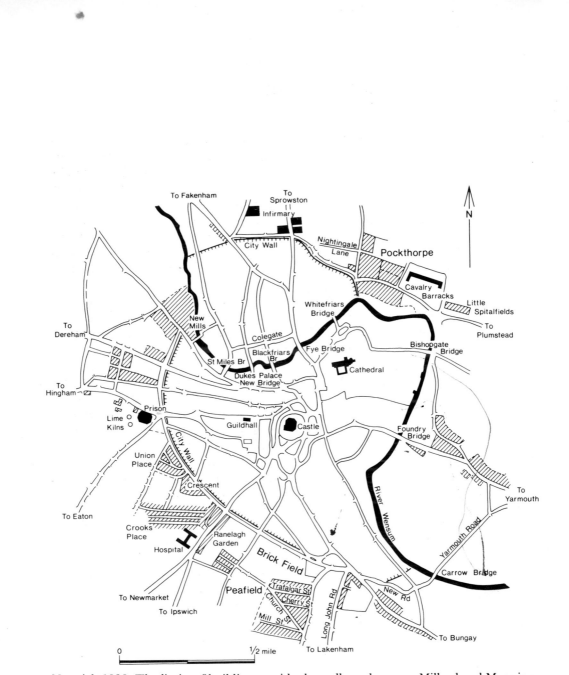

Norwich 1830. The limits of building outside the walls as shown on Millard and Manning Map of 1830.

Introduction
Christopher Barringer

William White in the 1845 edition of his *History Gazetteer and Directory of Norfolk* described Norwich, within the walls, as being in the shape of a cornucopia. He did not develop the metaphor but he might well have done. The cornucopia full, at least in part, of a lively, interesting society started to overflow as its population rose rapidly between 1811 and 1821 and it ceased to contain all that was Norwich. White also quoted the frequently used cliché of Norwich being a 'city in an orchard' but noted that though its 'sylvan ornaments have given place during the present century to new streets . . . it still retains much of its former rural aspect.' It was a growing and changing city as Maps I and II show.

In his *Victorian Cities* Asa Briggs pointed out that travellers arrived at the railway station of the fast growing towns. In many of these the station was central to the town: the marginal position of Thorpe Station, and the now defunct City and Victoria Stations, reflects the size of pre-nineteenth century Norwich. Nevertheless the traveller arriving at Thorpe Station, which was first built in 1844, crosses Foundry Bridge (1810), walks up Prince of Wales Road (1860) to the three buildings shown on the cover of this book. They are Harvey's Crown Bank (1865), the Agricultural Hall (1882) and the Royal Hotel (1897). As he goes on from there the traveller passes the Shirehall and the Castle walls, both designed by William Wilkins in the 1820's and follows the defensive ditch of the Castle which was made into the Castle Meadow in the middle of the Century. A nineteenth century route has led the visitor into the middle of a medieval city. Martin Creasey had no difficulty in finding much nineteenth century detail for his drawings in a city that is famous for its medieval churches and later medieval buildings. The century made a strong imprint on the visible fabric of the City.

A city is not however just a collection of buildings. It reflects the sum total of the lives of the many generations of its citizens and the people of the City of Norwich form one of the most fascinating aspects of its story during the nineteenth century. James Bell in his *Comprehensive Gazetteer* published in 1838 listed only three famous Norwich men—Archbishop Parker, Dr John Kay (Caius) and Dr Samuel Clarke. He lists none for the eighteenth and early nineteenth centuries! Bayne in his *History of Norwich* significantly starts his eighteenth century list of Norwich notables with the names of thirty-four merchants and manufacturers "lest their very names be forgotten!". Many of the men, no women are mentioned, of the arts and sciences whom he lists bridge the two centuries and are key figures in the study of the artists and writers of the nineteenth century in Norwich by Marjorie Allthorpe Guyton in the first

Chapter. A great flowering of cultural interests appears, growing perhaps in part from the fertile soil which these very merchants, such as the Gurney and Harvey families produced in the earlier part of the eighteenth century. Perhaps too the doubts and debates stemming from the flow of new ideas absorbed by those who could afford to travel also were forces at work—the awareness of slavery, of radical thought from France and America and of the deteriorating conditions of the poor in the fast growing cities of England together with the rise of new Nonconformist sects and the later revival of the Church of England were all at work.

The Gurneys in their big houses at Earlham and Keswick, were patrons of artists. Joseph John Gurney was an influential 'Friend', a scholar, a supporter of the first Lancasterian School in Norwich. On the day of his funeral, 12th January 1847, business in the city was suspended. The Harveys, a family which produced nine Mayors of Norwich, owned Crown Point, Catton Hall and Thorpe Lodge. John Harvey of Thorpe started the famous Thorpe Water Frolics and Thomas Harvey of Catton was a patron of Crome.

The role of Richard Mackenzie Bacon, editor of the Norwich Mercury, who was a key thread in the complex fabric of the cultural life of the city in which he drew together the theatrical, journalistic and literary strands of Norwich life is an important theme that is developed in the section by Marjorie Allthorpe Guyton. Rachel Young has stressed in conversation how closely all the artistic figures and indeed other principal figures of the city were linked. Dr Edward Rigby, who introduced smallpox vaccination into Norwich was:

> second cousin to Harriet Martineau, related and apprenticed to Harriet's uncle David Martineau and first cousin to John Taylor. Edward Taylor was involved with Philip Meadows Martineau in the first Norwich Music Festival and Rigby was a nephew of Mrs John Taylor.

Conversation in these circles could range widely across many fields of interest.

In stark contrast to this side of Norwich life is that led by the poor of the city. John Pound has drawn on a variety of official reports and major newspaper articles to give a picture of the interlocking problems of poverty and health in the city in the mid-century. Asa Briggs in *Victorian Cities* suggested that "perhaps their outstanding feature was . . . their hidden network of pipes, drains and sewers . . . a sanitary system more comprehensive than a transport system". The details of life in Peafield or St Paul's underline why this side of a city's provision was so important. This section also shows that despite many efforts the problem of bad housing in Norwich was not solved during the nineteenth century.

A city as proud as Norwich which was ahead of its times in some ways, for example in its treatment of the poor before the Poor Law Amendment Act of 1834, was not going to take kindly to being re-organised from outside by Central government. J. K. Edwards shows how the influence of Central government was increasingly felt as it nudged the city, along with others, into a greater variety of social provision.

Stefan Muthesius introduces the detail of the changes that were taking place in the form of houses as the city grew and as state legislation established minimal criteria for new housing and as new systems of the financing of housing evolved.

The revolutions in transport and the decline of the worsted industry form major themes in the two further sections by J. K. Edwards. The attempt to by-pass the old rival of Yarmouth by linking Norwich to Lowestoft by water was superseded by the impact of the railways. The rapidly expanding shoe industry and a host of other manufacturing industries, especially brewing and food processing, gradually replaced the textile industries. The two lives that J. K. Edwards has chosen—that of a Chartist weaver and that of a craftsman glass stainer give interesting vignettes of two very different but roughly contemporaneous lesser figures of city life.

As well as work, religion was a very important theme in the lives of many people in the nineteenth century although the 1851 Religious Census does remind us that very many were in no way involved in any religious activity at all. The descriptions of the liberal Bishops Bathurst and Stanley, the one at the end of a long reign the other reviving the Diocese give another facet of the life of the city in the century. The curious story of Father Ignatius contrasts with the detailed picture of the parish priest, the Rev. John Durst and the grim tasks faced by Mr Ross in St James' parish.

Richard Hale then introduces the wide range of beliefs held by the Nonconformist communities. Here of course were very strong links back to many of the major characters already met in the first chapter. A spate of chapel building took place much of which was linked with the important developments in elementary education in the city as described by David Smith. He picks up this theme in more detail and shows us something of the extraordinarily complex variety of provision that was developing and was almost always instituted by one or other of the parish churches or chapels.

As has been said in the preface these are but some of the themes that can be picked out in attempting to give an introduction to the physical, social, economic and political organism that was Norwich in the nineteenth century.

CHAPTER ONE

Artistic and Literary Life of Nineteenth Century Norwich
Marjorie Allthorpe-Guyton

When, in old age, John Callcott Horsley, the Royal Academician looked back some sixty years from 1903 to his first visit to Norwich in 1836 he recalled with deep affection his host, Richard Mackenzie Bacon (1775-1844): 'He lived at Cossey, near Norwich, that most interesting and picturesque old city, which in those days was famous for the number of interesting and highly cultivated families resident there.' Bacon and his daughters Louisa Mary and Rose, were among a remarkable group of families and individuals who promoted, for their own pleasure and the city's benefit, activities that were catholic in their range and often courageous in their conviction. They staged exhibitions, concerts and lectures, published books, pamphlets and newspapers dealing not only with the arts but with controversial questions of popular education, Catholic emancipation, Baptismal regeneration and political corruption and reform. They were of the professional middle class but often had close friendships with the aristocracy and landed gentry. They were, more often than not, nonconformist and even radical in their religion and politics. Their conviction and energy shone most brilliantly in the first half of the century when with all confidence, they could call their city 'the Athens of England'. The intellectual and philanthropic legacy they left was inherited by another generation which established a continuous record of community service founding most of the educational and cultural institutions of the city: the schools and colleges, the libraries, museums and theatres. No less significant was the major role some of them played in the history of the local press which they rightly regarded as a powerful means of securing their position and advancing their concerns and interests.

Literary Life
Amelia Opie (1769-1853) and Harriet Martineau (1802-1876)

Thomas Holcroft wrote of Norfolk that 'It has a rather distinguishing and paradoxical feature, if what I hear is true; it is said to be more illiterate than any other part of England, and yet, I doubt, if any county of like extent have produced an equal number of famous men'. And

1

women. Indeed, Holcroft fell in love with one of them, the darling of society in both Norwich and London, Amelia Opie. She became one of the most famous 'bluestockings' of her day, to the chagrin of her sister Norwich writer, Harriet Martineau who held her in some disdain, noting after Amelia had become a Quaker, 'a spice of dandyism yet in the demure peculiarity of her dress. She never interests me much, or makes me approve her highly.'

Amelia was undoubtedly the less formidable of the two women. For Benjamin Robert Haydon, the inspired but tragic history painter, she was at the age of seventy still 'a delightful creature' when she sat for his picture of the anti-slavery convention held in London in 1840. For Cecilia Lucy Brightwell, whom she entrusted with her papers, it was no 'wonder if she early loved and was beloved!'. She was blessed with vivid good looks 'Her countenance was animated, bright and beaming, her eyes soft and expressive, yet full of ardour; her hair was abundant and beautiful, of auburn hue, and waving in long tresses; her figure was well formed; her carriage fine; her hands, arms, and feet, well shaped: —and all around and about her was the spirit of youth and joy and love.' No wonder that her 'avowed lover' and later husband, the portrait painter John Opie, was smitten at first sight. But Amelia Opie was doubly blessed with a benevolent personality, 'extraordinary powers of conversation' and a

Amelia Opie (1769-1850). Etching by Mrs Dawson Turner (1774-1850) after J. Opie 1798. Norfolk Museums Service (Norwich Castle Museum).

talent for writing which led the literary lions of the time to pay 'their tribute of admiration to her power of thrilling the heart and awakening the softer passions.'

Amelia was born in a house in Calvert Street, Norwich, the daughter of James Alderson, a much loved Norwich physician, and Amelia Briggs, who was descended from Augustine Briggs, a Mayor of Norwich who gave his name to Briggs (now Brigg) Street in the City. At the age of fifteen, after the early loss of her mother, Amelia took over her father's household in Colegate and became hostess to his friends, among them Mrs John Taylor, William Taylor and Frank Sayers, whose interests, literary, political and religious her father shared. From childhood Amelia showed an intense curiosity and love of drama which led her not only to indulge her fears of black beetles, frogs and Bedlam lunatics but to a love of attending trials at the Norwich Assizes. She wrote ballads and poems and played the heroine in her first written tragedy at the age of eighteen. In 1798 she married John Opie who tried to curb her love of parties by encouraging her to stay at home and write—with some success.

In 1801 she published her novel *Father and Daughter*, which went into several editions, in spite of the *Edinburgh Review* which in 1830 dubbed it 'an appalling piece of domestic tragedy'. The novel was the first of a long series of tales and poems whose sentiment and moral tone appealed to a wide audience, although Harriet Martineau declared that the author wrote 'slowly and amidst a strenous excitement of her sensibilities'! The Edinburgh reviewer of her *Simple Tales* 1806 was hardly more charitable 'she does not reason well; but she has, like most accomplished women, the talent of perceiving truth without the process of reasoning'! The Rev. Sydney Smith, noted wit and writer, who praised one of her earlier poems *Go, youth beloved* 1802 in one of his lectures on moral philosophy, was both succinct and just 'Tenderness is your forte, and carelessness your fault'. Amelia Opie published her last novel in 1822. From her return to Norwich after the loss of her husband in 1807 she became increasingly influenced by Joseph John Gurney, 'the Quaker Pope', who formally received her into the Society of Friends in 1825. She could never, however, lose her love of fashionable society, of conversation, of music, of the theatre. Her acquaintance ranged far and wide. Her early visit to Paris in 1802 had brought her into contact with Napoleon's family and advisers, with the English statesman, Charles Fox, and with the artists Maria Cosway and Benjamin West. Her annual sojourns in London were a constant round of soirées where she enjoyed the company of French emigrés notably the legendary Madame de Stael and the Duc D'Aiguillon, of English radicals, writers, politicians and actors including William Godwin, Mary Wollstonecraft, Sheridan, Byron, Wordsworth and the Kembles, especially Mrs Siddons. It is in her letters and journals, where her extraordinary memory and eye for detail paint a brilliant picture of those evenings, that we find, perhaps, her true literary merit.

Harriet Martineau
(1802-1876). N.L.S.L.
Dalrymple Collection in the
Colman Collection.

Of an altogether different order was the work and the character of
Harriet Martineau. Her remarks about Amelia Opie are echoed by a
scathing attack on London and Norwich society written when she was in
her thirties in 1837; the attention adored by Amelia Opie Miss Martineau
considered nauseating flattery—from those 'whose aim it is to have
brilliant parties and celebrated acquaintance.' She considered that the
drawing room was the grave of literary promise. Born into an old
Huguenot family in Norwich, Harriet Martineau was brought up among
the same circle of literary Unitarians to whom Amelia Opie returned as a
widow in 1807. Harriet was a sickly, introverted child who began writing
and reading in earnest at an early age. In adolescence she was almost deaf
and she became engrossed in religious and philosophical works which
nourished her deeply serious mind. She published her first article on
Female Writers on Practical Divinity in 1821 in the Unitarian paper, the
Monthly Repository, whose editor, William Johnson Fox, later became a
valued support when her family were left penniless in 1829. Harriet then
had to write in order to live; she wrote prize-winning essays and
embarked on her first stories published as *The Illustrations of Political
Economy* which illustrated the political economy of Malthus, Ricardo, Mill

4

and Bentham and which exactly suited contemporary taste. In 1832 she moved to London, writing and publishing with remorseless energy and moving among statesmen, literary celebrities and philosophers who uniformly admired and respected her intellect and staunch opinions. She became one of the most remarkable and courageous women of her day, suffering personal abuse and facing physical danger when attending abolitionist meetings during her visit to America in 1834. She cured herself of illness through Mesmerism, a popular form of hypnosis whose advocates included Charles Dickens and the Bishop of Norwich (Henry Bathurst). One of its proselytisers was the Rev. George Sandby, Vicar of Flixton, Suffolk. She travelled widely, including the Middle East—by camel to Mount Sinai and Petra and on horseback to Damascus. In later life she built a house in the Lake District and started a farm with the help of a farmworker from Norfolk.

Harriet Martineau held a modest view of her own talents as a writer; she had 'small imaginative and suggestive powers', and therefore no approach to genius but 'earnestness and intellectual clearness within a certain range'. According to Maria Weston Chapman who edited her *Autobiography* she had 'probably the best woman's library extant . . . consisting of between two and three thousand volumes . . . books of art, biography, education, general literature, geography, history, morals and politics, political economy, theology and works of reference.' She became robust and handsome in old age until heart disease finally claimed her. Hawthorne described her as having 'so kind, cheerful, and intelligent a face, that she is so pleasanter to look at than most beauties. Her hair is of a decided gray, and she does not shrink from calling herself old.' Even at the end a visitor could describe her presence as so life-enhancing that 'I see what it is to have lived,—not under the exhausted receiver of ladyhood or mere womanhood,—but the life of a human being.'

Throughout her life, Harriet Martineau expected the same high standards and devotion to work from others as she expected from herself. Her memories of her first thirty years in Norwich are sharp with trenchant comment on its literary life. She considered Norwich 'a rival of Lichfield itself . . . for literary pretension and the vulgarity of pedantry. William Taylor was then at his best . . . before the vice which destroyed him had coarsened his morale, and drained his intellect.' She and her sisters, still as yet children, made 'capital subjects' out of the bluestockings especially one 'who sported youthful vivacity, and political enthusiasm with her scanty skirts and uncovered head to past seventy'! Such dissipation she thought should have been beneath Mrs Opie and Mrs John Taylor. She considered Dr Enfield, the Octagon Minister, 'a feeble and superficial man of letters', Sir James Edward Smith, the botanist, 'not pedantic and vulgar like the rest, but weak and irritable', Dr Alderson, Amelia's father, 'solemn and sententious and eccentric in manner, but not an able man in any way'.

William Taylor (1765-1836) and Frank Sayers (1763-1817)

Harriet saved her sharpest barbs for William Taylor who 'was managed by a regular process,—first, of feeding, then of wine-bibbing, and immediately after of poking to make him talk . . .'. Whatever Harriet Martineau's views on his weaknesses—his drinking and his snuff—Taylor's strengths and influence as a scholar and critic did much to dispel the parochialism of English literary tastes. Taylor was a schoolboy friend of Thomas Martineau, Harriet's father. Both had been educated at Palgrave School run by Rochemont Barbauld and his wife Anna Letitia Aiken whom Taylor regarded as 'the mother of his mind'. William Taylor travelled widely on the continent in his youth and became an ardent enthusiast for German literature and culture. He met Goethe at Weimar in 1782. On his return he joined the several debating societies which were founded by radicals such as his father and William Enfield. These political and philosophical gatherings, the Tusculum and the Speculative, were followed in the early 1800's by the Norwich Philosophical Society whose members included the Cromes, father and son, and Dr Edward Rigby. In 1814 Taylor delivered to the Society a lecture on landscape painting which was published in the *Monthly Magazine*. By this time Taylor had established an international reputation as a translator of German poetry. His translation of Burger's *Lenore* so influenced Sir Walter Scott that he declared that Taylor made him a poet. Henry Crabb Robinson considered Taylor's translation of Goethe's *Iphigenia in Tauris* of 1790 as the best version of any of his larger poems. Taylor brought together his life's study of German literature in his three volume *Historic Survey of German Poetry* published 1828-30. His last publication, written in 1831, was a *Memoir of the late Philip Meadows Martineau*, uncle of Harriet, who was perhaps the most distinguished provincial surgeon of his day and a founder of the Norfolk and Norwich Triennial Music Festival.

Taylor's middle years were occupied by reviews of which almost two thousand were published between 1793 and his death. Madame de Stael gave warm tribute to his review in the *Monthly Review* 1814 of her famous *De L'Allemagne* published in English in 1813. Although he was severely criticized for his curious indulgence of making up words, many of which have since been absorbed into the vocabulary (*rehabilitation*, for example), he was praised by William Hazlitt for having introduced a style of philosophical criticism which became the boast of the *Edinburgh Review*. He wrote on a wide range of subjects, often with less conviction than ingenuity, which led Harriet Martineau to one of her more just criticisms—that he was a 'wild rover'—especially in the fields of politics and religion. She could not understand Robert Southey's friendship with him because she thought he 'did more mischief to young men (through his entire lack of conviction and earnestness and truth-speaking) than the Homes and Carlyles and others whom Southey abhorred as emissaries of Satan'!

William Taylor (1765-1836). Detail from engraving after a portrait by John Barwell (no date). Norfolk Museums Service (Norwich Castle Museum).

Frank Sayers (1763-1817) aged 37. Engraving of a portrait by W. C. Edwards (1777-1855) after J. Opie. Norfolk Museums Service (Norwich Castle Museum).

But the truth was that Taylor was an entertaining and a generous friend, particularly to his boyhood classmate, Frank Sayers, and later to his young pupil, George Borrow.

Taylor formed a lifelong friendship with Sayers when they were among the eight scholars at Palgrave School. He regarded the friendship as 'the dearest and proudest trophy of my life'. Rex Stedman has noted that as young men they would take walks with their friend, William Windham of Felbrigg, 'wandering over Mousehold and through the woods near Thorpe, discussing politics, philosophy and, above all, literature'. Sayers had abandoned medicine for literature and by 1800 he had a number of tragedies and poems published, notably his *Dramatic Sketches of Northern Mythology* 1790, which was well received in both England and Germany. Taylor called it an 'imperishable monument of English poetry'. Sayers delivered a lecture to the Speculative Society in 1791 on Aesthetic philosophy *In what does Beauty consist* which was published in three editions. Henry Reeve recorded that his scholarship was given warm praise by Sir Walter Scott who wrote that he 'united the patience of the antiquarian with the genius of the poet'. After his mother's death in 1792 Frank Sayers moved to the Close, Norwich, and gathered around him a circle of distinguished friends including Southey, Thomas Fanshawe and Thomas Amyot. In later life he published studies on archaeology, philology and history. He served on the Committee of the Norwich Public Library of which William Taylor was President and gave his own library to the Library of the Dean and Chapter of Norwich. Although Sayers was politically less radical than Taylor he supported agitation for the abolition of slavery and helped to fund a local hospital for the blind. Taylor paid him the warmest tribute by declaring him 'the first man in Norwich' and by publishing Sayers' work in two volumes in 1823 with a deeply felt biographical memoir which was embellished with an engraving after Sayers' portrait painted by John Opie in 1800. Until his death in 1836 the portrait hung in Taylor's library in King Street, Norwich.

After Sayers died in 1817 and after the family business declined Taylor turned more to the company of younger men. Harriet Martineau took a dim view of this coterie, 'but matters grew worse in his old age, when his habits of intemperance kept him out of the sight of ladies, and he got round him a set of ignorant and conceited young men, who thought they could set the world right by their destructive propensities.' One of his chief favourites was George Borrow.

George Borrow (1803-1881)

It is no surprise Taylor was attracted to Borrow who became the most original and exotic personality in Norwich's literary history. He was Byronic in appearance, dark-eyed and swarthy, yet with strange thick greying and soon white hair. Taylor taught him German, which he learnt with extraordinary speed, adding yet another tongue to his understanding of ten languages, gained before he was eighteen years old!

George Henry Borrow was the son of a Cornish soldier who was stationed with the Norfolk Regiment of Militia at East Dereham. In 1814 the family returned to Norfolk after a posting to Edinburgh and George was sent to Norwich Grammar School under the headmastership of the Rev. Edward Valpy. John Borrow, his elder brother, became a pupil of John Crome. After a short period in Ireland, where Borrow first learnt to ride, the family finally settled in Norwich in a small house in Willow Lane which at intervals was to be George Borrow's home until his marriage in 1839. Borrow's roving boyhood and his pugnacious, untamed spirit were a recipe for troubled schooldays. He was horsewhipped for truancy and left in 1818. Yet this was a period when Borrow learnt and read voraciously with the guidance of Thomas d'Eterville a French emigré priest and of Norwich's numerous second-hand bookshops. At Taylor's house he met John Bowring, the linguist and traveller who was later knighted for his public services, including advice on the setting up of the Government Schools of Design. Bowring's own success and Taylor's enthusiasm for his talents fired Borrow's ambition. He had tired of transcribing legal documents in the lawyers' office of Simpson & Rackham in Tuck's Court, St Giles, where his father had placed him. In *Lavengro* he recalled 'The scene of my labours was a strange old house, occupying one side of a long and narrow court, into which, however, the greatest number of windows looked not, but into an extensive garden, filled with fruit trees . . .'.

Through the introduction of his mentors, Taylor and Bowring, he published an article on Danish Poetry and Ballad writing in the radical *Monthly Magazine*. After his father died in 1824, his restlessness urged him to leave the limited prospects of Norwich. In 1824 he wrote to Roger Kerrison of his intention 'to live in London, write plays, poetry etc. abuse religion and get myself prosecuted'.

However, after a gruelling year in London working for the publishers of the *Monthly Magazine* on a six volume compilation of *Celebrated Trials* which was published in 1825, Borrow left the capital. He wandered the country living alongside gypsies and tinkers. By the middle of August he was back in Norwich, his ambition to publish his numerous translations rekindled. In 1826 he himself printed a collection of *Romantic Ballads* translated from the Danish and *Miscellaneous Pieces* which failed to meet with any critical acclaim. He was a poor translator of poetry but as yet unable to recognise his limitations. He travelled anxiously between Norwich and London, with trips to France, Spain and Portugal, returning always to his mother in Willow Lane to refresh his spirits with visits to Tombland Fair and plunges in the River Wensum.

It was through John Gurney of Earlham Hall, Norwich, who had befriended him as a young boy that Borrow's literary career was finally launched. Gurney introduced him to the Rev. Francis Cunningham, husband of Crome's lively pupil Richenda Gurney and a great advocate of the Bible Society. In 1833 Borrow became an agent and translator for the Society in Russia and Spain. His account of his travels, *The Bible in Spain*, published in three volumes in 1843, became one of the most famous literary successes of the nineteenth century—despite its suspect piety and fierce anti-popery. The book was written at Oulton Cottage after Borrow's marriage to Mary Clarke in 1839 and received the blessing: 'Gil Blas with a touch of Bunyan' from Richard Ford who spent four days with him in 1844. Over the next years, between fitful trips abroad and increasingly melancholy, Borrow wrote the two books of his autobiography, *Lavengro* and *The Romany Rye* published in 1851 and 1857. They were not a success: Edward Fitzgerald gently criticised them for lack of taste. They seemed curiously out of date with their wild romanticism. Today, however, they give us a rare insight into 'lowlife' Norfolk, its characters and their landscapes: the gorse-strewn heather, wooded lanes and riverbanks, the fens and marshes now changed irrevocably by modern agriculture.

George Borrow (1803-1881). Photogravure after Henry Wyndham Phillips 1820-1868. Norfolk Museums Service (Norwich Castle Museum).

As a boy Borrow's love of horses and of the Romany language led him to lifelong friendships and strange adventures with Norfolk gypsies whom he met at fairs and on Mousehold Heath. He writes in *Lavengro* of his encounter with Parkerson, the Norfolk Bard, the poet-laureate of farmers, corn-merchants and drovers. He leaves us memorable tales of Norfolk pugilism such as the great fight between Edward Painter of Norwich and Thomas Oliver of London which brought hordes of fans of England's 'bruisers' to the city in July 1820: 'the roads were alive with pedestrians, equestrians, Jews, Gentiles and Gypsies, in coaches, barouches and vehicles of every sort'. He gives a wry anecdote of Norwich civic life when the city fathers commissioned Benjamin Robert Haydon to paint the Mayor, Robert Hawkes. Haydon painted Hawkes, 'who was built like a dray horse', with disproportionately short legs. But Borrow saw the funny side of Haydon's misguided effort. He saw the painter more as a Hogarth than a Raphael and thought 'what a capital picture might have been made by my brother's friend, if, instead of making the Mayor issue out of the Norman arch, he had painted him moving under the sign of the "Checquers", or the "Three Brewers", with mace . . . likewise with Snap and with whiffler, quart pot and frying pan, Billy Blind and Owlenglass, Mr Petulengro and Pakomovna; then had he clapped his own legs upon the Mayor, or any one else in the concourse, what matter?' Borrow's disconnected, vivid narrative style gives the luminous sharpness of memories recalled. Yet he remains a strangely enigmatic figure. His last years after his wife's death were spent in Norwich, his evenings passed in solitary drinking in the Norfolk Hotel, without the consolation of friends or religion.

Mary (1797-1884) and Anna Sewell (1820-1878)

The story of Norwich's literary life does not quite end with the death of George Borrow in 1881. While Sir Henry Rider Haggard was settled in his Norfolk country house at Ditchingham writing his African fantasies, *She* and *Allan Quartermain*, Jarrolds of Norwich were bringing out in 1886 the *Poems and Ballads* of Mary Sewell (née Wright) who had died two years earlier in 1884 at her home, 125 Spixworth Road, Catton, Norwich. She had moved back to Norfolk in 1867 with her beloved daughter Anna, who wrote there her legendary life of a horse, *Black Beauty*. Mary Sewell herself wrote a number of successful works. The lives and works of Mary and Anna Sewell are marked by a strength of mind and spirit which makes it remarkable that neither mother nor daughter is recorded in the *Dictionary of National Biography*. Elizabeth Bayly wrote *The Life and Letters of Mrs Sewell* in 1889 and provides a valuable account of her life. Mary Wright was born in Sutton, Suffolk, although her mother's family were Quaker farmers from Tivetshall, Norfolk. She describes them in an autobiographical letter to her grandchildren rich with anecdotes of English country life in the first decades of the nineteenth century.

Quaker living then was sober in the extreme: 'Art and science, books and leisure, were not at home in the old farmhouse. Pictures on the walls were considered dangerous, as possibly leading to idolatry. Music was a vain amusement and hymns as well as songs were prohibited. The voice was not cultivated and a musical instrument was never seen in any Quaker's house'. Mary and her sisters, however, were sent to a Norwich Dame School, they also were taught drawing by a Norwich master, quite probably John Crome 'who taught many families in the county: and he sometimes took us out to sketch. He was a pleasant friendly man. He would bait his horse in my father's stable, take tea with us and then go on to someone else.' Like her fellow Norwich writer of children's books, Louisa Barwell, Mary Sewell later valued drawing from nature as indispensable in the education of young children.

The Wright family fortunes were destroyed when Mary's father joined his brother the ill-fated shipowner, Richard Wright, whose steampacket, which plied the River Yare between Norwich and Yarmouth, exploded with great loss of life in 1817. Mary became a governess in Essex and soon married. In 1820 her first child Anna was born 'an unclouded blessing, for fifty-eight years the perennial joy of my life'. After her son's birth in London, Mary Sewell wrote her first book for children and parents *Walks with Mamma* in words of one syllable. This was followed by several other children's books written often in verse and works for the poor, such as *Homely Ballads for the Working Man's Fireside* of 1858, together with *An Appeal to Englishwomen. By the Author of Mother's Last Words* published for the Anti-Slavery Association in 1863. Most of her works were written at her home at Wick, near Bristol, but several were published by Thomas Jarrold of Norwich, who 'took the warmest interest in all her writings, and his death, shortly before the appearance of *Black Beauty* (by her daughter Anna) was a heavy loss to her. She clung to old friends'. Mrs Sewell maintained also her contacts with the Norwich Friends, especially at their yearly meetings in London where 'many of the rich Friends kept open house and invited large companies to dinner between the meetings. Mildred Court, where Elizabeth Fry (1780-1845) presided, was very popular.' (She lived in London after her marriage in 1800). Mary Sewell later adopted Unitarian views and after much painful deliberation left the Society of Friends. Her work, with its underlying concern for the social ills of Victorian England, secured her a ready market; her *Mother's Last Words* of 1860 achieved 'a sale unprecedented in the history of ballads' of well over one million copies.

She wrote little after her return to Norwich where above all her energies were given up to her beloved ailing daughter whose 'hungry nature longed for food of many kinds—political, social, philanthropic—all these departments "teemed" with interest to her.' Anna had been lame since childhood but she was fearless and independent and became expert with her ponies and carriage. In November 1871 she wrote in her journal 'I am writing the life of a horse and getting dolls and boxes ready for Christmas.' Her mother's friend and biographer, Elizabeth Bayly, gave her an essay on animals by Horace Busnell which encouraged her work: 'she evidently believed in a horse having a moral nature.' From her sickbed she wrote intermittently over the years, first in pencil and later, weakened further by illness, dictating passages to her mother. Thomas Jarrold died while preparing the book for press and Anna Sewell died shortly after its publication in 1877. It was a resounding success, going into five editions by 1878; it has since been translated for publication world-wide and it became an Evergreen Classic in 1965. Contemporary readers were astonished at its unladylike quality and 'stablemindedness' exclaiming 'how could a lady know so much about horses!' Anna Sewell dedicated her book to her mother and is buried with her parents at the Friends burial ground near Buxton, Norfolk.

Music and Theatre

Richard Mackenzie Bacon 1775-1844

The Norfolk and Norwich Triennial Music Festival was founded in 1824. In the late eighteenth century Norwich's most successful composer, Dr William Crotch, the Musical Child was born. At the age of eleven, Crotch left the city to study in Cambridge and later became first principal at the Royal Academy of Music. His oratorio *Palestine*, first played in 1812, is one of the few oratorios by an English composer to have survived. Norwich is also the home of the Tonic Sol-fa system of teaching sight singing which originated with the work of Sarah Ann Glover born in the city in 1785. Miss Glover's method was propagated by the Rev. John Curwen and she herself published *A Manual of the Norwich Sol-fa system* in 1845 and *A Manual of Tetrachordal system* in 1850. Her work was largely responsible for the growth of choral societies; it enabled children and artisans to learn technical skills and become efficient choralists. It is no surprise, therefore, that the Norwich Festival was augmented by a new Choral Society directed by Professor Edward Taylor (who was not related to William Taylor) and the Rev. R. F. Elwin with Zechariah Buck as Organist. In the nineteenth century the six provincial triennial Festivals were 'the only direct stimulus to our best composers', they provided rare opportunities for the production of new work or 'novelties' as these pieces were called. The Norwich Festival followed that of Birmingham founded as early as 1768; Leeds followed in 1858.

The 'Founder of the Feast' in Norwich was Richard Mackenzie Bacon, writer, musician and proprietor and editor of the *Norwich Mercury*. Bacon was one of the most liberal and cultivated of men, his interests ranged widely, not only did he have a reputation as a good shot—he was on close terms with two of Norwich's biggest landowners, Lords Stafford and Leicester—but he had a passionate concern for

Richard Mackenzie Bacon (1775-1844). Oil attributed to George Clint. Private Collection.

theatre and music. He was the son of a grocer, attended Norwich Grammar School where he became head boy and in 1798 he married Louisa Mary, daughter of Augustine Noverre who had been brought to England from Paris by David Garrick. From 1816 the Bacons lived at Costessey in a house opposite the Falcon's Inn from whence Bacon rode to work in Norwich 'a small keen-looking man, dressed as a prosperous farmer'. In 1818 he began to publish in London England's first national music magazine the *Quarterly Musical Magazine and Review* which he edited for ten years. In August 1818 Bacon began campaigning for a Norwich Music Festival.

It was not an auspicious time; the annual Cathedral oratorio, sermon and dinner had been poorly attended that year. Norwich was also served with the weekly Hall Concerts and Grand Music Festivals were held occasionally in the Theatre, in St Peter Mancroft and St Andrew's Hall. Bacon, nevertheless, galvanised the support of Edward Taylor, musical critic for *The Spectator* and of the influential Norwich surgeon Philip Meadows Martineau. Despite opposition from the board of the Norfolk and Norwich Hospital, which was to benefit from the profits of the Festival, the arrangements were launched on 25th October 1823. There was a distinguished list of patrons headed by King George IV and St Andrews Hall was secured as the venue. The dates of 21st to 24th September 1824 were fixed, the programme being three evening and three morning concerts with the week's entertainment concluding with a Grand Ball. Sir George Smart was engaged as conductor and a committee selected with Taylor and Bacon appointed as advisors. 'A medal designed by Steel was struck to commemorate the occasion; a plate engraved by Cotman was freely advertised but does not appear to have been published, and lastly the *Norwich Mercury* printed an entire newspaper with a wood-cut frontispiece by Stannard, representing the interior of St

Andrew's Hall as it was when prepared for the festival'. The concerts included leading singers: Mr Lindley, Madam and Signor de Begnis. The programme contained works by Rossini, Handel's *Messiah*, Mozart and Haydn's *Creation*. The great Manuel Garcia, operatic tenor, also appeared. The Festival was a resounding success—despite the rain which leaked through the hall roof: 'The audience . . . the stupendous orchestra crowded with professors of the highest eminence, piled as it were upon each other to the very top of the organ,' Bacon noted in a Special Festival Supplement. Over eight thousand people attended and the profit to the hospital was £2,400.

Bacon presided closely over subsequent festivals and Legge and Hansell noted that at his death 'the English musical world lost an able, fearless and cultured critic', one who did not fail to pass rigorous judgement on the quality of each Festival. In 1827 he expressed reservations on the ball 'Dancing has been called the poetry of motion, but the present style is very, very prosy indeed.' He was perpetually in disagreement with Edward Taylor, especially in 1836 when Taylor's 'arrangement' of Mozart's *Requiem* was given its première. Taylor had taken outrageous liberties 'by way of introduction (he) took the andante from the overture to *Don Giovanni* and grafted it bodily on to the beginning of the *Requiem* . . . He also introduced an air from Mozart's *Tito*, a recitative from *Idomeneo*, another from Spohr's *Faust* and a chorale from a *Passion* by Bach.' Bacon condemned 'Laying the immortal legacies of genius on the Procrustes' bed of modern "arrangement" to be lopped or lengthened at the suggestion of a prudence that touches upon pusillanimity.' In all his musical work Bacon was assisted by his daughter Louisa Mary Barwell (1800-1885) who not only co-edited his magazine but in the 1827 Festival sang the sestetto from Mozart's *Cosi Fan Tutte* and joined the principal singer Madam Caradori in a scena from Weber's *Der Freischütz*. She was a close friend of the Swedish soprano Jenny Lind who, although she sang often in Norwich concerts, never appeared at a Festival. After her marriage to John Barwell in 1824 Louisa Bacon became a well known educational writer, an interest she shared with her closest friend Lady Noel Byron. She wrote many children's books and in 1880 a poem *Flora's Horticultural Fête* for the children's hospital which Jenny Lind had established in the city.

The Festival survived uninterrupted until the first World War in spite of periods of severe depression and of cholera in the 1830's; indeed *The Times* in 1842 found it 'a curious circumstance that a city of declining importance and decaying trade should have shown so unrelaxing and judicious support of music and have been able to not only take but also to keep the lead of all provincial festivals.' There were many triumphs. Through his friendship with Edward Taylor, Ludwig (Louis) Spohr's *Last Judgement* was played complete in 1833 for the first time in England. In 1839 the same composer's *Calvary* was also given its English première with the composer himself appearing. In his time considered by many a greater composer than Beethoven, Spohr referred to Norwich as the greatest triumph of his artistic career. In 1842 Taylor retired from conducting and directing the festival. Mendelssohn and Costa were invited and finally Sir Julius Benedict, Jenny Lind's director, accepted. The Norwich Festival had achieved national recognition; in 1833 Edward Taylor had given the city a backhanded compliment: 'placed in a corner of the kingdom, dirty, crooked, old-fashioned Norwich is never heard of or known to exist except when dragged into infamous notoriety by its corrupt electors, or held up to more honourable notice for its unrivalled triennial festival.'

After 1845 there was loss of confidence. The choral society declined; in 1836 it had comprised almost 300 voices 'more than 200 of whom are living in Norwich—weavers, dyers, tailors and shoemakers, who leave their looms and vats and shopboards to perform the most sublime of Mozart's compositions.' The director the Rev. R. F. Elwin 'tall and fine-looking, crotchety but amusing' fell ill and retired to Leeds in 1847. There followed a series of disappointments. In October 1847 Mendelssohn had written offering to conduct the 1848 Festival but he died a month later at the age of thirty-eight. Jenny Lind was offered the unprecedented sum of 1,000 gns. to appear but declined an engagement. The 1851 Festival was deferred until the next year because of the rival attraction of the Great Exhibition. The next three festivals had to contend with the threat of war, tax increases and cholera. Henry Pierson's oratorio *Jerusalem* was given for the first time in 1852 and was ridiculed in the local and national press. The Festival made a deficit in 1854 and in 1857 the press reported that the county families, who were substantial patrons, felt 'they could travel to London and hear better music for less money.' John Barwell thought the whole enterprise was antiquated. The fifties saw the nadir of the Norfolk and Norwich Triennial Festival; but the crisis passed and under the chairmanship of Hay Gurney the Festival attracted Royal patronage which could not fail to swell the attendance. In 1866 Handel's *Passion* was performed for the first time in England in the presence of the Prince and Princess of Wales, the Queen of Denmark and the Duke of Edinburgh. Richard Wagner was heard in 1869 for the first time in Norwich (The Tannhäuser) and the 1884 Festival was declared the best English Festival of the year. With the Prince and Princess of Wales again present, the public rose to their feet and pelted the orchestra with flowers after a performance of Gounod's *Redemption*.

In most ways the Norwich Festival reflected nineteenth century English bourgeois tastes. Although at least seventeen British composers conducted their own works, of which twelve had been specially written for Norwich, the influence of Handel and Mendelssohn predominated. The programmes were also characteristic of the period: made up of a curious assortment of selections, a whole piece was rarely played. The performances were also formidably long, the evening programme often finishing at well past midnight. The later festivals were undoubtedly less picturesque than those of the twenties and thirties when the perpetually leaking roof of St Andrew's Hall forced Mr Lindley to play a violincello concerto under an umbrella and John Sell Cotman jauntily appeared at the Fancy Dress Ball of 1830; 'as a chinese mandarin with a red coral globe on the top of his cap, from the verge of which were suspended two peacock feathers'! The balls, were discontinued in 1875. Nevertheless the Festival was the backbone of musical life in the city and attracted new business—in 1827 Richard Mackenzie Bacon estimated that over £50,000 had been spent in the city during Festival week. From its foundation until 1893 the Festival made a total loss of only £338 and benefitted local charities to the sum of £13,520 of which half went to the Norfolk and Norwich Hospital. Bacon would have been well pleased.

Theatre

Apart from his musical interests Richard Mackenzie Bacon was a great Shakespearean enthusiast. His young friend John Callcott Horsley even thought he might have 'had a great career on the stage as the impersonator of Shakespearean characters, especially as a refined interpreter of Falstaff.' It seems Bacon had a natural flair for comedy: Horsley recollected a hearty discussion of the merits of goose and Norfolk dumplings when Bacon mimicked the local farmers who thought 'the goose is an orkard bird, t'aint enough for two and a bit too much for one'! Bacon and his fellow enthusiasts held Shakespearean evenings when 'the unfathomable depths and heights of the poet were discussed and to these you were permitted to bring your friends and visitors.' The Bacon family also had close ties with the Norwich theatre. A Richard Bacon, who was one of the proprietors of the theatre in the 1780's and '90's, was almost certainly Richard Mackenzie's father. Other proprietors included Bacon's later rival, William Stevenson, editor of the *Norfolk Chronicle*. Richard Mackenzie Bacon himself became a proprietor by 1806. The Bacons and the Barwells were friends of John Brunton (1741-1822) the actor-manager of the Theatre Royal, Norwich during its heyday when, as Theodore le Gay Burley has noted, the Norwich Company served as 'rich recruiting ground for Covent Garden and Drury Lane'. And Sarah Siddons played for nine nights (in 1788) when the favourite fare was horror and tragedy such as *The Dumb Ward of Genoa* and *The Bleeding Nun of Lindenburg*!

The Norwich Theatre, the second oldest purpose built theatre in England, was built by the architect Thomas Ivory in 1758 at the corner of Theatre Plain and Theatre Street. Dorothy Eshleman recalls that in 1799,

17

William Wilkins, the architect, proposed alterations to enlarge the cramped facilities of the old theatre where 'a lady must be separated from the Arm of her protector both on entering, on leaving the Lobby . . . it really is otherways impossible that Ladies can reach their carriages without danger of spoiling their Dresses and being squeezed perhaps between Doorkeepers, Porters and prostitutes . . .' The theatre, rebuilt and renovated in 1801, was embellished by the Company's Imperial Arms painted by Robert Dixon, later a member of the Norwich Society of Artists, who was appointed scene painter to the theatre in 1800. The Theatre Royal was a formidable rival to the old White Swan Inn near St Peter Mancroft which, nevertheless, continued as a playhouse showing variety performances until March 1820. Robert Dixon's scenery at the Theatre was a major draw for the spectacular effects of melodramas such as *The Miller and his Men* of 1814 for which he designed a ravine and rocky gorge complete with drawbridge and explosions. Dixon died in 1815 at the early age of thirty-five and the Theatre held a benefit for his widow and children. His successor was Francis Thorne, trained at Covent Garden, whose scenery became even more inventive with the use of gauze and mechanical devices which, in *The Flying Dutchman*, of 1827, presented the 'phantasmagoric appearances' of a vessel under sail.

In the early years of the nineteenth century the Theatre Royal played more serious drama with some distinguished players: Charles Kemble as Cato, King Lear and Macbeth in 1816 and in 1817 Edmund Kean, then but thirty, took the Norwich stage for eight nights opening as Richard III and delighting the audience with his Othello: 'the Affecting tone in which he delivered his concluding speech before he stabs himself, drew tears from many.' The Garrick tradition was dying and Kean's naturalistic innovations prompted a column and a half from the critic of the *Norfolk Chronicle*. Kean played Norwich again in 1819 and 1830 and his son, Charles, first came to the City in 1828. There were also local productions. In 1815, the year before the East Anglian agricultural revolt of 1816, *The Rebellion of Norwich in 1549* was staged with scenes of 'Kett the arch rebel' and 'the awful catastrophe which closed the curtain on his infamous career.'

In 1818 the sensational Eliza O'Neill played five nights in *Romeo and Juliet*, *The Stranger* and Thomas Otway's republican play *Venice Preserved*, a sure success in the Jacobin city; indeed, it was a sell out 'no law prevailed but that of the strongest. There were shrieks, reproaches, lamentations, bonnets were cramped up, hats squeezed flat, gowns torn . . . motley mob . . . to the highest state of exasperation, fermentation, and desperation. The house was crowded in every part . . . families of the highest respectability were in inconvenient situations. Even the orchestra was occupied by the public'. In 1820 a new melodrama by Edward Fitzball, *Giraldi*, based on a tale by Amelia Opie, had its première at the theatre. Fitzball was born in Cambridgeshire and after an attempt at printing in

Norwich was encouraged by Amelia Opie to write for the theatre. He became a prolific dramatist for the Adelphi and Covent Garden and wrote librettos for opera.

The Norwich Theatre inevitably suffered from the slump of the 1820's: in February 1821 the *Norwich Mercury* lamented the poor houses where 'London actors perform to almost empty benches.' In 1825 the last performance was given in the old theatre which had become sadly dilapidated. William Wilkin's son, also William and architect of the National Gallery, who had acquired the lease from John Brunton in 1799, proposed to provide for a new theatre, an idea which was unanimously accepted by a relieved committee. The new Theatre Royal was built at a cost of £6,000 a few yards from the site of the old theatre. It opened on Easter Monday, March 27th, 1826, with *The School for Scandal* and *Youth, Love and Folly, or the Female Jockey*! The evening was enlivened by the usual rowdiness when 'vulgar blockheads committed a cowardly assault upon the peaceable individual who vends refreshments.' A new era of Norwich theatre had begun! Fortunately it was not discovered until 1883 that the licence to perform plays was granted to Thomas Ivory *personally* in 1768 and ceased to have validity upon his death in 1779. Both the old and the new Theatres Royal in Norwich were run for over one hundred years 'without patent, licence or permit of any sort'.

In 1839 James Smith, Actor-manager of the theatre for thirty years, handed over to his son George Smith, regretting the decline of the theatre which he saw as the result of an 'increase of dissent and fanaticism'. What would he have thought of the 'pretty but invertebrate French trifles' of Leslie's Opera Bouffe Company which played in 1873! There were, nonetheless many fine performances. In 1830, three years before his early death, Edmund Kean played Lear and Norwich saw what Bosworth Harcourt noted as 'the end of perhaps the most wonderful genius that every donned the "sock and buskin" in England'. Macready, Fred Vining, Fanny Kemble and Emily Brunton also appeared. In 1831 Harriet Constance Smithson, a beautiful Irish actress, played Norwich as her first engagement on her return from Paris—shortly before she married Berlioz—and in 1836 Harriet Gurney Grundey made her debut at the age of nineteen as Belvidera in *Venice Preserved*.

The programme was varied with musical performances often scheduled in the Assize or Festival week when Festival singers such as Madam Malibran and Clara Novello appeared in the theatre. There were many independent concerts staged; Paganini 'the fascinating but by no means fair dealing foreigner' played in 1831 and Liszt in 1840, when Weber's *Der Freischütz* was also performed as a benefit to Thorne the scene painter and Reeves, a vocalist. In the 1850's Edward Fitzball declared that in Norwich plays were 'much better performed than they are at the present day in any theatre in London.' The company even tackled in 1852 Webster's *The Duchess of Malfi* for the benefit of Fred

New Theatre, Norwich. James Sillett (1764-1840). Pencil and greywash. No date. Rebuilt by William Wilkins in 1800, it survived until 1825. Norfolk Museums Service (Norwich Castle Museum).

Theatre Royal Norwich. 1828. Rebuilt by William Wilkins in 1826. Bayne noted 'the building is only a piece of patch-work and has no pretensions to architectural design'. From James Sillett's *Views of the Churches, chapels and other public edifices in the City of Norwich.* John Stacy 1828. From a copy in the Norfolk Local Studies Library. Hereafter these prints are referred to as Sillett 1828.

Phillips who had broken a leg while playing Macgregor in *Rob Roy*. He left the stage and became the first editor of the *Norwich Argus*.

It was in 1852 that the Norwich circuit came to an end. The Theatre Royal's company had from the beginning toured their productions throughout the smaller towns of Norfolk, Suffolk and Cambridgeshire. In 1792 David Fisher, an actor-member of the Norwich company, left with his wife and joined with William Scraggs to form the Norfolk and Suffolk Company of Comedians which toured independently of the Norwich Theatre Company's circuit. The Fisher family eventually built several theatres of their own. Their famous company disbanded about 1844. David Fisher and his son both also played at the Theatre Royal in Norwich. The last actor to have toured with both the Norwich and the Fisher companies was Frederick Charles Burton who also played and sang in the Festivals. He died in 1917 at the age of ninety-five. With the passing of the stock company a chapter closed on the Norwich theatre. The actors no longer played their city—much to the regret of Bosworth Harcourt: 'They formed associations with ourselves and became part and parcel of our social life . . . now we have Monday to Saturday visits from different kinds of "shows" troupes of every sort. The Theatre is simply a lodging house.' There had always been the need for sensational attractions from London: Barmin's Tom Thumb in 1866, Blondin the acrobat in 1869. After the appointment of Fred Morgan as manager in 1885 the theatre provided fully for new public tastes. Although he declined a booking of the boxing kangaroo, the variety show and the 'high kicking business' now beckoned from the wings.

The Theatre saw great changes over the century. The Victorian taste for melodrama persisted but the stage had had from the beginning to compete with more bizarre entertainments: panoramas and travelling exhibitions, waxworks, circuses and freaks of all description. Messrs. Marshall's *Grand Historical Peristrephic Panorama of the Battle of Trafalgar* was in Norwich in 1823; Wombwell's *Royal Menagery* was a regular attraction and the Norfolk and Norwich Bazaar, later an amusement hall, offered Madame Chia a bearded lady from Switzerland! Pleasure gardens were an additional threat. The Norwich Ranelagh gardens, on the site of the future Victoria station offered full blooded dramas in its own theatre, the Adelphi. The great attraction in 1837 was a piece called *Etheldrida, Princess of Norwich, or the Kings of Mercia and East Anglia and the Wild Woman of Mosswold Heath*.

In 1848 the Adelphi offered a local drama *The Spirit of the Loom* showing 'Norwich as it is' with 'Effects of Vice, Drink and Misery, Burning of the Cotton Mill and dreadful conflagration'! The Theatre Royal proprietors had tried to influence the city magistrates to refuse the Adelphi a licence because the 'theatre is immoral in the highest degree as leading to dissipation and vice'! It closed with the building of the new Victoria Station in 1849. The last years of the century brought further problems when the shortlived Vaudeville Theatre opened in 1876 in St Giles Street offering a roller-skating rink, cycling, performing dogs and music-hall. It closed, however, in 1882 and became the city's Salvation Army headquarters. The decline of the theatre was sorely felt by some, especially Bosworth Harcourt who mourned the days of the heroine 'who when she goes mad always goes into white satin'. And the passing of 'The Lank Man in the pit . . . who sold nuts, cakes and oranges and those three apples for a penny . . . Lemonade too which with oranges seemed especially more in demand during Tragedy than at Comedy or Farce.'

The Fine Arts: Painters, Patrons, Institutions and Collections

Norwich has a quite remarkable record of achievement in the visual arts during the nineteenth century. One that, with the exception of the Middle Ages, has not been equalled by the city before or since. It was the birthplace of several artists and architects of national importance, it founded one of the earliest provincial schools of art in England, and made a significant contribution to the early history of photography. Some of the most distinguished antiquarians, collectors and naturalists of the period also have close links with Norwich and Norfolk.

The Norwich Society of Artists

The Norwich Society of Artists, established in 1803, was the earliest and most important of the provincial artists groups of nineteenth century England. It was founded in the wake of the vigorous artistic life of eighteenth century Norwich, when eminent London artists such as Beechey, Reinagle and Cipriani were frequent visitors to the city. It was not an isolated phenomenon, other societies quickly followed, particularly at Leeds, Birmingham and Manchester. None of these, however, survived as long as the Norwich Society which spanned three decades ending with the last exhibition in 1833. In its first Articles it is described as an 'Academy for the Lovers of the Arts, or A Society instituted for the purpose of an enquiry into the rise, progress and present state of Painting, Architecture and Sculpture'. It began with fortnightly meetings 'to chat on Art or anything else' in a room in Little Cockey Lane and in 1805 held its first exhibition in Sir Benjamin Wrenche's Court when it received a warm welcome from the *Norfolk Chronicle* on the 10th August:

> 'Among the novelties of the week was an exhibition of paintings and drawings by several professors and amateurs of this city many of which possess considerable merit.'

In the first year of which there is a record in the Society's catalogue, 1806, we see that nine of the sixteen members were not artists. The president was William Clayton Leeds, a civil servant, the vice-President was Arthur

Sir Benjamin Wrench's Court, Norwich. Pencil, watercolour and brown ink. By Henry Ninham 1793-1874. Norfolk Museums Service (Norwich Castle Museum). This was where the first exhibition of the Norwich Society of Artists was held in 1805.

The Corn Exchange: built 1828. Sillett 1828. Built on the site of Sir Benjamin Wrench's Court the Exchange continued as a display centre for the Norwich Society of Artists. Exchange Street was cut from the Market Place to St. Andrews Street and it was completed in 1832.

Browne, an architect; there were two collectors, the Rev. William Gordon of Saxlingham Nethergate and Michael Beale Crotch, a musical instrument maker and brother of Dr William Crotch. Throughout its history the Norwich Society of Artists included among its members men whose contributions to the literary, theatrical and musical life of the city have already been discussed, notably Richard Mackenzie Bacon, John Barwell, Henry Robert Bowles, the Rev. Robert Fountaine Elwin, Edward Rigby and William Wilkins. The role of these amateurs in the Society probably caused the quarrel which prompted three of the professionals, the drawing masters—Robert Ladbrooke, John Sillett and John Thirtle—to break away and form their own short-lived Society in 1816-18. The serious minded Ladbrooke seemed to favour the purchase of casts and books in preference to the convivial gathering of the gentleman amateurs and artists but as Henry Ladbrooke recalled, 'Crome being the more popular carried the day in favour of the night suppers.' None of the minutes of the Society seem to have survived even though the last secretary, John Barwell, did not die until 1876 and we know little more of the Secession or of any other intriguing crisis in the life of the Society.

The relationship between the Norwich Society of Artists and the three generations of artists, who, by their common aims and close master-pupil and family ties form the Norwich School of Painters, also remains unclear. Several artists in particular: Henry Ninham, the Stannard brothers, Joseph and Alfred, and the talented amateurs Robert Leman and Thomas Lound, exhibited with the Society but never became members. In spite of its longevity the Norwich Society of Artists failed to secure patronage for its artist members. It had the wholehearted support of the press, of gentleman patrons and members and of the Corporation who even granted the Society £100 for the purchase of casts in 1829. Artists nevertheless found it difficult to sell their work. Even fresh initiatives after 1828, when the Society changed its name to the Norfolk and Suffolk Institution for the Promotion of the Fine Arts and when Cotman and J. B. Crome organized a series of *conversazioni*, failed to save the Society.

The foremost artist-members of the Society and the most significant painters of the Norwich School were John Crome and John Sell Cotman. Both have an international status as landscape painters. Both exerted a profound influence on their contemporaries and pupils and, to some extent, on each other. The inevitable professional rivalry between the two and their sharp differences of character gave fresh vitality to Norwich artistic life. By all accounts Crome was amiable, even rascally. Richard Noverre Bacon remembered him as 'my mirth-loving, kind and earnest teacher'; while Cotman was intensely ambitious, mercurial and given to periods of black despair especially towards the end of his life. The two men came closest in their work, particularly in the earlier years of the Norwich Society from 1806 when Cotman had returned to Norwich from

London. Both were influenced by the active role they took in the intellectual life of the city. Crome and his son John Berney Crome were, like William Taylor and his friends, members of the Philosophical Society and Cotman joined the Society of United Friars, a philanthropic society with quasi-medieval rituals. Both artists had libraries and print collections which reflect the antiquarian and aesthetic interests which they shared with the Norwich *literati*. While Cotman left a voluminous corres- pondence which has greatly contributed to studies of his work, there are only five extant letters of John Crome and precious few papers of other Norwich School artists. Because of this paucity of material, research on Norwich School painting, its subjects and their meaning both for the artists and their patrons, rests, of necessity, on hypothesis. Unhappily, some recent research is unbalanced by current ideological prejudices.

John Crome 1768-1821

Even in his lifetime John Crome was considered to be the founder of the Norwich School. It is Crome's evocation of the Norfolk landscape—its heaths and commons, rivers, woods and windmills, its coastline, cliffs and jetties and the gabled buildings and riverside of Norwich itself—that eluded imitation by even his most talented pupils, James Stark and George Vincent. Son of a journeyman weaver and publican, Crome worked first for Norwich's distinguished physician, Dr Edward Rigby, and, in 1783, was apprenticed to Francis Whistler a coach and sign painter of Bethel Street. By 1790 he had been introduced to Thomas Harvey, a master weaver of Catton, Norwich, who, according to Dawson Turner, the Yarmouth patron of both Crome and Cotman, was 'the intimate friend of Mrs Siddons, of Kemble, of Beechey and of Opie, passionately fond of the Arts and himself no despicable artist'. Harvey was related by marriage to Sarah Siddons, who was a frequent visitor to Catton. William Windham of Felbrigg records in his diary 12th October 1793 'in the evening to Catton, having first drank tea with Unthank, and called at Mr Harvey's at Catton, where Mrs Siddons was finishing the reading of Jane Shore'. Harvey had amassed a fine collection of old master and modern paintings: English, Dutch and Italian, including works by his friend Thomas Gainsborough, by Richard Wilson and the seventeenth century Dutch masters, Ostade and Hobbema, which especially influenced Crome. Harvey's activities as a collector are well documented by letters from dealers in London, Rome, Antwerp and Amsterdam. He also owned several Cromes as well as works by Crome's early friend, Robert Ladbrooke. His patronage of John Crome may well have extended to as late as 1813 and at his house Crome almost certainly met Sir William Beechey and John Opie, whose conversation and advice gave him the social ease and confidence to become the most successful Norwich drawing master of his day. Kitson, Cotman's biographer, noted

John Crome (1768-1821).
Oil on canvas by John Opie
(1761-1807). Norfolk
Museums Service (Norwich
Castle Museum).

that in 1827 Hudson Gurney of Keswick wrote to Dawson Turner 'Old Crome had everything here, and while he lived there was but a bad chance in Norwich for another Drawing Master'.

Crome's nonconformist mind, he was a Baptist and a Liberal, probably found him favour with the Gurney family of Earlham whom he taught from 1798 and with whom he made one of his few trips from Norfolk, to the Lake District in 1802. The journals of the lively Gurney girls, quoted by A. J. C. Hare, suggest a warm, even close relationship with their drawing master; the most talented, Richenda, writing on the 17th January 1798 'I had a good drawing morning, but in the course of it gave way to passion with both Crome and Betsy—Crome because he would attend to Betsy and not to me and Betsy because she was so provoking.' The Gurneys, being strict Quakers, did not approve of picture collecting, but they did acquire two of the most beautiful and important Crome oils: the *Boulevard des Italiens* and the *Fishmarket at Boulogne* painted after his only journey abroad, to Paris in 1814. Along with many other British artists Crome went to see the rich collections freshly looted by Napoleon, then on public exhibition in the Louvre. Through their friendship with Crome the Gurney family also supported the Norwich Society of Artists; Daniel Gurney was a patron and subscriber while Richard Hanbury Gurney was also a member between 1815-1817.

As well as teaching other Quaker families in Norfolk, Crome taught the daughters of the Catholic Jerninghams of Costessey Hall near

Norwich. The family lent three works to his memorial exhibition organised by the Norwich Society of Artists in 1821. By 1828 Sir William Jerningham was also the owner of Crome's *Postwick Grove*. However, apart from the Harveys and Jerninghams, Crome found no ready market for his pictures in Norwich. Great Yarmouth provided more enthusiastic patronage; indeed Dawson Turner remarked that there 'a sum little short of £25,000 has within the last thirty years been expended on this one branch of the arts'. Crome found it worthwhile to make the long ride to Yarmouth to teach Samuel Paget's wife and daughter and the family of Dawson Turner, indomitable banker, bibliophile and collector, who was, according to Benjamin Robert Haydon, 'an immense living index', his mind 'ever on the lookout but never on the look *in*'. Paget and Dawson Turner both owned Cromes, Turner buying eleven works in all. Next to Thomas Penrice, Dawson Turner acquired the most distinguished picture collection in Yarmouth.

Crome would also have known Daniel Coppin, a painter tradesman of Norwich, President of the Norwich Society of Artists in 1816, whose activities as a connoisseur and dealer attracted a visit in 1812 from the influential Joseph Farington of London. Farington recorded in his famous diary that he had 'not met anyone who appeared to be more devoted to works of art and took more genuine pleasure in contemplating them'. Like many artists of the day Crome was also a dealer; he even tried to sell Dawson Turner paintings by the old masters. Crome largely supported his family of at least nine children by his dealing and teaching. His own work yielded a less reliable income. Although he was kept busy with commissions in later life, his early works such as the magnificent *Slate Quarries* in the Tate Gallery and *Carrow Abbey* in the Castle Museum, now highly regarded for their strength and simplicity, were criticized for lack of finish. He had slack periods when he cleaned the Civic Portraits in St Andrews Hall for the city council. When London artists such as Lawrence and Turner were charging as much as 500 guineas for a picture Crome could only command between 15 and 50 guineas. At Crome's funeral which was attended by an 'immense concourse of people', Dawson Turner paid him the warmest tribute 'I had the highest regard for him when living. I enjoyed his society: I admired his talents: I valued the man.'

After his death his sons and pupils found sales even more difficult in a period of recession. Dawson Turner wrote to John Sell Cotman on 22nd June 1826 'the times are wretchedly bad. They are unfavourable to everything; but particularly to the luxuries of life with which retrenchment first begins!' Cotman had moved back to Norwich from Yarmouth in 1823, to a grand house in St Martins Palace Plain which he could ill afford. The next ten years he devoted to establishing his position in Norwich's artistic life, a position which he had found difficult to achieve while Crome was alive.

John Sell Cotman
(1782-1842). Etching: Mrs
Dawson Turner (1774-1850)
after J. P. Davis 1818.
Norfolk Museums Service
(Norwich Castle Museum).

John Sell Cotman (1782-1842)

John Sell Cotman's work, in oil, watercolour and etching, place him as
one of the most original of British artists. Next to Turner, he has no
equal in the mastery of watercolour; indeed Laurence Binyon went so far
as to write 'the most perfect examples of pure watercolour ever made in
Europe'. His prodigious output and his sensitivity as an etcher still await a
just assessment. While Crome's critical measure is frustrated by the many
fakes and copies after his work, Cotman's is obscured by the mass of
drawing copies which he and his family churned out for his pupils. His
temperamental personality led him constantly into difficulties with his
patrons. In 1806 he was also mysteriously blackballed by the London
Society of Painters in Water-Colours. But his lack of success in his native
city was also the result of the failure of patronage which affected all the
Norwich artists. Cotman had returned to the city in 1806 having spent
the previous six years in London where he achieved some success as a
watercolourist. By this time he had produced his fine series of Greta
watercolours, the result of his long visits to the Cholmeley family of
Brandsby, Yorkshire, where he spent 'the happiest and blithesomest
Hours' of his life. He made great efforts, however, to launch himself in
Norwich: he held a one-man show in his lodgings in Wymer Street in
1806-7 and exhibited two hundred works with the Norwich Society of
Artists between 1807 and 1812. He became its Vice-President in 1810
and President in 1811, positions which Crome had held in 1807 and

1808. He had received kindness and financial help from his early patrons, Sir Henry Englefield, Vice President of the Society of Anti-quaries and a relative of the Cholmeleys, and Dawson Turner who bought, among others, one of his earliest watercolours that of Covehithe Church, Suffolk, which is now in the British Museum.

Yet by 1808 Englefield was approached for more assistance and writing to Francis Cholmeley he feared that Cotman 'must essentially want prudence as well as application or with his talents he could not have failed so totally. I am sure he might have stood far above Varley if he had chosen to do so.' Cotman had experimented with oil and had shown many of his Yorkshire watercolours and sketches which, while they undoubtedly influenced Crome and other Norwich artists such as Robert Dixon and Cotman's future brother-in-law, John Thirtle, failed to secure him sufficient sales or pupils. His watercolour style changed and took on a greater intensity of colour and strength of composition to compete with oils at exhibition, but superb drawings such as *Greta Bridge* 1810 in the Norwich collection were criticised for their classical 'old master' qualities. Cotman painted some of his finest Norwich subjects, of *Mousehold Heath*, the *Marl Pit* and *Bishop Bridge*, but these nevertheless failed to find buyers. His move to Yarmouth in 1812 was a desperate attempt to establish a new market for his prints as well as a steady income from Dawson Turner.

By the 1820's the climate in Norwich had worsened and in 1827 James Stark was quoted by the *Norwich Mercury* of 26th May, 'It is but too true that Norwich stands at an infinite remove below most other places in offering encouragement to art'. Norwich artists were forced to show their works elsewhere—in the provinces and in London. Some artists though, notably Joseph Stannard, were more popular with local collectors. Stannard's large narrative painting of *Thorpe Water Frolic* exhibited in 1825 had an immediate appeal for, as the *Chronicle* exclaimed on the 6th August 'of all the gay, the bustling and delightful scenes in nature, we know of no more refreshing and enchanting than a Water Frolic.' The painting commemorated an annual local event when John Harvey of Thorpe recreated a Venetian regatta where as many as 20,000 spectators lined the river at Thorpe, the gentry on the north bank and the populace on the south 'so happily blended without being confounded with each other'!

In 1830 Stannard, talented and successful, died at the age of thirty-three. A chapter was closing on Norwich's artistic life. Stark and Vincent had left the city, J. B. Crome went bankrupt in 1834 and went to Yarmouth, John Sell Cotman moved to become Drawing Master at King's College, London. It was left to a younger generation to embark on new ventures: to establish a School of Art, organise new exhibitions and new art societies which enriched the city's art scene until the end of the century.

Art and Photography

Thorpe river, the 'Richmond of Norfolk' which had been the subject of so many earlier Norwich School paintings, continued to be the haunt of Norwich artists. Some met for nine-pin suppers at Hinsby's gardens where the Norwich glass stainer James George Zobel spent many a jolly evening (see also Chapter VI). On such an occasion, in 1832, when J. B. Ladbrooke, son of Robert, presided and Alfred Stannard was present, Zobel wrote in his diary 'Supper on table at 10 minutes past 7 o'clock . . . rump steak with pickled onions and walnuts, cucumber sliced in vinegar peppered and salted, a dish of mashed potatoes, two pots of ale and two of Porter during supper . . . the result of this supper . . . caused me to pass my own home and wandered into St Stephen's. There I was sufficiently silly and regardless of expense and probability of venereal disease to lay with a prostitute all night. Whole expense with her 6/6d. Lost ¾ of the next day by idleness and drank an ounce of Epsom salts at 4 o'clock p.m.'! John Berney Ladbrooke (1803-1879) became one of the most prosperous of Norwich Drawing masters, running his school from Ketts Castle Villa, Mousehold, an imposing house which he designed and built himself. Most provincial drawing masters, however, were

J. B. Ladbrooke with some of his pupils. Norfolk Museums Service (Norwich Castle Museum).

threatened by two new developments: art underwent the momentous impact of the invention of photography and between 1838 and 1852, the Government established the provincial Schools of Design.

Daguerreotypes and landscape photography achieved such popularity that some provincial artists abandoned their teaching and their brushes for the camera. Several Norwich artists experimented with the new art and were among a circle of amateurs with literary and scientific interests who became significant innovators in the early history of photography. They included Dr Hugh Diamond, who experimented for record purposes with photographs of the insane, Thomas Damont Eaton, a Norwich solicitor and W. J. J. Bolding, a farmer and merchant from Weybourne, North Norfolk. Bolding was a friend of the brilliant young Norwich watercolourist, John Middleton (1827-1856), who took landscape photographs of which a set of calotypes is in the Norwich Castle Museum. Other artist-photographers included the brewer Thomas Lound and the insurance agent Robert Leman, both of whom had cameras and equipment in their posthumous sales. Lound was on the committee of the first photographic exhibition held in Norwich in 1857. Earlier interest in the subject was shown by Louisa (Bacon) Barwell in her lengthy and informed foreword to the Norwich Polytechnic Exhibition of 1840 in which she also promoted her husband's campaign for a Norwich School of Design.

The Barwells and the Norwich School of Design

John and Louisa Barwell made a vital contribution to the artistic life of Norwich. From the eighteenth century the Barwell family had run a wine business in St Stephen's Norwich. John Barwell (1798-1876) led a full public life as a councillor and Alderman, but refused the honour of the Mayoralty. He was also a talented artist, musician and singer; an exhibitor, member and last secretary of the Norwich Society of Artists. His impressive portrait of William Taylor is in the collection of Norwich School in the Cathedral Close. In 1837 he lectured to the Mechanics Institute 'on the study of the Fine Arts as connected with Manufactures' and recommended the establishment of a School of Design in Norwich. He and Louisa later organised the Polytechnic Exhibition which gave them a platform to point out the inferiority of British design in comparison with the French. The exhibition was a great success; from power looms, steam engines, Norwich shawls to shrunken heads and pictures, it combined a didactic function with the diversion of the grotesque and the bizarre. The publicity it gave to Barwell's cause also encouraged the Town Council, who were concerned with the decline in the Norwich textile industry, to seek government approval and grant aid to set up a School of Design. In 1845 Norwich received £300 from the

31

£10,000 which Parliament had allocated for the provincial schools. On 21st January 1846 the Norwich School of Design was officially opened by its President Sir John Boileau of Ketteringham Hall, Norfolk.

The Barwells' contacts in London and abroad were instrumental in the founding of the Norwich School of Design. Both were at the forefront of English interest in foreign educational theory and held progressive views on art education. Above all, Louisa's sister, Rose Bacon, married Richard Redgrave, one of the 'great Triumvirate' with Dyce and Cole, who promoted the cause of art education in England. The Barwells maintained their prominence in Fine Art activities in the city throughout the century. The year 1839 had seen the establishment of the first Norfolk and Norwich Art Union and the revival of *conversazioni* which had begun in 1830 when Barwell, Bacon, Lound and Leman had been members. The Honorary Secretary of the Art Union was Robert Leman and the subscribers included Barwell and Thomas Lound. Both Leman and Lound later became committee members of the School of Design. The Barwells' connection with Norwich School of Art spanned several decades. Their son, Henry George Barwell, was its secretary for twenty-five years and died whilst still a committee member in 1898. Their younger son, Frederick Bacon Barwell, one of the most successful genre

John Barwell (third from left). Detail from painting by C. L. R. W. Nursey (1820-1873). Oil *The Officers of the Norwich Battalion of Rifle Volunteers on Mousehold Heath*. Norwich 1862. Norwich Brewery Ltd.

Mrs Louisa Barwell. Oil by Richard Rothwell 1800-1868. Norfolk Museums Service (Norwich Castle Museum).

painters of his day, became Senior Inspector in the Department of Science and Art and completed his father's work by persuading the Norwich City Council in 1898 that a School of Art had an essential role in its educational provision.

Exhibitions and Conversazione

The Norwich School of Design was first housed in the Royal Norfolk and Norwich Bazaar, elegant, three-storeyed and colonnaded, built at 24 to 26 St Andrews Broad Street by Samuel Lovick in 1831. It was also the venue of the Art Union exhibitions and the 1840 Polytechnic Exhibition. The teaching of the Norwich School of Design, later the Norwich School of Practical Art, departed little from that of a traditional academy. This emphasis on fine art was promoted by exhibitions organised between 1848-1855 by the Norfolk and Norwich Association for the Promotion of the Fine Arts. These shows of contemporary paintings, including works by the Norwich School artists, Middleton, Lound and Leman, were accompanied by *conversazione* and Art Unions.

Royal Norfolk and Norwich Bazaar 24-26 St Andrews Broad Street (above road works). Photograph (c.1896) N.L.S.L.

The School of Design became the venue of fashionable *soirées*, especially under the fourth headmaster, the energetic Claude Lorraine Nursey. These elegant evenings prompted criticism from the *Mercury*, 4th November 1854, 'For whom is the school intended? Is it for the "Special Class", the Aristocratical or the Middle and Artizan Classes . . .' and undermined the School's purpose of serving the cause of industrial design. Even the school's contribution to the Great Exhibition of 1851, an elaborate painted ceiling containing portraits of the great Renaissance artists with the arms of the City of Norwich, had no industrial purpose. The unfortunate Nursey was eventually forced to resign in 1859 after a scandal which revealed that he had allowed students to *trace* drawings for the National Competition! Nonetheless, Nursey stayed on in Norwich and in 1862 completed two paintings of the Norwich Battalion and the Norfolk Yeomanry of which the former includes portraits of Barwell and fellow committee members of the School of Art. The picture is now in the collection of the Norwich Brewery. Under Nursey the Norwich School of Art left its cramped quarters in the Bazaar for the top floor of the Norwich Free Library in St Andrews Broad Street, which opened in 1857. The School of Art and the Library remained unhappy bedfellows until the building of the new Norwich Municipal Technical Institute in St Georges in 1901. Not only was the library building unsuitable, but art school life proved tiresome to the librarian who more than once had to complain 'of the bad behaviour of the Boys upon leaving the School of Art every evening . . . turning out the Gas, throwing the Mats in the Street and Shouting and Shrieking' and of the School porter for his 'neglect of duty, dirtiness, several acts of insubordination and drunkenness'!

New Art Societies and The Technical Institute

Although the School of Art failed ever to fulfill its original purpose it was the mainstay of amateur art activities in Norwich in the last decade of the nineteenth century. The School survived a virtual invasion of middle class ladies who won most of the National prizes and medals. One distinguished pupil was Catherine Maude Nichols (1847-1923) who in 1889 was made the first (and for ten years the only) woman Fellow of the newly formed London Society of Painter-Etchers. She showed frequently in London and abroad where she received greater recognition than she did in Norwich. She also wrote copiously, theological works as well as local favourites. *A Novel of Old Norwich* 1886 and *Haunts of George Borrow*. She founded the Woodpecker Art Club in 1889 which, with the East Anglian Art Society (1876) and the Norfolk and Norwich Art Circle (1885) was closely associated with the staff and students of the School of Art. A fellow past student was James Reeve (1833-1920), later Curator of the Norwich Museum for over fifty years, who was responsible for the collections of the East Anglian Art Society coming to the Castle Museum in 1897. Reeve's friendship with many of the younger Norwich School artists, especially John Joseph Cotman, led him to advise the Colman family on the purchases for their magnificent Norwich School collections which eventually were bequeathed to the Castle Museum in 1894 and 1947. Apart from Miss Nichols other distinguished women artists in Norwich who became also pupil teachers at the School, were Margaret Holmes, Ethel Buckingham and the Offord sisters, Gertrude and Georgina. They showed at the Royal Academy and at Women's Exhibitions in Paris and Chicago.

Alfred Munnings (1878-1959)

Gertrude Offord was later remembered by one of her pupils in the 1890's who was destined to become one of the most successful British artists of the twentieth century, Alfred J. Munnings. Munnings worked at the art school in the evenings from 1873 to 1898. After a nine-hour day as a lithographic artist at Page Brothers, he could not wait to get back to the cast; 'the never-to-be-forgotten horse's head from the Parthenon . . . I lived only to go on with that splendid horse's head in sepia from seven to nine'! Munnings' oil painting of the life room at the art school won him the National Bronze Medal in 1898: 'the faded grey colouring of the rooms was a perfect background to everything—students in blouses working at easels, large casts of Greek and Roman fragments with slight dust settlement on to surfaces, aged castor oil plants in green tubs.'

In 1894 the students of Norwich School of Art took the bold and unprecedented step of sending a petition to the School of Art committee for 'some concerted action being taken towards providing a new building'. Munnings was among the signatories. During the 1890's there was mounting pressure on the City Council to provide improved facilities for higher education in science and art and the council agreed to the building of a new Technical Institute designed by W. Douglas Wiles under the direction of the City Engineer, Arthur Elliston Collins. The School of Art moved from the Free Library to its new quarters on the River Wensum, St George's Street, in March 1901. Noel Spencer, retired principal of the school recorded: 'It must have been a momentous day when the great plaster casts of Venus of Milo, Ilissus, Theseus and all the others came down the narrow staircase and were loaded onto horse drays to be trundled along to the new Technical Institute beside the river.'

Architecture: George Skipper 1856-1948

One of the finest Edwardian buildings in the City, and, for its time, incorporating a number of progressive features, the Norwich School of Art has a robust simplicity exemplified by Arts and Crafts ideals. It is a fitting tribute to a former pupil and an outstanding Edwardian architect,

George Skipper. The late Sir John Betjeman referred to Skipper as 'altogether remarkable and original. He is to Norwich what Gaudi was to Barcelona'. Skipper joined the school for just one year in 1872-3 and won prizes for excellence in 'freehand, geometry and model'. After training in London and a few years in Dereham, Norfolk, he returned to Norwich in 1880 and ran an intensely busy practice, completing, apart from competition work, his splendid hotels in Cromer, of rich carved stone and terracotta. The next fifteen years saw the building of his major Norwich works: his new office at 7, London Street (1896) and one of his masterpieces, the Royal Arcade, between Gentleman's Walk and the Back of the Inns. Opened in 1899 it was hailed as 'a fragment from the Arabian Nights dropped into the heart of the old city' and dubbed by Pevsner as 'perfectly innocent in the front but very naughty when its back is turned'! The Arcade was soon followed by the Norwich Union Life Insurance building in Gurney Street which competition Skipper won in 1901. Skipper surpassed even himself in this magnificent Palladian building which stands under the satisfied gaze of Talbot, Bishop of Oxford and Sir Samuel Bignold, son of the founder of the insurance society and a long serving and influential committee member of the Norwich School of Art.

Skipper is one of a distinguished line of architects associated with the city whose work has national significance: from Thomas Ivory, who built the City's Assembly Rooms and the first Theatre Royal, to Sir John Soane and William Wilkins, both honorary members of the Norwich Society of Artists, to Thomas Jekyll who built the Chinese Pagoda which stood in

The Royal Arcade. 1899. Architect George Skipper (1856-1948).

Chapelfield Gardens until 1947. Designed for the Philadelphia Exhibition of 1876 Pevsner gleefully described it as 'one of the most gorgeous Victorian cast-iron monstrosities of England . . . not looking in the least like a pagoda nor indeed like anthing else'! Jekyll designed his fine sunflower fireplaces which are now coveted collectors' pieces for the Norfolk ironworks of Barnard, Bishop & Barnard. Among the medieval, Elizabethan and Georgian riches of the city centre, Norwich building of the last century tends to be overlooked. There are, nonetheless, exceptional examples of industrial architecture; one such is Jarrold's printing works on the River Wensum at Cowgate, built by the County Surveyor, John Brown, as a yarn mill in 1839, and rightly called 'the noblest of all English Industrial Revolution Mills'.

Antiquarianism and Collecting

The nineteenth century was the age of the public institution in England; it was also the greatest period of private and public museum building and the founding of scientific and literary institutions. Norwich was no exception; indeed the city is associated with men and women whose collections and achievements have more than local significance.

One of the major influences on the work of some Norwich artists in the early 1800's was the growth of antiquarianism. Several of the Norwich School artists produced etchings and publications of Norwich and Norfolk antiquities and architecture which had a national as well as local market. Between 1810 and 1821 John Sell Cotman's main output was in etching, culminating in his major publications *The Architectural Antiquities of Norfolk* completed in 1818 and *The Architectural Antiquities of Normandy* 1818-21, the result of his three trips to France. Cotman was encouraged by Dawson Turner and two of the leading antiquarian writers of the period: Hudson Gurney, banker and partner of Dawson Turner, and John Britton an honorary member of the Norwich Society of Artists and co-editor with Edward Brayley of *The Beauties of England and Wales,* to which he contributed the Norfolk section. Hudson Gurney (1775-1864), the eldest son of Richard Gurney of Keswick Hall, Norwich, became the head of the Norwich Gurneys. He was immensely wealthy yet generous to his friends and causes, of which he embraced many. He was unfailingly helpful to Cotman in his architectural projects and printed for the benefit of Samuel Woodward's widow the *Norfolk Topographers Manual* and the *History of Norwich Castle* based on Woodward's collections. A poet, a prolific writer and scholar and a benefactor to the Society of Antiquaries, Gurney was a mainstay of the Norwich Literary Institution and the Norwich Museum. The Literary Institution was founded in the Haymarket by Simon Wilkin in 1822 to compensate for the shortcomings of the Norfolk and Norwich Subscription Library, founded by Philip

Meadows Martineau in 1784, which 'did not include enough works of learning and transactions of societies'. The Subscription Library, although called the Norwich Public Library, was a private circulating library 'a club for the comfortable study of books admirably housed in a dignified and commodious building in quite the best site that could be chosen for it'—it moved to the elegant doric building by the Guildhall in 1838. The Library and the Literary Institution amalgamated in 1886 when the collections amounted to some 70,000 volumes. A disastrous fire, which broke out in Dove Street in 1898, destroyed most of the contents but some reparation was made from the libraries of Dean Goulburn and Hudson Gurney whose library had grown to over 10,000 volumes.

Hudson Gurney (1775-1864). Etching: Mrs Dawson Turner (1774-1850 after J. Opie 1797. Norfolk Museums Service (Norwich Castle Museum).

During his lifetime Gurney also contributed to the collections of the Norfolk and Norwich Museum which opened in adjoining rooms of the Literary Institution in 1825. Gurney was largley responsible for the collection of Samuel Woodward, geologist and antiquary, joining the museum after Woodward's death in 1838. The Gurneys' contribution to the Museum, later housed in Exchange Street and then Museum Court, St Andrews Street, was sustained by the generosity of John Henry Gurney who became its President in 1849. His outstanding collection of birds of prey was sold to the British Museum in 1950. Another spectacular collection which left Norwich was that of Sir James Edward Smith (1759-1828), the distinguished Norwich born botanist and founder of the Linnaean Society. Smith's collection included the great Linnaean collection of plants, insects, shells and minerals which remained at Smith's house in Surrey Street until his death, when it was purchased by the Society. Smith was the most influential botanist of his day and the central figure of a circle of Norfolk naturalists which included Sir William Jackson Hooker, the founder of Kew Gardens and son-in-law of Dawson Turner who was himself an assiduous botanist. Like many of his Norwich friends Smith was a Unitarian and a deacon of the Octagon Chapel at the time of his death.

The private collections of the Norfolk and Norwich Museums were enriched in 1891 by the antiquities of Robert Fitch (1802-95), a geologist and antiquary, many years secretary of the Norfolk Archaeology Society. Shortly afterwards in 1893 the Museum collections became public and were rehoused in the newly converted Norwich Castle which was opened by the future King George V and Queen Mary in October 1894. They were given lunch by the Mayor in the Picture Gallery, which was resplendent with the Norwich School collections of the East Anglian Art Society and of J. J. Colman, secured through the tireless efforts of James Reeve. Exactly one year before Lady Elizabeth Eastlake, the daughter of John Crome's early patron, Dr Edward Rigby, had died in London. The wife of Sir Charles Eastlake, director of the National Gallery, Elizabeth Rigby became one of the most prolific and important nineteenth century writers on the fine arts. She also prepared her father's early letters from France for publication in 1880. Lady Eastlake: 'intellectual and courageous, impervious to bores, highly esteemed and looked up to in the best society in London for nigh on fifty years' was the last of Norwich's *grande dames* who achieved a status and influence that would be envied by many of their successors today.

The Norwich Press

While Leeds and Manchester led the field as provincial press centres, Norwich can claim no little attention for the literary and intellectual merit of some of its editors and proprietors, notably William Taylor and

William Stevenson, Esq., F.S.A. Lithograph: William Sharp after W. Hilton. Norfolk Museums Service (Norwich Castle Museum).

Seth William Stevenson. By Thomas Wageman (1787-1863). Norfolk Museums Service (Norwich Castle Museum).

Richard Mackenzie Bacon (whose contribution to the cultural life of Norwich has already been stressed), William Stevenson and his son Seth William Stevenson, Simon Wilkin and Thomas Starling Norgate. Their controlling interest in the Norwich press during the first decades of the 19th century provided not only a powerful force in the formation of public opinion on commerce and politics, but indispensable support and publicity to the literary, musical and artistic interests which they wished to promote. William Taylor had been a contributor to *The Cabinet*, a fortnightly radical magazine which appeared in 1794-5. Other writers included J. S. Taylor, Dr Rigby, William Dalrymple, Amelia Alderson (Opie), Thomas Starling Norgate and William Enfield, all of them luminaries in Norwich's literary life in the early nineteenth century.

In 1803 William Taylor (see also the Literary Life section of this chapter) became the editor of a new radical weekly, *The Iris* or *Norwich and Norfolk Weekly Advertiser*, printed and sold for 6d. by Samuel Kitton and John Shalders of London Lane who were probably also the proprietors. Taylor tried to get his friend, the poet Robert Southey, to move to Norwich and become editor, but Southey was doubtful of the success of the venture. When Taylor himself undertook to edit the first issue Southey replied regretting that Taylor 'who should be employed in preparing dishes for the daintiest palettes should be making wash for the swine'. Indeed, when he received the first two issues Southey was unrestrained in his criticism of Taylor's inappropriate editorials: 'You have ruined your style by Germanisms, Latinisms and Greekisms . . . you are sick of a surfeit of knowledge . . . your learning breaks out like scabs and blotches upon a beautiful face . . . faults they are, faults anywhere, and tenfold aggravated in a newspaper. How are plain Norfolk farmers—and such will read the "Iris"—to understand words which they never heard before, and which are so foreign as not to be even in Johnson's farrago of a dictionary?' In spite of Taylor's high flown classical and metaphorical language *The Iris* did meet with some success. It had agents throughout Norfolk, Suffolk, Essex and London and managed to attract the three hundred subscriptions needed to keep it afloat; but at the end of 1804 Kitton's partnership broke up and publication ceased: 'She came from heaven on her rainbow, but the earth seemed too gross for her footsteps and she retired in disappointment.' Nevertheless, *The Iris*, and *The Cabinet* before her, aired the independent and radical views of a distinguished group of intellectuals and, in challenging the *Norfolk Chronicle* and the *Norwich Mercury*, laid the foundations of a free press in the city and county.

In 1830, Simon Wilkin, founder of the Norfolk and Norwich Literary Institution, published *The East Anglian:* or *Norfolk, Suffolk, Cambridgeshire, Norwich, Lynn and Yarmouth Herald,* a weekly which was run by scholars and modelled on the defunct *Iris*. The editor was Thomas Starling Norgate, former contributor to *The Cabinet* and to several national magazines, including the *British Critic*, the *Analytical Review* and the *Monthly Magazine*. The *East Anglian* and later the *Norfolk News* and the *Eastern Counties Daily Press* served local dissident opinion so effectively that by 1900 they eclipsed the long established papers, the *Norfolk Chronicle* and *Norwich Mercury*. These more conservative organs, while less intellectual and more moderate in their profile, gave unusually wide and perceptive coverage of the arts due to the literary calibre and sensitivity of their respective editors: William Stevenson, Seth William Stevenson and Richard Mackenzie Bacon.

From 1785 until the turn of the nineteenth century the Stevenson family were responsible for the journalistic side of the *Norfolk Chronicle*. William Stevenson (1741-1821) was a proprietor until his death in the same year that saw the passing of John Crome, founder of the Norwich Society of Artists (discussed earlier in this Chapter) of which Stevenson had been a patron in 1819 and 1820. A student of the Royal Academy, Stevenson began his career as a miniature painter and by 1784 had opened a Drawing Academy at 100, Pottergate Street, Norwich. He became a friend of the London portrait painter, Sir William Beechey, who lived in Norwich from 1782-7, and of the extraordinary Ignatius

Sancho, the friend of Sterne and Garrick, who wrote to him in expectation of a Norfolk turkey 'the grand Turk of Norfolk, if it comes, we will devour it—my dear Stee'.

Stevenson became a Fellow of the Society of Antiquaries and his literary and antiquarian interests led him to republish Bentham's *History of Ely Cathedral* in 1812, to edit Campbell's *Lives of the British Admirals* and to write frequent contributions to Nichol's *Literary Anecdotes* and to the *Gentleman's Magazine*. He sponsored the Norwich poet, Elizabeth Bentley and ensured that the *Norfolk Chronicle* reported the annual exhibitions of the Norwich Society of Artists.

His son, Seth William Stevenson (1784-1853), part proprietor of the *Chronicle* in 1808 and proprietor in 1844, succeeded his father as editor in 1818 and devoted whole columns to the Society's exhibitions which are invaluable indicators of the critical taste of the day. On 29th July 1820 the Chronicle stated 'We have a most decided preference for the chaste and sober style over everything, however elegant and captivating, which partakes in the slightest degree of gaudiness and flutter.' Seth William also supported the Norwich artists by becoming both a patron and a subscriber to their Society. His knowledge of the Fine Arts was enlarged by extensive tours on the Continent of which he published travel diaries in 1817 and 1827. The first, a journal of *A Tour through Part of France, Flanders and Holland in the Summer of 1816*, was dedicated to the Society of United Friars of which Seth William Stevenson was one of the last surviving members, along with his contemporary, John Sell Cotman, who followed Stevenson to France in 1817. Stevenson's later life was dedicated to the study of Roman coins; his magnum opus was finally completed and published posthumously in 1889 as *A Dictionary of Roman Coins, Republican and Imperial*. Like his father, Seth William became a Fellow of the Society of Antiquaries and held office as sheriff and mayor of Norwich. The Stevensons were staunchly protestant and high Tory. The *Chronicle* held 'Church and State as its watchword'. When controversy raged in Norwich over the Reform Acts in the 1830's Seth William Stevenson gave support for the status quo: 'If England may be saved at all . . . she will be saved by the conservatives. Now is their day—now is their hour' (*Norfolk Chronicle*, 17th November 1832).

More sensitive to liberal opinion and more wide ranging in his interests was Richard Mackenzie Bacon, proprietor and editor of the rival paper, the *Norwich Mercury*. Bacon's cool sense answered the hot blooded radicalism of the followers of Paine and Cobbett in a series of pamphlets which he published on the aristocracy, election bribery, stack burning and the prevailing distress of the poor. Bacon's knowledge of the problems of his city and county, his interests in new printing technology, in classical learning, in music and the fine arts gave his editorials national status. He was a strong advocate for the fine arts and reported the exhibitions of the Norwich Society of Artists, of which he was both a member and subscriber, in great detail. His papers in Cambridge University Library include letters from J. B. Crome and James Stark thanking him for his support. Bacon's son, Richard Noverre Bacon, became sole proprietor of the *Mercury* in 1853. His inflexible approach led to fluctuating sales and once, when he crossed swords with the architect restoring St Andrews Hall, Norwich, to some loss of dignity. The architect caricatured Bacon in two carvings on the small South door: one shows a pig (Bacon) playing his organ (*The Mercury*), with devils blowing the instrument and a row of imps peering over the top of the organ pipes: the other depicts a pig with a horn—blowing his own trumpet! Nonetheless, Richard Bacon was enlightened enough to engage the scholar and writer John Wodderspoon who wrote articles for the *Mercury* on Crome and Cotman as well as on antiquarian subjects.

Later editors of the *Mercury*, Henry Francis Euren and his son, continued to lace the solid business of the paper with arts reports but of more significance was the newer *Eastern Counties Daily Press* and its predecessor, the *Norfolk News*, which achieved far wider circulation. The *Norfolk News*, was launched at the home of Jeremiah Colman in 1844 by the Norwich reformer Jacob Henry Tillett, known by his opponents as the Norwich Robespierre. Its first editor was the amateur artist and friend of John Joseph Cotman, Joseph Geldart, and its printer was Thomas Jarrold who published Mary Sewell's *Mother's Last Words* and Anna Sewell's *Black Beauty*. Jeremiah James Colman joined the Committee of the *News* in 1858 and thence began a controlling interest in the local press held by a Norwich family whose collections fill the galleries of the Castle Museum and whose libraries form the rich local antiquarian and theological collection of the city's library. J. J. Colman and Thomas Jarrold launched the *Eastern Counties Daily Press* in 1870.

The paper not only gave wide music coverage under the music editor, Charles Noverre, but long, detailed reports of the vicissitudes of the Norwich Public Library. The rainbow that brought *The Iris* in 1803 did not return, but its reflection continued to enrich the Norwich press throughout the nineteenth century.

Conclusion

The renaissance of the arts in a city with no university, a mere manufacturing town whose most lucrative industry after 1840 was brewing, begs more questions than it answers. Contemporary visitors to the city found the variety of activity astonishing and in spite of much recent research a full and objective analysis of the social and political context of Norwich cultural life remains to be published. That the lively, intellectual climate of the city was associated with those who adhered to local nonconformist and radical tradition is acknowledged. Many of these men and women enjoyed a liberal education which was broadened by frequent and extensive foreign travel. They also escaped the confines of provincial life by a continuous contact and correspondence with friends in London and abroad. In many ways the city's cultural life, especially in the first half of the century, was less insular than it is today. By the mid century Harriet Martineau thought that Norwich had had her day. She was equally convinced of the reasons for decline: 'railways, free trade, and cheap publications have much to do with the extinction of the celebrity of ancient Norwich, in regard both to its material and intellectual productions. Its bombazine manufacture has gone to Yorkshire, and its literary fame to the four winds.' The revival of activity in the last decades of the century proved her wrong; but there is no doubt that the early 1800's were exceptional years not only in the life of one provincial city but in English intellectual and cultural history.

Acknowledgement

I am indebted to Dr Miklós Rajnai for allowing me free use of his research material on the Norwich School of Artists, sponsored by the Paul Mellon Centre for British Art; Dr Rajnai also offered useful criticism of the text; to Rex Stedman F.L.A. for his kind permission to publish material from his thesis on the Norfolk Newspaper Press; to Norma Watt for help always freely given; to John Mullis for keeping an eye on my syntax and for helpful comments on the text.

End piece. The present Norwich School of Art. Built as Norwich Technical Institute 1899 by A. F. Collins.

Sources

Footnotes have been avoided in the text. However, to help readers locate the origin of a quotation used in the text, page numbers have been added to sources which are given in the order used in the text.

Literary Life

Dictionary of National Biography. A major source.

Horsley, John Callcott, *Recollections of a Royal Academecian.* Ed. Mrs Edmund Helps, London, John Murray, 1903, p. 75, 83.

Martineau, Harriet, *Biographical Sketches* 1852-1875. 4th ed. London 1976 pp. 331, 336.

Brightwell, C. L. *Memorials of the life of Amelia Opie.* Norwich 1854, p. 35, 36, preface v and vi, 128, 129.

Martineau, Harriet, *Autobiography,* Vol. III, 1877. Pp. 202, 268, 299, 283, 469, 268, 275, 277, Vol. 1 pp. 297-301.

Sandby, G. *Mesmerism and its Opponents with a History . . .,* Henry Price Library Senate House, London.

Stedman, R., F.L.A. *Vox Populi. The Norfolk Newspaper Press 1760-1900,* unpublished thesis, Library Association, 1971, p. 50, 56, 58, 162.

Sayers, Frank M. D. *Collective Works to which has been prefixed some biographical particulars by W. Taylor of Norwich.* 2 Vols. 1823.

Reeve, Henry, attributed to, 'The Worthies of Norwich', *Edinburgh Review,* July 1879, p. 64.

Borrow, George. *Lavengro,* New Edition. London 1900, pp. 114, 115, 122, 562, 225, 226.

Sewell, Mary. *Poems and Ballads with a Memoir by E. B. Bayly.* 2 Vols. Jarrold, 1886.

Bayly, Mrs, *Life and Letters of Mrs Sewell,* 3rd Edition, London 1889, pp. 9, 36, 53, 141, 72, 73, 135, 271, 249, 276, 277.

Music and Theatre

Legge, Robin H. and Hansell, Walter E. *Annals of the Norfolk and Norwich Triennial Music Festivals* 1824-1893. 1896 preface, pp. vi, 15, 100, 27, 62, 110, 43, 116, 154, 39.

Burley, Theodore le Gay. *Playhouses and Players of East Anglia.* Jarrold, 1928, p. 16, 10, 20, 57, 10, 167, 169, 67.

Eshleman, Dorothy A. Ed. Proposals of William Wilkins 1799, *The Committee Books of the Theatre Royal Norwich 1768-1835.* The Society for Theatre Research, 1970, Appendix B. p. 152.

Harcourt, Bosworth, *Theatre Royal, Norwich: the Chronicles of an Old Playhouse,* 1903, p. 13, 86, 89.

Fitzball, E. *Thirty-Five Years of a Dramatic Author's Life* 1859, Vol. 1 p. 39.

The Fine Arts

Fawcett. T. *The Rise of English Provincial Art 1800-1830,* Oxford Studies in the History of Art and Architecture, Clarendon Press 1974. p. 99, 18, 138.

Rajnai, Miklós, *The Norwich School of Painters,* Jarrold, 1978.

Rajnai, Miklós and Stevens, Mary, *The Norwich Society of Artists 1805-1833,* Norfolk Museums Service 1976.

'New Light on Crome. Some Ladbrooke Memories, The Reminiscences from a Notebook of Henry Ladbrooke', *Eastern Daily Press,* 22nd April 1921.

Hawcroft, F. W. 'Crome and his Patron, Thomas Harvey of Catton', *Connoisseur,* cxliv 1959. pp. 232-7.

Kitson, Sydney D. *The Life of John Sell Cotman* 1937. p. 251.

Rajnai Miklós, Ed. *John Sell Cotman 1782-1842*. The Herbert Press, 1982.

Clifford Derek and Timothy, *John Crome*. Faber and Faber, 1968.

Clifford, Derek, *Watercolours of the Norwich School*. Cory, Adams and Mackay, London, 1965.

Hare, A. J. C. *The Gurneys of Earlham* 1897, Vol. I. p. 74.

Anderson, Verily, *Friends and Relations*, Hodder and Stoughton. n.d.

Turner, Dawson, *Outlines in Lithography* 1840. p. 24.

Fawcett, T. Thorpe Water Frolic, *Norfolk Archaeology*, Vol. XXVI part IV, pp. 393-8.

Edwards, J. K. Ed. *The Diary of James George Zobel, Glass Stainer, Lady Lane, Norwich. December 1827-November 1858*. February 1964.

Allthorpe-Guyton, Marjorie, *A Happy Eye, A School of Art in Norwich 1845-1982*. Jarrold, 1982.

Munnings, Sir Alfred, *An Artist's Life*. 2 Vols. Museum Press Ltd., London, 1950 pp. 58, 59.

Architect Exuberant George Skipper 1856-1946. Exhibition Catalogue. Norwich School of Art 1975. Exhibition organised by David Jolley. p. 14.

Hepworth, Philip, The Norfolk and Norwich Subscription Library, *East Anglian Magazine*, Vol. 14. Aug. 1955. No. 10, pp. 575-579.

Durbin, Gail, *The Past Displayed, a picture history of the Norwich Museums*, Norfolk Museums Service, 1984.

Sancho's Letters, ed. Joseph Jeckyll, M.P. 1781.

CHAPTER TWO

Poverty and Public Health in Norwich
1845-1880
John Pound

In 1844-45 the reports of the Health of Towns Commissioners 'revealed the startling fact that when Britain was leading the world in industrial development the living conditions of the majority of her people were so bad that the annual death rate from typhus fever alone was double that of the fatalities of the allied armies at Waterloo'.[1] What was true of London, Manchester, Liverpool and York was equally true of the textile towns of the Midlands, small towns like Tonbridge in Kent and declining industrial towns such as Norwich, varying only in intensity and in the reasons which may have exacerbated such conditions.[2]

Squalor and overcrowding had been prevalent in Norwich since at least the reign of the first Elizabeth, but the living conditions of the poor had deteriorated steadily since the ending of the Napoleonic wars. Economic decline, combined with the activities of speculative builders who had not anticipated such decline, had made the conditions of all classes of the labouring poor bad, and those of the handloom weavers bad beyond belief. In 1844 three-quarters of the recipients of poor relief in Norwich were weavers. By 1848 one-fifth of the entire population of the city were described as paupers. In that year the District Visiting Society (which, itself, had relieved between eight and nine thousand people in each of the preceding three years) noted that 'the poor have parted with their furniture and goods to such an extent as to leave them little or nothing to fall back upon in times of emergency . . . From want of employment and other causes, (they) are scarcely able to provide their families with bread and much less able to supply them with fire and sufficient clothing.'[3]

The link between economic decline and human deprivation was clearly stated by the Commissioners themselves:

> Norwich, it is feared, has seen its best days as a place of commerce, and would appear to be in that painful state of transition from a once flourishing manufacturing prosperity to its entire decline, and must, ere long, revert to its original condition as a capital of an extensive agricultural district. A large portion of its inhabitants are therefore poor, their labour becoming daily lowered in amount of recom-

pense; . . . Neglect and decay are now conspicuous in the streets and quarters occupied by the working classes, so as to render them places of the most dismal aspect.[4]

The working class quarters were mostly to be found in narrow streets and lanes where courts and yards were linked by a single opening or doorway, some three feet wide, which led into the adjoining thoroughfares. They housed anything from a single family to as many as the forty-six found in St John's Head Yard in Coslany.[5] Between them, they formed a veritable maze for the traveller and it was 'next to impossible for a person not born in the place to find his way about without the assistance of a guide'.[6] The yards were closed at the end, the houses frequently built back-to-back, and both were erected without any regard for ventilation. Toilet facilities were wholly inadequate and were consequently a prolific source of typhoid fever, a situation made worse where houses were built onto the city walls and the privies or bins placed close to their fronts. Possibly the worst living conditions of all were those where the houses were situated in yards or alleys which were actually below the level of the adjoining streets.

These places are appropriately named 'holes', such as 'Dyble's Hole' and others. Many of these 'holes' are to be found in the lower parts of the city, abutting on the river where the ground is constantly damp and moist, while heaps of filth and rubbish, open bins or privies, decaying vegetable and other matters, are constantly contaminating, by their offensive malaria, the unwholesome atmosphere in which the wretched inhabitants live.

Outside the city boundary every species of irregularity existed. Houses were built back-to-back, four inch brick work or lathe partitions separating houses or rooms of buildings. They were of such low quality that on one occasion sixty of them, together with the freehold land, were sold for as little as £600. The interior accommodation was limited and poor, with four or five families often occupying a single house. In one case, ten people were found sleeping in the same room. Many houses were in a wretched condition, being in bad repair, seldom whitewashed, crowded together in great numbers, deficient in light and ventilation and having no ready supply of water. While matters were usually outside their control, the poor did not always contribute to their own well-being. Referring to the yards and alleys, one doctor commented: 'Here reside the most dirty in their habits, personal and domestic; here the combing of wool, carried on in close rooms, by the use of charcoal stoves, is a frequent cause of disease; here the want of water, of drainage and of proper receptacles for refuse most obtains.' Another observed that 'from the negligence of the inhabitants refuse matter was often deposited close to their own doors'.

Very many houses—and not just those in the poorer districts—were totally without any form of drainage communicating with the common sewers. A majority of these were in areas, whether courts, yards or even new streets, which were entirely outside the control of the Paving Commissioners. In the worst districts, where there were 'cottages closely packed together and numerously occupied by very poor persons', surface drainage gutters ran down the middle of the thoroughfare and the liquid refuse was allowed to remain stagnant. The soil of 'necessaries' and the muck of pigsties were carried into the yards to accumulate within a few feet of the doors. There it remained until a sufficient quantity could be collected for sale. In the main, no scavengers were appointed by the public, the refuse being removed by the occupants of the courts and yards. When it *was* removed by an outside source, it was usually done in the daylight by a local farmer in common carts which were far from watertight. Any residue was allowed to sink into the subsoil, causing appalling smells when heat followed heavy rain. The public sewers, such as they were, were very poorly constructed. Consequently, offensive, decomposing, substances accumulated in the receptacle below the level of the sewer, giving off offensive gases which often entered the houses. Such sewers were not trapped and in hot weather their smell was abominable.

A generally bad situation was made worse by a proliferation of public nuisances, including slaughter houses which adjoined people's houses; decaying and decomposing animal remains heaped up in masses and causing an appalling stench; and osier's pits with osiers decaying in stagnant water next to a public road. The situation was summarised thus:

> The system of building outside the town in more prosperous times, and in the most unprepared grounds, cottages for working class accommodation of the very worst description, has proved at all times, but since the decline of its commerce especially, most prejudicial to public health. Here is a concentration of all the evils that can afflict the manufacturer; want of employment and its consequent poverty, crowded and badly constructed habitations, filth, want of sewerage and drainage, an impure air, and want of water. It is here that epidemics make their earliest seizure, that they remain the longest, and that prove the most severe; here also that all other forms of disease appear in their most aggravated forms.

It is not without significance that in the years immediately preceding the investigation the Norwich death rate was higher, on average, than that of England as a whole, the annual figures being 2.5 and 2.2 per cent respectively.

The report of 1844-5 was both confirmed and reinforced by the visit to Norwich in May 1850 of William Lee, a government health inspector, as a prelude to the proposed introduction of the Public Health Act which

Sources of pollution in the River Wensum 1850.

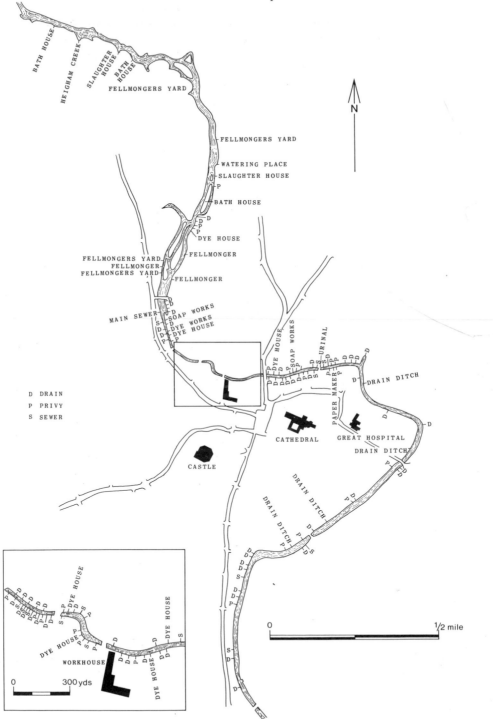

BATH HOUSE

HEIGHAM CREEK

SLAUGHTER HOUSE

BATH HOUSE

FELLMONGERS YARD

N

FELLMONGERS YARD

WATERING PLACE

SLAUGHTER HOUSE

P

BATH HOUSE

D
P
P

DYE HOUSE

FELLMONGERS YARD
FELLMONGER
FELLMONGERS YARD

FELLMONGER

FELLMONGER

MAIN SEWER
SOAP WORKS
S
DYE WORKS
DYE HOUSE

DYE HOUSE

SOAP WORKS

URINAL

PAPER MAKER

DRAIN DITCH

D DRAIN
P PRIVY
S SEWER

GREAT HOSPITAL

DRAIN DITCH

CATHEDRAL

CASTLE

DRAIN DITCH

DRAIN DITCH

DRAIN DITCH

0   1/2 mile

DYE HOUSE

DYE HOUSE

DYE HOUSE

WORKHOUSE

DYE HOUSE

DYE HOUSE

0   300 yds

had been passed two years previously. Lee systematically toured the city over a period of eight days, visiting middle class areas as well as those of the poor, and everywhere finding evidence of a total lack of hygiene and the proper provision of public health facilities. He was able to confirm all that the Health of Towns Commission had reported and more. In particular, he commented on the gross overcrowding of the city's churchyards where there were a great number of bones and fragments of bones scattered over the surface.[7] His major concern, however, was with the city's water supply which he described as 'very bad and very defective—bad in quantity, bad in quality and bad in every thing that should constitute a water supply'. He was equally scathing about the totally inadequate drainage, commenting that 'the city, upon the whole, would be about as well off, or better, without any drainage at all'.

Both drainage and water supply were subsequently the subject of considerable debate, as is discussed below, and Lee's more detailed comments and suggestions for improvement can be more appropriately dealt with when discussing the water controversy and the improvements which were eventually made. Before these debates took place, Norwich was visited by a reporter of the London newspaper, the *Morning Chronicle*, as part of that paper's investigations into the living conditions of the labouring classes in England and Wales as a whole.

The *Morning Chronicle* Reports are effectively a Domesday survey of the conditions of public health in England and Wales in the mid-nineteenth century. Reporters were sent to all parts of the country, both rural and urban, and sent back reports in the form of letters to the newspaper concerned. Norwich was dealt with in two letters which were printed in December 1849 and which were the subject of comment in the local press. They provide a unique and detailed picture of working class life in early Victorian Norwich, and are particularly important for the detailed survey of local factory conditions, the comments on workhouse and lodging house provision and, above all, for the detailed interviews with individual weavers in their own homes.

The reporter visited no fewer than twelve Norwich factories.[8] Between them, they provided employment for some 3,900 people at the time of his visit, whether in the factory as such or, in the case of the handloom weavers and woolcombers, in their own homes. The descriptions he had been given of the manufacturers before his visits were far from good, ranging from accusations of apathy to suggestions that they were at least partially responsible for the enormous poor-rate in the city.

There are not more than a dozen manufacturers, and the majority of these are inert and apathetic. There is nothing in them of that 'go-a-headism' which is to be found in the other large manufacturing towns in the country. Knowing full well that there is always an abundant supply of labour in the market, they delay till the latest moment giving out the work, and until they 'can safely feel their way' as they call it—that is, till they know that some particular kind of fabric will 'take'. The evil arising from the adoption of this course falls with tenfold force upon the unfortunate workpeople. Day after day, and week after week, they are compelled to drag attendance at the different factories, for the purpose of obtaining a supply of work. The manufacturer declines to give out the 'shoot'; there is nothing like constant employment for the people; they are driven to the parish for relief, and the enormous poor-rate of the city—at present not less than £40,000—is the burden imposed upon it owing to the want of energy on the part of the manufacturers.

The reporter was not prepared to rely on second hand information alone, he preferred to see for himself both the type of employment and the working conditions of the operatives. In almost all cases he was offered every facility, and was able to comment in detail on the type of work done, the wages paid to both adults and children, and the conditions in which they worked. Children were employed from as young as ten years old. The very youngest and the learners seldom got more than two shillings a week and in many cases were described as being 'dear at that price'. Older girls could earn up to 4s. 6d., boys up to 9s. 0d a week. Women's earnings varied between 4s. 6d. and 8s. 0d. and men's from as little as 4s. 0d. on average up to 13s. 0d. a week, the latter being paid to 'the best weaver in the city'. Manufacturers varied in their use of the 'domestic system'. The firm of Grout, Martin and Co., in Lower Westwick Street which dealt in silk imported from Italy, India and China, had all its work done on the premises. As the reported noted:

> Every part of the establishment was remarkably clean, and the condition and appearance of those employed were calculated to remove a great many of the unfavourable impressions which some persons might be led to form of the injurious effects of factory employment.

Middleton's factory in Calvert Street, in contrast, employed a number of young people in their homes where they had to pay for winding, beaming, candles and other expenses, costs which reduced their earnings by some twenty per cent. Over a period of some six months, weavers were employed for as little as three weeks to as many as twenty-three, with the average wage, after deductions, varying between 4s. 6d. to the 13s. 0d. referred to above.

Two factories—those of Geary and Sultzer—are worthy of special note for the very obvious care that was taken of the operatives, whether children or adults. Geary's factory in St Augustine's Street which employed about 520 people, was concerned with the production of netted shawls, braces, webbing for shoes, belts and miscellaneous articles of a similar character. His employees included a number of children, and although anxious to avoid taking them too young, was 'constantly pressed by their parents to take the children and give them work'. Many of them had been brought to him 'when . . . scarcely fit to be left without a nurse'. Nevertheless, 'the whole of the children appeared to be perfectly contented, and to all appearance were in excellent health and spirits'. In contrast to many of the weavers in the city, the boys in this factory were assured of regular employment and a reasonable wage while they were learning their trade. The usual practice in Norwich was to take a boy for four years, on payment of a £5 premium, and to pay him a shilling a week for his first year, rising by a shilling a week throughout his apprenticeship to a maximum of four shillings in his final year. Geary's system was infinitely more generous.

> The plan pursued by Mr Geary is to take the boys, without any premium, for four years, teach them their business, and pay them for whatever amount of work they may perform. The boys are regularly indentured and undertake to remain four years; Mr Geary undertaking, on his part, to teach them the trade, and to find them employment during that period.
>
> At the expiration of the term they are at full liberty to stay with their employer, or to seek employment elsewhere. The boys are all kept in constant work, and during the first year many of them earn from 3s. to 4s. per week, while the best and oldest hands earn from 12s. to 14s.

Both Geary and his nephew Sultzer provided an evening school for the adults at their factories, Sultzer, if anything, being an even better employer than his uncle.

> There is no manufacturer in Norwich who exerts himself more laudably for the promotion of the comforts of his workpeople than Mr Sultzer. He has recently built several comfortable cottages in the neighbourhood of the factory for the accommodation of the persons employed by him, and he is now erecting warm baths for the use not only of his own workpeople but for the workpeople generally. In the whole of Norwich there is no such thing as a public bath, and it is intended to give a warm bath and a clean towel to every person for one penny . . . Provident habits are encouraged, as far as they can be, among the workpeople, by the formation of coal clubs and provident societies. Upon the payment of a small sum per week to the coal club, a quantity of coals is sent at cost price to the subscribers at the cheapest time of the year. The object (of) the provident society or club is that of inducing the workpeople who can spare it to deposit a portion of their earnings with their employer, who invests it in separate accounts, and in the names of the individual depositors, in the savings bank. Mr Sultzer (said) he had known great benefit to be derived from this system, as the workpeople were enabled to lay by a few shillings without the risk of its being discovered by their more

improvident relatives who would be certain to obtain it from them when they felt they wanted any little assistance.

A generally favourable account of the factories was concluded by noting that they were remarkably clean, the floors of nearly all of them being cleansed once a week; and that 'there was an air of comfort and cleanliness about the whole of them that contrasted strangely with the wretched habitations of some of the handloom weavers' subsequently visited.

After going on to describe the general sanitary condition of the city in words which suggested a familiarity with the report of the Health of Towns Commissioners, as well as his own observations, the reporter turned his attentions to the living conditions of the people themselves.[9] He provided detailed accounts of nine families, all of whom lived in the poorest areas 'across the water', and apparently also visited 'several others' who lived in similar circumstances. All of the families were united in their appalling living conditions and in the tremendously long hours they had to work to obtain anything approaching a reasonable living. The examples given below are typical of the many.

The first person visited was a gauze weaver living in White Lion Court, St Paul's, a court containing twelve houses, a stable and a slaughter house, with a common privy. Beside it was an open bin into which all the refuse of the court was thrown. The soil from the adjoining privy drained into it and after rain had fallen tended to ooze through the walls, sometimes entering the house as the floor was a foot lower than the ground outside. The weaver who lived here was obliged to work from daylight until eleven o'clock at night. If uninterrupted she could weave 'eleven dozen pieces' per week for which she was paid 11s. 11d. As she had to pay a girl 2s. for winding and had to pay a further 10d. for incidental expenditure, she actually received 9s. 1d. for her week's work. She described herself as a 'privileged person' who was usually able to get work if it was available, but for all that she was usually unemployed for at least four months of the year. Nevertheless, she was able to maintain her four children at school, although at the cost of tremendous physical labour.

A person unacquainted with the process of winding could scarcely form an idea of the quantity of manual labour performed for a penny. The 'dozen' referred to is a dozen skeins, each containing 560 yards, or 6,720 yards in the dozen; and this quantity has to be transferred from the hank or skeins to small bobbins for the shuttle, by means of a small wheel, turned by the hand of the winder. A great loss of time constantly takes place in consequence of the threads of silk breaking, and of the constant change of the bobbins required when full. At the winding it is physically impossible to earn more than 2s. to 3s. per week. Of course, the great proportion of this kind of work is done by young children or old persons; but that is not always the case. The person employed as winder in the above instance was a young woman of eighteen years of age, and she received 2s. a week and her dinner; but in addition to winding she was expected to assist in the household duties, in taking care of the children, and other matters, while the woman was at work.

The reporter subsequently visited a weaver living in Light Horseman Yard, Pockthorpe, a square court containing eight houses. His house consisted of three rooms, one above the other, with a staircase open to the court. The lowest room was occupied by his married daughter, the second was used as a living room for the whole family and as a bedroom for the weaver, his wife and two children, and the upper room was occupied by the loom and used as a bedroom for the rest of the family, eight in number. In this room there were two 'stump' bedsteads side by side. One had a few cords stretched across it, and on both were a coarse kind of sack filled with straw. There were no blankets but each had an old 'coverlid' and one had a dirty sheet. In this instance, the weaver could earn 14s. a week if the children did the winding, but his average earnings were 8s. a week. Expenditure on bread alone came to 7s. or 8s. a week, if the family had all they could eat, and never less than 6s., and, in addition, he had to pay 1s. 9d. a week for rent. Inevitably, this meant relying on credit from time to time. The man's eldest son was unemployed but his daughter, who worked in a factory, was able to contribute something from her earnings. Work was very irregular, and in the week that he was visited the weaver estimated that he would earn sixpence.

The gauze and crape weavers were the worst paid by far, receiving, apparently, three-halfpence per yard while the selling price ranged from 3s. to 4s. per yard. Weavers working in other spheres were marginally better off, but only in the most relative of senses.

The best paid weavers were, apparently, those concerned with 'havel work', which consisted in preparing the havel for the weaver, but when their expenses were deducted their overall earnings were pitifully small. A female weaver summed up her working conditions.

I get for drawing havels for nets or bareges 1s. 6d. per 1,800. I can do two of them in a day with my little boy helping me. That of course is 3s. a day—when you can get it. I pay a girl sixpence a day out of that to give me the 'ends'. But, Lor' bless you, sir, we play more than half of our time. (i.e., are unemployed). Since Christmas I haven't played so much as I did before, because we are always busier after than before Christmas. When I have got no work I am obliged to keep my end-drawer, and pay her just the same as though I was in work. If I wasn't to keep her I shouldn't p'r'aps know where to find her when I wanted her. Take all the year round, I suppose I can earn 7s. or 8s. a week, but then you must take the 3s. off that for the girl, and that only leaves 5s. for myself. When the work comes in I am obliged to work a good many hours—a long time after my husband and children have gone to bed. Ah, then there's extra candles and fire—you must reckon them. I can't tell you how much to set down for them because I don't keep any account.

The weaver concerned was more fortunate than some for her carpenter husband was in fairly constant employment, but her own relatively low earnings were confirmed by visits to other people working in the same sphere.

Shawl weavers had other problems. There was no guarantee that a finished shawl would be liked and this meant that some alteration would have to be made in the pattern, a time-consuming and costly business.

There is no end to the time that is lost in putting the things in harness and altering them . . . The masters appoint a certain time in the day to receive the work, and unless you can get it in by that time, the rest of the day will be lost. Sometimes it takes two or three weeks to put the loom in order, and you are not allowed anything for the loss of time. Sometimes, if you beg and pray of the master, when the pattern doesn't turn out well, they'll give you a couple of shillings perhaps, but that's only as a kind of charity; they won't allow that we ought to get anything for putting the loom in harness.

Under such circumstances, unemployment was inevitably high with corresponding pressure on the poor-rates. Workhouse accommodation at St Andrew's in Bridge Street, (now St George's) part of the old Blackfriars Street, was totally inadequate, with provision for little more than 350 people, young, able-bodied and old being found together in the same ward. Outdoor relief rose steadily from an average of 2,015 people a week in 1847 to a weekly average of 3,389 receiving help in 1849.[10] Many of those on outdoor relief would have refused to enter the workhouse if given the opportunity to do so. Those that did were better fed than many outside its confines. Men received 6 ounces of bread, an ounce of cheese and half a pint of tea for their breakfast, and a similar diet, without the tea, for their Monday and Saturday dinners. Tuesday and Thursday were meat days, each man receiving 4 ounces of meat together with 5½ ounces of yeast dumpling and 12 ounces of potatoes. On Wednesdays 6 ounces of bread were supplemented by 2 pints of soup or milk broth; on Fridays they were given twice the amount of yeast dumpling (11 ounces) while on Sundays they sat down to 16 ounces of suet pudding. Women and children received proportionately smaller amounts. Suppers normally consisted of 6 ounces of bread, half an ounce of butter and half a pint of tea, varied on Tuesdays and Thursdays by 2 pints of meat broth in place of the butter and tea. Such 'lavish' fare irked at least one of the assistant poor law commissioners who asserted that he had 'never seen bread of such fine quality in any other workhouse; it is equal to any provided for my own family.'

The reporter was able to speak in similar positive terms about the Boys' home in St Faith's Lane which provided accommodation for workhouse boys 'entirely removed from the contaminating influence of such an establishment'. All of the boys he saw were looking remarkably well, with sleeping apartments well ventilated, clean and comfortable, and with a diet which was both good and substantial.

In contrast, the lodging house provision in the city was abominable, a fact confirmed by Lee during his visit the following year. The *Morning Chronicle* reporter visited several of these, some during the day, some at night. One which he visited during the day was a public house.

> The house itself was in the most wretched state of dilapidation; one of the windows and frame were entirely gone from the staircase, and as you ascended the rickety and crazy stairs some care was necessary to avoid falling through the large space which was thus left open in the walls. In one of the rooms, used as the sleeping room, were six beds and a 'shake-down' or two on the floor. The window of this room was broken in several places and old pieces of paper, rags, and other materials were used to stop up the holes. The adjoining room to this was occupied by the landlady . . . Two other beds, besides that of the landlady, were in this room, and in one corner, on the floor . . . what seemed to be another bed. Above these rooms was an extensive loft, extending the whole length of the building, the access to which was by means of an old ladder. Upon inquiring, I was told that no person ever slept there, for the end of it had fallen away, and the roof was in such a state as to leave it entirely exposed to the weather. As I could not exactly reconcile the fact of the ladder being there with the statement that it was never used I ascended into the loft to see for myself. So far as the condition of the place was concerned, it was even worse than the description which I had heard had led me to suppose. Upon going to the further end of the wretched place towards what I at first thought a heap of rags, I was surprised to see some movement among them, and upon approaching somewhat nearer I found to my astonishment an old woman lying there. Upon announcing my discovery to the daughter of the landlady, she feigned to express complete surprise, and after a short pause she recollected that 'there was an old woman went up there the day before yesterday, but she thought she was gone'.

Men and women slept together in the same apartments and the place was totally lacking in toilet facilities, a large hole dug in the ground being the sole receptacle for all the filth and refuse of the house. Nearly the whole surface of the yard was covered with night-soil. In the city as a whole, rather more than one-third (220) of the 656 licensed public-houses and beer-shops were known to the police as common brothels, and many of the so-called lodging houses were clearly in this category.[11]

The report of the Health of Towns Commissioners and the observations of the *Morning Chronicle* reporter had painted a stark picture of the living conditions of a majority of the city's inhabitants. They had exposed a proliferation of problems, but common to all of them was an inadequate water supply and a totally inefficient drainage system. (Agreements of 1584 and 1790 had established the city supply of water from the New Mills by a system of leasing the Mills to lessees who undertook to supply the water supply as stipulated in the lease.) Some improvement was made in both of these areas during the next two decades, albeit tardily and, in the case of the latter, under external pressure.

The deficiencies of the Norwich water supply became particularly noticeable in 1848 when fear of approaching cholera focussed the attention of the inhabitants on questions such as drainage and flushing. It soon became apparent that many of the poorer inhabitants obtained their water supply from a polluted river, and that it was from a polluted section of the river that the Water Company obtained its own supply at New Mills. Water was supplied by the existing Company to part of the city only. It was intermittent, unfiltered and consequently impure, and it was noticeable that five of the city's ten public pumps were situated close to adjoining church yards, with all that this implied.

Consequently, a group of citizens proposed to form a new Water Company and the old Company, not being in a position to extend the supply themselves, agreed to sell their works to them. Opposition to the scheme arose, however, not least in some sections of the press, and the promoters agreed to give up their plan to the Norwich Corporation, provided that they would give a guarantee to undertake the work. The Corporation offered money but no guarantee and the promoters therefore determined to proceed with their original Bill.

The whole issue was debated vigorously in the local press, with the *Norfolk Chronicle* supporting the Bill and the *Norfolk News* opposing it. There were issues other than the Water Bill at stake, however. The *Norfolk Chronicle* was violently antagonistic towards the adoption of the Public Health Act in Norwich and supported the Bill in preference to this, while the *Norfolk News* was equally whole-heartedly for the Act.

The *Norfolk Chronicle* argued that the adoption of the Public Health Act of 1850 would be very expensive, and that once introduced 'every sanitary measure would be under the control of three gentlemen residing in London who would see with the eyes of their inspector, and act with his hands'. The paper asserted that the citizens would have to meet much of the cost of any measures initiated by the Act, and that matters would soon be as bad again in the worst districts even if a temporary remedy was effected. The editor acknowledged the need for improved drainage and a better water supply, but considered that these measures could be carried out 'without resorting to the Public Health Act which should never be called into operation anywhere until every other means had totally failed'.

The editor was so antagonistic towards the Act that when dealing with the water supply he made totally contradictory statements within a seven week period. In articles in the Spring of 1850, he initially praised the river, asserting that 'in those parts of Norwich inhabited by the poorer classes . . . an ample supply of water can be obtained from our valuable river, without any expense whatsoever, and it would be unjust to tax either the occupiers or the owners of property in those localities for a necessary of life which they can get with no other cost than a little trouble'. Seven weeks later he stated that 'no subject can be more important as regards the sanitary state of the town than that of a plentiful supply of pure water . . . Without water, it is impossible that cleanliness can be observed, and unless it is pure it is most injurious to health'. He referred to the fact that many of the poor felt the deprivation of water acutely, and that 'during the late visitation of cholera the patients attacked nearly all, if not all, resided in localities where the water they drank was deeply impregnated with the impurities which flow into our river'. The condition of the river was amply illustrated in a later edition of the paper which referred to people taking water from the river near a dye-works. They were said to know what colours were being dyed as well as the dyers. 'They think the brown the best; they say that the black spoils their tea, and so does the scarlet.'

The *Norfolk Chronicle* insisted that a supply of pure water should not be 'clamoured down merely on the grounds of expense', claiming that the highest increase in water rates they had heard asserted would be a trifle compared to the Health of Towns Act. They wholeheartedly supported the proposed Bill.

In contrast in February 1850 the *Norfolk News* was equally strongly against it, considering the measure far too expensive. In their view, the expenditure could only be met by a greatly increased number of consumers or by heavy additions to the rates. It was claimed that there was no satisfactory provision made for those parts of the city which most needed a supply, and that there was nothing to compel the Company to supply water to a new locality until they were guaranteed a return of 10 per cent on their capital. Referring to the Bill's stipulation that a sufficient supply of water would be available to householders able and willing to pay for it, the paper commented that 'money will always command a sufficiency of the luxuries, much more of the necessaries of life. But how are the poor, the very poor, to be secured in the enjoyment of that element to which they are as much entitled as to the air they breathe?'

In April 1850 David Stevenson, an engineer appointed by the Commissioners of Woods and Forests, was sent to report on the Norwich water supply. After reporting that he had seldom seen a place worse supplied with water, he commented favourably on the proposed new Company. The new supply was to be obtained from a place above all pollution, the analysis of the water was favourable, it would afford a sufficient supply for the increased population and the proposed charges were moderate for the locality. He considered that if the proposed measure were carried into effect a 'great benefit would be bestowed on the inhabitants of Norwich'.

The case for a better, and more widely distributed, water supply was brought forcibly home during Lee's investigations a month later. He was particularly concerned with this aspect of the city's public health, and he spent several days touring various parts of Norwich and noting its deficiencies in this respect. In Peafield in New Lakenham for example, (an area built outside the walls after the Napoleonic wars: see map), some

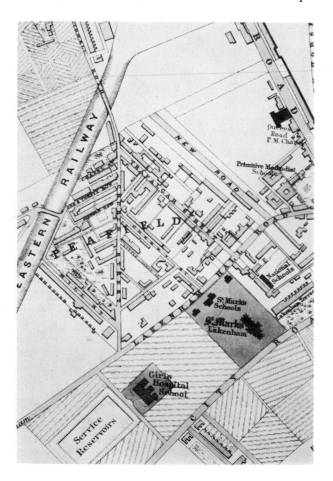

The Peafield area 1873.

2,000 people were provided with only eight pumps and two draw wells. If one pump was out of repair, the others were locked to prevent their use. In the King Street area of Norwich, 19 of the yards had neither pump nor pipe water, the inhabitants being compelled to use the river into which 'all the privies, drains and washings from dye offices, fellmongers, brewers, butchers and water closets had by this time emptied themselves into it'.

The river apart, the worst sample of water analysed during Lee's visit came from the Marquis of Granby public house in Bishopsgate, being described as of a dull, thick and dirty colour with a nauseous taste. Almost as bad was a sample from Cock Yard, St Paul's which had a cloudy colour and a flat and nasty taste. There were exceptions however. The public pump at Hay Hill provided bright and sparkling water with a pleasant and brisk taste while that in Lown's Yard, St James's, was of a bright colour with a tolerable taste.[12]

Lee would have preferred to see the water supply under the control of the local Board of Health; he was opposed to a profit making concern. Nevertheless, the Bill was duly given parliamentary sanction, and although not providing a perfect supply of water was a great improvement on the previous conditions. Samuel Clarke, the Norwich Sanitary Inspector, described it as being very good indeed when examined before the Royal Sanitary Commission in 1869, and he was a reliable witness as will be seen. The *Norfolk News*, defiant to the last, objected to 'having compulsory blessings crammed down our throats', but most people were well satisfied with the turn of events. Even so, as one doctor pointed out to Lee, nothing less than a compulsory supply of water to the cottages would be of any use, for the people would not take it unless forced to do so.

He was probably referring to the expense involved, but it is not insignificant that the Norwich death rate from cholera in 1853-4 was higher, proportionately, than in 1832, the figures being 28.30 per 10,000 and 21.11 respectively, whereas in the country at large there had been a steady decline in deaths from this cause.[13]

Lee made a number of suggestions to improve the state of public health in the city, including the drainage of the meadow land in the Wensum valley to remove the damp and humid atmosphere around it. His main recommendations were that there should be an abundant supply of pure water for every house; efficient drainage of the courts, houses and other buildings; the remodelling of privies and the construction of additional ones where necessary; improved paving of the streets and courts; and improved sanitary cleansing. He also recommended widening of the public thoroughfares, erection of public baths and wash-houses, the closing of the existing burial grounds and the application of the sewerage to agricultural ground to produce a large public revenue.

The only immediate response to Lee's recommendations was the extension of the existing water supply. It took six years to provide a new burial ground between Earlham and Dereham roads and eight before the northern part of the city was drained, but the pollution of the river Wensum remained a potential source of contagious disease until the city's hand was forced by external events.[14]

It should, perhaps, be emphasised that just as Norwich was one of a number of towns with an inadequate water supply, so it was one of the many, throughout the entire country, with a river which was thoroughly polluted. The river Aire in Leeds, for example, was described as being 'full of refuse from water closets, cesspools, privies, common drains, dung-hill drainings, infirmary refuse, wastes from slaughter houses, chemical soap, gas, dye-houses, and manufactures, coloured by blue and black dye, pig-manure, old urine wash'; while the Irwell at Manchester was said to be rising by two or three inches a year because it was so silted up with filth.[15]

The situation at Norwich was made worse by the steady increase in the number of factories after 1850. In 1864 White's Norfolk Directory recorded the presence of extensive establishments for dyeing and finishing manufactured goods as well as several iron foundries, tanneries, breweries, maltings, soaperies, chemical works and brick and tile works. By the same date some 3,000 of the city's 18,000 houses had water

Typical mid nineteenth century housing in north Norwich with outside water closets.

closets and, although this was small by contrast with Manchester where fewer than one-sixth were without this facility, all of them emptied their contents into the river. Not surprisingly, when the City's Surveyor inspected the Wensum in that year he found it to be 'thoroughly and irremediably polluted, presenting all the features of a large sewer . . . All attempts to cleanse it . . . must leave the river essentially unchanged until the causes of its contamination are removed.[16] Between the New Mills and Carrow 120 sewers poured into the river as well as the residue of the manufactories referred to above, these were shown on a map printed in Lee's report (Map II.1). All that was dirty and worthless was thrown into it and surface drains, which continued to predominate in the poorer districts, carried all their animal and vegetable matter into the sewers or into the river itself.

The increased use of water closets, whether in private houses or factories, tended to make a bad situation worse. According to the Norwich Surveyor, the water closets would not ordinarily pollute fresh water, but the Wensum was inclined to be sluggish and slow moving and was incapable of removing such an accumulation of sewage. He urged the erection of two intercepting sewers large enough to receive the whole sewerage of the district, which could then be carried to the marshes into proper depositing tanks prepared for the purpose.

Whatever improvements might have been undertaken, in 1866 the city's hand was forced by being threatened with an injunction from the neighbouring village of Thorpe.[17] The Wensum joins the river Yare just outside Norwich and near the village, and its inhabitants complained that the Wensum was polluting the Yare, and threatened court action unless the matter was remedied. The city sought expert advice, calling Joseph Bazalgette who as Engineer to the Metropolitan Board of Works had had considerable experience in dealing with London drainage problems. It was subsequently decided to undertake a large-scale drainge scheme, at an estimated cost of £100,000, and to use the high land of Whitlingham Farm for sewerage irrigation. On 3rd October 1866 the Corporation applied to Parliament for permission to carry out the work.

When the estimated cost, with the implied increase in rates, became generally known, considerable opposition to the scheme arose, led by a group calling themselves the Memorialists. They used every legal means of opposition—placards, broadsheets, public meetings and letters to the press—and they concentrated their attack on the water closets themselves. They deduced that if an alternative could be found to the water closet system the river pollution would cease, the residents of Thorpe would be satisfied and the necessity for an expensive drainage scheme— and an increase in rates—would no longer exist. The suggested alternative, the earth closet, was hardly new, but it was pointed out that any waste matter could be sold to farmers, thus benefiting the city financially as well as solving the sanitary problem. The City's Surveyor referred to sources of pollution other than the water closet, which would make a drainage scheme imperative irrespective of the use of earth-closets, and he pointed out that in Manchester the installation of earth-closets had led to a loss of £8,000 a year.

The most powerful supporter of the water-closet system was the *Norfolk Chronicle*, and it systematically demolished the Memorialists' arguments, point by point, in a well-argued editorial in March 1868. It pointed out that a congress held at Leamington two years previously had come out overwhelmingly in favour of irrigation; that a Royal Commission, appointed to decide the best way of removing town sewage, had declared that 'dry closets of every form are necessarily a social abomination in a town' and that 'compared with privy and cess-pit the water-closet is a vast improvement'. The Commissioners noted how water-closets had improved the health of towns such as Salisbury, Worthing and London, and how the capital city, in particular, (sewered and water-closetted throughout) had a lower rate of mortality than Liverpool, Manchester, Birmingham, Leeds and Sheffield. Privies, cesspools and cess-pits had been systematically abolished there, and tubular drains and water closets substituted in their stead, but 'in the other large towns named, the local civic authorities have not yet learned so much of sanitary science'. The paper concluded by providing evidence of increased crops grown under irrigation by town sewage at Barking, effectively disproving the Memorialists' arguments to the contrary, and declaring itself to be wholeheartedly in favour of the scheme.

Protests notwithstanding an *Act for the Better Sewering of Norwich* was passed in 1867 and the scheme was carried out and completed at a cost of £110,000 and the delivery of sewage to Whitlingham Farm began on 14th August 1871. The sewers had been badly constructed, however, and instead of being water-tight as they should have been they allowed spring water to make its way through the brickwork. Within a short time the farm was receiving 5 million gallons of sewage a day instead of the 2½ million anticipated, and the whole scheme collapsed. Later the old sewer was repaired at a cost of £18,000 in July 1877 an essentially temporary measure for it had to be replaced at an estimated cost of £78,000 ten years later. Nevertheless, the river had been largely freed from pollution and a drainage scheme, however imperfect initially, had been finally established, albeit one that was still far from perfect where the poorer areas were concerned.

The improvements in water and drainage which had taken place in the two decades since Lee's original recommendations must be regarded as positive achievements, and ones which would have raised the living standards of a majority of the citizens of Norwich. For the very poor, however, conditions remained abominable. Few people appreciated their dilemma, and when occasional light was cast upon them they were almost invariably blamed for the situation in which they found themselves. The

Morning Chronicle reports, for example, were regarded with incredulity by sections of the local press and the *Norwich Mercury* on 19th January 1850 was quick to suggest that the examples provided were wholly untypical.

> '... who would have gone to St James or St Paul's for a generally fair specimen of the Norwich Weaver or his abode. It is true that he would there find the most wretched squalor and poverty—but why? Because it is the resort of the lowest of the low, and the most idle, and the beggars of the city.'

The *Norfolk Chronicle* was similarly sceptical and just as inclined to blame the poor for their own living conditions. At the time of Lee's visit it commented.

> 'On Saturday last we visited several yards and courts in one of the worst parts of the city. We found many of the houses perfectly neat and clean and nothing whatever offensive—but the contrary—about them or their immediate localities—whilst others with the same advantages were complete receptacles of dirt and filth and scarcely fit for a decent person to enter. The former required no sanitary interference, whilst no measure that could be adopted could improve the latter.'

If the conditions of the poor were bad in 1850, whether self-imposed or not, they were immeasurably worse a decade later. By the 1860's the decline of the handloom weaver was absolute and the poverty of the most badly off among them was almost indescribable. Nobody had bothered to investigate their living conditions since the *Morning Chronicle* reports of 1849, and their suffering would have remained largely unknown but for the campaigning activities of the Norwich Sanitary Inspector, one Samuel Clarke. It was Clarke who had provided Lee with much of his information in 1850 and it was to Clarke that Dr Johnson, at least, attributed much of the improved health of the lower part of the town. He now undertook what amounted to a personal crusade against the conditions of the poor and in a series of letters to the *Norfolk Chronicle*, which were published between November 1863 and March 1864, he revealed to an incredulous public just how bad their conditions had become. Over the six month period he provided fifty examples, of which the following are typical.

A family of five had only one straw bed between them. One child was paralysed, another nearly blind. In a similar situation in Coburg Street, a 17 year-old girl and her two brothers slept on a small heap of dirty, loose straw, which was matted underneath like the bottom of a pig-sty, and was rotting the floor through into the room below.

Elsewhere a man, his wife, a son aged 21 and daughters aged 29 and 15 all slept in one room measuring 12 feet by 7 feet 9 inches. The woman and her son were ill with typhus fever, the son dying on a Sunday but being kept in the bedroom until the following Tuesday. The father and sick mother slept in the same room during this time.

In a few cases, the families were at least part responsible for their own plight, and Clarke made this absolutely clear. In Old Barrack Yard, Coslany, for example, he came across a mechanic with a wife and six children. The man earned £1 6s. 0d. a week and gave his wife £1 of this, but the place was indescribably filthy, with the children shoeless, nearly naked and with hair matted and covered with vermin.

In due course, the *Norfolk Chronicle* felt constrained to investigate for itself. As its reporter pointed out on 9th April 1864:

> The condition of the labouring classes, and the means of increasing their scanty share of home comforts, have of late occupied a prominent position among our social problems. Within the past few months the question has undergone a large amount of discussion; it has been talked of at public meetings and argued in the columns of the press, but although enquiry has thus been stimulated, and many startling facts have been brought to light, the question still remains an open one, and we have as yet barely got beyond the confirmation of the saying, "One half of the world is ignorant of how the other half exists".

The *Norfolk Chronicle* reporter attempted to dispel some of this ignorance by systematically touring the city with Clarke and providing much more detail than Clarke had been able to do in his letters. In virtually every case, the reporter came across extreme poverty, with people being underfed, inadequately clothed and with almost a total want of bedding and firing. The examples quoted are too numerous to refer to here, but one may be taken as typical of the many:

> We . . . visited the house of a weaver, named Alden, in Bett's Yard, St Mary's. Here were father, mother, and six children occupying three rooms, for which the weekly rent was 1s. 9d. This was a case of extreme destitution. The husband, who had refused out-door relief, had gone away in search of employment, which he was unable to get in Norwich. The wife and family had received a note for the workhouse; but the woman refused to go there for several reasons: first, that she would be obliged to abandon the few articles of furniture she possessed, so that in the event of her husband returning to Norwich and procuring work, the family would have no home to go to; secondly, because in the workhouse she would be separated from her children; and, thirdly, because if she took the relief so offered, her husband would probably be apprehended and sent to gaol on a charge of neglecting to maintain his family. The straw beds, the scanty clothing of the children, and the generally wretched appearance of the house, made up a scene of more than

ordinary misery. The woman earned a trifle by charring, and said she had been assisted from Mr Clarke's fund. I asked her how she fed the children, and was told that she got them a bit of bread when she could, and sometimes a neighbour would give them a help. She had no idea whether they would have any dinner on the morrow (Sunday); they had none on the Sunday previous; but she added, turning to her little ones, and showing them a half crown which the inspector gave her, "Thank God, you shall have a dinner tomorrow". She had previously received a blanket from Mr Clarke, which she exhibited with some little pride.

While acknowledging the appalling living conditions of the Norwich poor, the newspaper, nevertheless, questioned the necessity of having to provide them with monetary assistance. In the editor's view, this suggested that either poor relief, for which the citizens were being so heavily taxed, was being imperfectly administered, or that the destitute state of the poor was due to their refusal to accept parochial aid. The paper commented that those refusing the workhouse test had only themselves to blame if they were reduced to the verge of starvation.

Clarke noted this aversion when referring to the surviving weavers in Norwich, most of whom were in a pitiable state, particularly those with large families. They were willing to work, but dreaded the workhouse with its separation of father, mother and child. He summed up the position in a letter to the *Norfolk Chronicle* on 23rd January 1864:

'. . . Norwich is filled with poor . . . not merely the lazy and dissolute, but those who would willingly work, could they obtain it, and would eagerly exchange the shuttle for the spade if their exhausted strength permitted, or if they were adequately skilled for the task.'

The shuttle had indeed already been exchanged for the last, if not the spade, some time before. As early as 1840 many were leaving the textile industry to enter the boot and shoe trade which seemed to offer better prospects of a decent livelihood. In 1862 there were 3,000 shoe operatives in Norwich, divided almost equally between men, women and children, and by 1868 the number had doubled. The shoe trade enjoyed a 'boom' period at this time, the Norwich manufacturers making the types of shoe that both public and buyers, in the home and overseas markets, required. In contrast to their predecessors in the textile industry, they did not hesitate to use machinery. Wages, however, were by no means high. As late as 1886 women could only average 3s. per week, and men no more than 12s. In addition, they were obliged to work in old, over-crowded buildings—a fact which accounted for the high incidence of tubercular fever at this time. J. K. Edwards describes the shoe industry more fully in Chapter VI.

Many of the unemployed local weavers made efforts to help themselves. In 1863 a Weavers' Association was formed, and J. H.

Gurney contributed £100 to it from a fund left by his father, J. J. Gurney, to assist in improving conditions of unemployment in Norwich. The weavers negotiated for work, and succeeded, in some cases, in obtaining employment in villages immediately outside Norwich. Inevitably, however, the handloom weaver gradually disappeared, and was absorbed either into remaining silk-weaving factories or into other industries.

The poor continued to be helped by such bodies as the Norwich District Visiting Society, whose activities in the 1840's have already been referred to. The Society relied entirely on voluntary contributions but in the winter of 1862-3, for example, succeeded in giving relief at the rate of £60 per week over a ten week period; all of it to the casual poor who they preferred to help rather than have permanent pensioners. Another association, which was operating early in 1863, proposed to buy up badly drained, ventilated and lighted houses, renovate and improve them and then rent them to the poor. They also hoped to provide a model lodging house. Unfortunately, there is no further record of their activities, which suggests that the project may have been still-born.

The living and working conditions of the poor in Norwich were not ones to hold the permanent attention of the press, and after Clarke's revelations interest in the subject was negligible for a further decade. In 1873, however, under the provisions of the Public Health Act of the previous year, Norwich appointed T. W. Crosse as its first Medical Officer of Health at a salary of £200 a year; and his reports make it abundantly clear that life for the very poor was as grim as ever.

In his first report in 1873, Crosses concentrated particularly on infantile mortality, noting that children under five made up more than one quarter of the total deaths. He attributed this to insufficient and unsuitable food, bad management, indifference to cleanliness, scanty clothing and ill-ventilated houses and the administration of opiates. Where the latter was concerned, cases decreased considerably when parents were informed of the peril. Deaths from diarrhoea were commonplace among children, partly due to the fact that many of them had their food diluted with polluted pump water. Another cause of disease was parental reluctance to vaccination against smallpox, a reluctance which led many of them to avoid registering their children's births.

Two other factors adversely affected the children's health. Wages in Norwich were below the national average, a fact which led many mothers to leave their children at home while they contributed towards the family income. In some cases the children were locked out of the house until their parents returned, in others they were left in the care of an older child who could scarcely look after itself, facts which, at least indirectly, adversely affected their health. The second factor concerned the current policy of compulsory education. Cases of scarlet fever had increased alarmingly, rising from five in 1873 to seventy-eight in 1877. Crosse considered the elementary day school to be a prime factor in spreading the disease. He particularly indicted the system of payment by results, a system in which attendance at school, as well as scholastic achievement, affected the teacher's salary, noting that:

> The fact that the Education Authority makes no allowance for absence from sickness, and that the attendance of children has a direct bearing on the government grant, causes direct pressure to be brought upon teachers and parents to have children at school irrespective of their sanitary conditions.

The problem was not peculiar to Norwich, the South Durham Medical Society, for example, had recommended that the medical certificate system should be adopted, and that children in the same room as sick children should not be allowed to return to school without a certificate to say that they may safely do so. The Society also proposed that a School Board Medical Officer should be attached to, and paid by, every School Authority.

Back of the Norwich Technical Institute (now the School of Art) built in 1899: drainage and hygiene dominate architecture.

Two years later Cross's pressure at national level was rewarded by the passing of the Norwich Improvement Act on 22nd July 1879 under which Norwich, in common with twelve other English and two Scottish towns, enjoyed the power of enforcing compulsory notification of the existence of infectious diseases. In the first year of its operation alone, 858 notifications of ill-health were received, and it led to the detection of many impure and imperfect water supplies and of unemptied bins and other sanitary defects, defects which must otherwise have escaped notice, at least for a time.

The improvements came none too soon. The *Lancet* noted that Norwich had the highest mortality rate in twenty large towns dealt with by the Registrar-General during the period 1870-78. Bye-laws concerning the erection of buildings in the city were frequently broken, unlicensed slaughter houses operated but were never inspected, cottage accommodation was insufficient and privies worse.

There were still hundreds of densely populated yards where the drainage was most imperfect, and where refuse accumulated in choked gutters and badly constructed gratings and gullies. Many districts were ill-sewered and in some there was no provision for drainage at all. The deaths from diarrhoea, already referred to, bore a clear relationship to filth, Crosse commenting that 'in proportion as the sewering and scavenging of any city are well and efficiently done, so will the mortality from this disease become diminished, for it is a disease most characteristic of, as it is most prevalent in, filthy districts'. The paved streets and the footpaths were also in a very bad state. The interiors of the courts and alleys not repairable at the public expense were infinitely worse, being soaked with water and filth throughout the winter. It was noted 'that these evils are very much felt in the lower and poorer portions of the town, and must tell severely on the health of the young who are so much in the streets'.

In 1880 both scarlet and typhus fevers were epidemic in the city, both being directly related to the crowded and dirty conditions referred to above. In the densely populated Coslany district alone, the mortality from scarlet fever averaged 27.26 persons per 1,000. In Platfoot's Buildings in the Heigham Road typhus fever was endemic, attributable solely to the fact that every sink communicated directly with the sewer, allowing noxious gases to escape into the houses from the defective drains, and to the fact that the inhabitants were supplied with impure water from two pumps.

All of the above suggests that the very poor, at least, were affected peripherally, if at all, by the improvements in the city's public health between 1850 and 1900. Somewhat ironically, the health of children may even have worsened for a time with the advent of compulsory education, with pressure being put on them to attend, irrespective of their fitness to do so. The efforts of Clarke and Crosse eased the situation initially, and those of the Medical Officer, in particular, ultimately led to lasting benefits, but the city had to wait until the twentieth century, and wholesale schemes of slum clearance, before anything like a satisfactory system was to emerge.

Public lavatories St Andrews Plain built in 1902.

Notes and Further Reading

The main source for more detailed information and further sources is Pound, J. F. *Norwich Public Health, 1845-1880,* Unpublished B.A. dissertation, University of Birmingham 1960.

1. Gregg, P. *A Social and Economic History of Britain.* 1760-1955, pp. 192-3.
2. Ginswick, J. ed., *Labour and the Poor in England and Wales, 1849-51: Vol. II Northumberland and Durham, Staffordshire, the Midlands* 1983, pp. 141-200, for Nottingham, Derby and Leicester; M. Baker-Read, 'The Public Health Question in the Nineteenth Century: Public Health and Sanitation in a Kentish Market Town; Tonbridge, 1850-57' in *Southern History* IV, 1982, pp. 167-89; see also P. E. Razzell and R. W. Wainright, eds., *The Victorian Working Class: Selections from Letters to the Morning Chronicle,* 1972, pp. 91-323, for *inter alia* Manchester, Halifax, Bradford, Liverpool and Birmingham, and, for an overview of the whole question of public health in nineteenth century. England, Wohl, A. *Endangered Lives,* 1983.

3. Digby, A. *Pauper Palaces,* 1978, p.136.

4. *Second Report of the Royal Commission for inquiring into the State of Large Towns and Populous Districts 1845.* Appendix: Norwich.

5. Numbers of families in yards derived from Page R. A. F. and Palgrave-Moore in Vol. VIII, 1975 & Vol. IX n.d., of *Norfolk Genealogy:* Beverly A. Mead, *Coslany 1851: A Study of the Social and Economic Conditions in a Norwich Ward,* A dissertation submitted in 1978 as part of the requirements for the Certificate in Education.

6. The Morning Chronicle Reports. *The Rural Districts: Norfolk, Suffolk and Essex,* Letter XVI, 12th December 1849. The whole series will eventually be reproduced in Ginswick, op. cit., but the Norwich material has yet to appear in print.

7. Report of an enquiry held before William Lee Esq., Superintending Inspector, of the Sanitary conditions of the City and County of Norwich, with a view to ascertaining the desirableness of the application of the Public Health Act, 1850, p. 62.

8. *Morning Chronicle,* Letter XVI, 12th December 1849, for what follows on factory conditions.

9. *Ibid.,* Letter XVII, 15th December 1849, for the living conditions of the Norwich Weavers.

10. *Ibid.* for lodging and workhouse conditions. According to the Morning Chronicle reporter, there was provision for 355 people in the workhouse. Digby, op. cit., p. 128 gives a figure of 380.

11. Razzell and Wainwright, *op. cit.,* p. 57.

12. Pound, J. F. Appendix B.

13. Lee enquiry, p. 25; Sixth Report of the Rivers Pollution Commissioners, p. 471.

14. Mackie's *Norfolk Annals,* 1900 Vol. II under 1856 and 1858.

15. Wohl, *Endangered Lives.* 1983, p. 235.

16. *Norfolk Chronicle,* 3rd September 1864.

17. For what follows on the drainage dispute, see Pound, *op. cit.,* pp. 58-73.

CHAPTER THREE

Developments in Local Government in Norwich 1800-1900
J. K. Edwards

Foreword

In the hundred years of the Nineteenth Century the population of Norwich, in company with those of many other towns and cities in the United Kingdom, roughly trebled: from 36,000 in 1806 to 110,000 in 1901. The expansion derived largely from the tremendous increases in production which took place in industry and agriculture, allied to new forms of transport (steam power applied to railways, ships, and in a minor way to road haulage), collectively entitled 'the Industrial Revolution'. By these means new employments were created, living costs reduced, and standards of living raised, all highly beneficial developments. Yet, because these innovations collectively increased the rate of social and economic change to an unaccustomed degree, they brought with them many problems—unregulated housing, inadequate water supply and sanitation, an urgent need for better law enforcement, the sheer size of urban populations—each of them a separate facet of 'the social problem'.

To ameliorate their effects, the Central Government with its comprehensive national view had to lead, persuade and coerce the many local governments and city councils into new attitudes and activities. Later in the Century, when some successes had been registered, the local governments maintained the momentum of change by meeting the developing wants of urban peoples—for baths, libraries, museums, parks and gardens—wants that were natural extensions of the earlier needs.

So urban society, and indeed the urban framework, underwent what was in fact, the social equivalent of the Industrial Revolution. In this transformation, the local authority (in our specific instance, Norwich City Council) was both the instrument of the Central Government and also a local (and sometimes unwilling) innovator.

It was often a difficult position for subsequent City Councils and little has previously been written of the ways in which they coped with local needs and with external pressures.

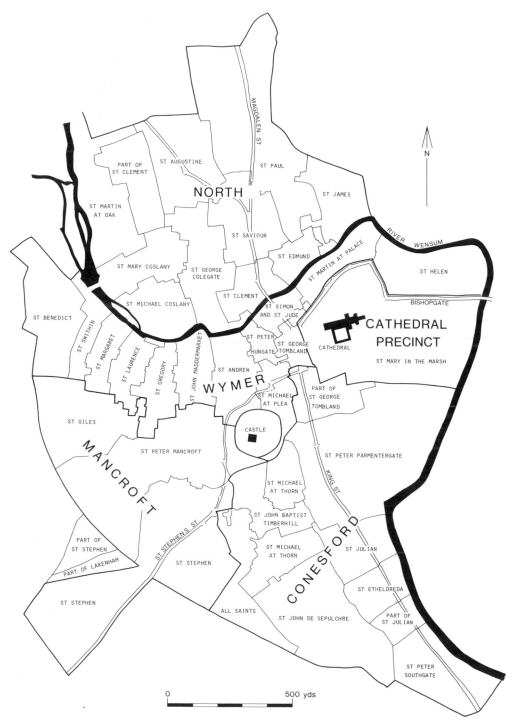

Parishes and Wards in the City of Norwich c.1800.

1800-1850 City Administration

(a) *Before 1835*

In 1800, the governance of the city was in the hands of 'the Corporation' which meant, in essence, that as a body it could collectively own land (mainly within the city walls); could levy tolls in a variety of ways and so derive an income; and it could apply this income as it thought fit to maintain and improve the physical fabric of the city, the walls, gates, bridges, roads, public buildings and so on. As a legal entity, the Corporation was made up of some 3,500 freemen, persons who were 'free' of all tolls, customs and other payments imposed or levied by the Corporation and they were the only citizens, out of the total population of some 36,000, able to vote at local and national elections—for local officers of the Corporation and for Members of Parliament. Freemen, in fact, were superior citizens and very proud of their superiority. It was a distinction they gained either through inheritance as the son of a freeman or by having served an apprenticeship to a freeman, though necessary conditions were that they had to be self-employed (i.e. a master-craftsman) and not dependent on poor-relief.

The elected officers of the Corporation—the Mayor, two Sheriffs, twenty-four Aldermen and sixty-four Common Councillors—formed the two executive bodies: the Mayor's Court, comprising the Mayor, Sheriffs and Aldermen assisted by the Town Clerk; and the Common Council Chamber, presided over by a Speaker with proceedings being directed by the City Chamberlain. The two bodies normally sat monthly but were reinforced, when the importance of the issue warranted it, by Special Assemblies involving the whole freeman body. Clearly, for the time, there was a considerable element of democracy at work.

The appointment, by election, of the officers of the Corporation was also a democratic affair. Within each parish in the city, the freemen elected two Common Councillors for a three-year period, one-third retiring each year. The Mayor's Court elected all new Aldermen (a nice example of a 'self-perpetuating oligarchy' at work) to serve for life, their main duties—as true Senior Citizens—being to elect the Mayor each year, to sit as magistrates, and to exercise patronage over candidates for entry into the many charitable foundations of the city.

From the ranks of the Aldermen, the offices of the two Sheriffs and the Mayor had to be filled, the Mayor being 'the first citizen' and chief administrator and who, after 'passing the chair' became a magistrate for life. To be elected Mayor was, of course, an honour; but it was nevertheless something of a mixed blessing for mayoral expenses were usually high (the compulsory election feast might cost anything up to £1,000) and the official allowance of some £300 was low. Naturally, some thrifty Aldermen opted out of election, preferring to pay the £100 fine instead; but generally the brewers, wool merchants, textiles manufacturers, bankers and insurance-men who were elected proved very well able to bear the financial burdens of mayoral office and may well (it was, indeed, highly likely) have managed to recoup themselves, for after all that was what local government was then all about.

To maintain law and order was perhaps the first requirement of the Corporation's officers. Twelve elected ward constables acted (usually unwillingly) as the city's police force together with a separate night-watch, a small troop of men employed by the Corporation to patrol the city between dusk and dawn each day to ensure the keeping of the peace. There were several Courts: the Guildhall for petty offences; the Quarter Sessions for more serious cases; and the Norfolk Assizes, then held surprisingly at Thetford, for the most serious. Apart from these, the Mayor's Court was endlessly involved in its customary regulations—the Assize of Bread, determining the size of the loaf at the accepted standard price; setting the wages of journeymen weavers, almost an anachronism by 1800; administering the many City charities such as that of the Great Hospital and stimulating and extending charitable endeavour in the city at times of dearth or more seriously, famine. All were then very much a part of everyday life.

The principal activity of the Corporation however, was to maintain the physical structure of the city to ensure that it functioned adequately

The Guildhall. Sillett 1828.

for citizens' needs. Included in this, was the proper upkeep of the banks of the river Yare as far down-stream as Hardley Cross, for many of the essentials for the trade and industry of Norwich came and left by way of the river.

All goods coming by sea into Yarmouth paid a toll to the Norwich and Yarmouth Navigation and, of this, the part received by Norwich Corporation was applied by the River and Street Committee endlessly to the 'depthening' and otherwise clearing the river bed and banks of deposits. Additionally, all goods entering Norwich by the river also paid a toll as established by the Tonnage Act of 1725/6 and received by the Tonnage Committee to be applied to the repair and improvement of roads, streets, walls, bridges etc. Since there was then no such thing as a general rate, these were the only ways in which the Corporation could gain the necessary revenues, which were by no means large—some £1,200 for the year 1800 and varying little during the next thirty-five years.

Financially, however, there was one far greater item of corporative concern. This was the levying of the Poor's Rate (£24,000 was raised in 1800) and the application of the proceeds to the support of the poor—the sick, the aged, the infirm, the feeble-minded and the able-bodied poor, the unemployed. It was a system which penalised the wealthy and provided, surprisingly generously at times, for the 'disadvantaged'. The executive body The Guardians of the Poor set up by an Act of Parliament in 1711 was legally autonomous and separate from the Corporation. Hence, it has to be mentioned but need not concern us further here.

Such, then, was local government in Norwich (and in most other cities in Britain which enjoyed corporate status) at the beginning of the Nineteenth Century, very much as it had been for the hundred or so past years. Revenues, expenditures and corporate administration were all (comparatively) slight. But, then, the population was small, individual effort met most needs, and the thriving textile industry provided both the democracy and the corporate revenues. It was an effective system for its time, one suited to those particular conditions. Nevertheless, it had to adapt as the Century wore on because conditions changed, as in fact they always do. What follows is, in essence, an account of that adaptation.

The first of these changes affected—revolutionised in fact—the Corporation itself and in this the local situation was that of the entire country writ small. Economic developments during the first thirty or so years of the 19th Century created many new groups of well-to-do people anxious for a share in the electoral processes (and, of course, in the perquisites and power which these provided) but who, because of ancient law and custom, were as yet barred from voting. At the same time, a part of the existing electorate, while sharing in the power system, had become degradingly poor and hence unworthy, in the values of the times, of the vote. A concomitant of the existing system was that poor voters became quite as willing to sell their votes to the highest bidder as were the candidates for office willing to bid; electoral corruption, in fact. One example: at one Parliamentary election in Norwich in the early 1830's, £44,000 was alleged to have been spent by candidates on 'pecuniary temptations'. Seeking to remedy the twin faults of the system—unrepresentativeness and corruption—the government set up a Municipal Corporations Commission which investigated electoral affairs in all the corporate towns and this, in 1834, came to Norwich.

Conditions in the city during the early 1830's certainly warranted investigation. The hand-loom weavers, as self-employed craftsmen, were largely freemen; but, alas, under the rigour of economic circumstances were no longer the proud bearers of electoral privilege they had been thirty years earlier. Many, indeed, had been reduced to the utmost poverty and of these there were a fair number—not all, by any means—who were willing to sell their votes. There were, also, in this city that was changing from a heavy dependence on the manufacture of textiles to enjoying a much broader economic base, many affluent people who had no vote and who resented the fact. The city's electoral conditions, in truth, exemplified some of the worst defects in the entire country, as the Commissioners in their Report made clear, while the administration of the Corporation itself was found wanting. So much needed to be changed and was changed.

The Shire Hall. Sillett 1828.

(b) *The Municipal Reform Act 1835*

The Commissioners' Report was published in 1835 and its recommendations passed into law in October, the same year. The privileged status of the freemen was removed, a harsh blow for the many to whom the £5 or £10 collected in electoral corruption made independent living, free of poor relief, possible. Voting lists, polling booths and voting papers were introduced instead of verbal voting in public. All citizens who paid a £10 a year rent obtained the vote, these electing Councillors who, in turn, elected Aldermen and, with them, elected also the Sheriff and the Mayor. Perhaps more important, though, than these democratic changes was the fact that the Council (no longer the Corporation) was empowered to levy a 'Borough Rate' on property, so as to bring in greater revenue and was also compelled to ensure that the Borough Fund Account was regularly audited. Additionally, a Watch Committee had to be constituted with the aim of introducing a police force and finally the new Council gained the power to make bye-laws as part of their stronger powers needed for the better administration of the city.

All told, there is little doubt that the changes in Norwich, as in so much of the rest of the country, had been sorely needed, although there was little apparent recognition of the fact locally. Indeed, there was a considerable and vehement public protest which the government simply shrugged off. It needed only the passing of a few years to demonstrate that the implementation of the Commissioners' Report had ensured the far better government of the city; that it had become, in consequence, far better able to cope with the economic and social changes which were then all too quickly taking place.

* * * *

Improvements and Changes 1800-1850

In its general configuration, Norwich in 1800 retained many of the features of a medieval city, based on and encircling the castle although a number of major improvements had been made after 1750. Most streets were crooked, narrow and cobbled—where they were covered at all—with sea-shore flints, as were the open public areas or plains. Recently completed, a major improvement ensured that many of the principal city-centre streets now had name-plates and their houses numbered; but pavements for pedestrians—'walk ways'— were non-existent as yet except that Gentleman's Walk, to the pride and probable relief of the citizenry, had just been paved 'with good Scotch granate'.

Could we view them today, we should consider the city centre of those times to be grubby if not filthy, even though streets were cleaned fortnightly. The old, narrow, hump-backed bridges were part of the same scene, tending to divide rather than link the inner city parishes. A public water supply from New Mills provided by the Norwich Water

Company existed but it supplied only the houses of people able and willing to pay (and then only for a few hours daily) and there was a scattering of rising mains particularly in the market places. Principally, though, the mass of people depended on the several hundred wells sunk into the chalk underlying the sands and gravels on which the city had been founded, wells dangerously liable to be infected by sewage in places. Even so, Norwich in 1800 typified, both in its better and in its less salubrious elements, the ancient provincial cities of Britain of the day, where no-one was far from, or liable to be forgetful of, the surrounding agricultural hinterland and which were all the healthier for that.

These, then, were the features of the city that the Corporation had to administer and improve. The sources of revenue, the tolls from the river traffic and the rents from land and property, were already by 1800 proving inadequate, even for mere maintenance. To make matters worse, a great urge for urban improvement had begun to grip the country, 'a general spirit for correcting errors and establishing improvements' and had already produced enormous benefits in London and in several major provincial cities.

Since Norwich was one of the most affluent towns in the provinces, a number of its leading citizens clamoured for the same benefits and eventually the idea of improvements gained general acceptance.

To make extensive alterations to the city meant being able to raise much greater income and also to engage in long-term borrowing and for this a special body had to be constituted, a Board of Improvement Commissioners, by Act of Parliament. So in 1805, the Corporation applied for an 'Act for the Better Paving, Lighting, Cleansing, Watching and Otherwise Improving the City of Norwich' and in 1806 were able to set up their Board, each parish in the city electing a member.

When constituted, the Improvement Commission had an enormous task confronting it which meant, of course, spending very large sums of money. Soon after they began work, much of the initial enthusiasm for improvement, alas, disappeared for the textile industry had entered on a period of trading doldrums. Changes were therefore entered on hesitantly and cautiously, very differently, in fact, from the manner in which proposals had been voiced in 1805.

However, some changes were undoubtedly made and in the matter of road improvement one can note an advertisement of the Commissioners detailing the work to be done: 'The present street pavement, which is of concave form with a channel in the middle is to be taken up and re-laid convexedly, with a channel on either side.' For this purpose, 'cobbles from Cromer and the adjacent coast' were to be used while footways were to be built of Yorkshire stones with curbs of Aberdeen granite. A month after the advertisement appeared, contracts had been concluded for paving St Stephen's Street, Rampant Horse Street and Brigg Lane, probably the most used of any in the city. Hence quite a lot may be said for the resolution of the Commissioners in tackling their task, in this respect at least.

To improve road surfaces was only one of their activities and the rebuilding and reinforcement of the ancient bridges, heavily battered by the ever-increasing trade and transport of the late 18th Century, was another, equally important. So one finds that Coslany, Carrow, Foundry, Hellesdon and Fye bridges were either extensively renewed or entirely re-built during the next fifteen years or so, improvements which must have made very heavy demands on the financial resources available.

This was not all. The lighting of the central area had to be improved. At the beginning of the 19th Century, the city centre was lit by some 900 oil lamps, mainly provided by the Corporation (which levied a 'lighting Rate' to cover the cost) or alternatively were displayed by individuals who objected to the levy. The result was a curious (to modern eyes) combination of municipal and individual provision, aspects of which persisted until well into the second half of the Century. Within six months of their first meeting, the Board had not only increased the number of lights to 1,200 but also the hours of illumination and the number of 'lighting nights' in the year. At the same time, the city 'Watch' was expanded to a body of thirty-six officers with improvements in both the powers and the efficiency of the force. This was not a police force, since it operated at night only, but clearly, when added to the improved lighting of the city centre, it helped better to combat night-time crime and to increase citizens' security.

To pay for all these improvements, a rate was levied to raise £5,000 a year; but this would have been grossly inadequate were it not for the 'voluntary subscriptions' made towards the cost of improvements by those householders who benefited largely from them. Thus the paving of Cockey Lane, Little Cockey Lane and London Lane (all of which formed the present London Street) at a cost of £2,040, and the paving of St Giles from the Gates to the Market Place only went ahead when the householders affected had raised, or promised, appreciable contributions.

Despite all this very good work, it gradually became evident that the task of modernising the medieval nature of the inner city was beyond the abilities of the 1806 Improvement Commission. Consequently, in 1825, a new Improvement Act was obtained giving the Commissioners powers to levy higher rates on property and compelling householders to clean the streets fronting their houses. It was at this time, incidentally, that drivers of vehicles were first compelled to keep to the left of the road, a regulation from which one can gain a picture of what the traffic-crowded streets were like beforehand.

Despite the new Act, improvements were introduced at much the same rate as formerly, for the merchants and manufacturers in the city were still passing through a bad period economically and collective resistance to the rate being levied was considerable and frequently bitter. But one improvement did eventuate successfully; the introduction of gas (it was then called 'oil gas') lighting provided by courtesy of the Norwich Gas Company, a private company; and by 1830 some four miles of gas main had been laid to bring a radical and much needed transformation of the urban night scene.

One other aspect of the work of the Improvement Commissioners in those years, hygienically very important although by no means costly, was the improved cleaning of the main streets, although improved clearing might be a more accurate term. This dumping of rubbish, filth, offal and all types of excreta in the gunnels and gutters was perhaps the aspect of urban life which would revolt us today more than any other, with shopkeepers being prime offenders. But little was ever said, for the simple reason that everybody then living had grown up with the custom whereas, we today, in looking back, have known better conditions. Only when it came to be realised that such dumping had gravely deleterious effects on the health of the community, and after the Local Board of Health had been introduced by 1850 at the instigation of the Central Government, was much done to reduce effectively this obnoxious nuisance in city life.

Altogether, if one would dare to pass judgment on the operations of the Improvement Commissioners in Norwich during the period 1806-1850 one would have to note that there was great initial enthusiasm for better things and thus, had economic circumstances been more favourable (and had some leading citizens been rather more far-sighted) then many more urban amenities could have resulted. Economic reality, however, had greater force than enthusiasm and not until after 1850 did it relax cramping rigidities and permit a fuller realisation of the 'improvers'' ideal. The record, in fact, does seem to suggest lost opportunities in some respects. Even so, the city was a better place to live in by 1850 than it had been in 1800 and this we must put, with all their admitted inadequacies, to the credit of the Norwich Board of Improvement Commissioners.

We have noted that as a result of the 1806 Improvement Act the city Watch had been expanded and made more effective while twenty-four petty constables maintained day-time law and order. Little was done by way of building on this foundation during the next thirty years. With the passing of the Municipal Corporations Act in 1835, however, a new Watch Committee was set up and early in 1836 the City Council decided to found a true police force (these were very troubled times) modelled on that introduced in London seven years earlier and held to be highly effective. So it was that, on March 1st, 1836, 'The new police force, in an uniform dark blue dress with waterproof capes similar to those worn by the police in London, went on duty in Norwich for the first time, a force of eighteen men under a single superintendent'.

This still left the maintenance of civil order at night in the hands of the Watch (the council paid for the police, the Improvement Commissioners for the Watch, a curious arrangement!), but even so, for the first time in its history there was 'an efficient force, well disciplined, constantly on duty the whole twenty-four hours'. From the viewpoint of the Twentieth Century, it seems little enough to applaud, yet it was truly a revolutionary departure from ancient custom. So much so that police constables of impartiality and integrity were initially hard to find and the Annual Reports of the Watch Committee during the first years of life of the new force contained not infrequent examples of constables being drunk on duty, of assaulting private persons, as well as of wilful neglect of duty. To some extent, though, this was only to be expected for the concept of a restrained, orderly, disciplined force, doing a job that the army or the local militia had previously done, often with considerable bloodshed, was entirely novel, at a time, too, when heavy drinking was far more widely prevalent than now.

A year later, in 1840, organizational logic prevailed and the 'night watch' became 'night constables', subsequently to be incorporated into the police force proper. At the same time, new regulations were introduced by the Council and for his 17/6 a week the constable had henceforward to demonstrate 'coolness, firmness, promptitude and a perfect command of temper'. And since it was also expected that a constable should 'never suffer himself to be irritated or moved by any ill-language or threats' it may be presumed that his was no sinecure.

Be that as it may, within two or three years after its inception, the police force had come to be recognised locally as something of a beneficial instituion. During the next ten years, its scope, size and efficiency seem to have steadily increased, to number some eighty men by 1851; and it seems clear that the amateurism of the late 1830's had given way to well developed professionalism by mid-Century very much to the benefit of the populace at large.

One last introduction in those years was that of a paid fire-fighting force. Innovation here was much slower than with the police. Partly, this was due to the fact that the fire insurance companies, having an understandable interest in keeping fire damage to a minimum, employed their own machines and crews (on a part-time basis) and provided excellent bonuses for speed and efficiency—30/- for the crew of the first engine at a fire, 20/- for the second, and 10/- for the first person to give warning. Since company crews went only to the premises of that company's customers, and since each of these had to be clearly distinguished, the city has been bequeathed a considerable number of attractive leaden plaques in consequence.

Perhaps more important, however, was the fact that radically improved fire-fighting methods had to await the introduction of a better water-supply and a system of rising mains. Indeed, throughout the entire period 1800-1845 little change took place and it comes as no surprise when reading the Report on the state of Large Towns of 1845 to learn that 'The state of the city's fire engines (there were only two) has long been a great source of complaint'.

Fortunately, pressures from a group of civic leaders were soon to ensure a major change and in 1847 the Council set up a fire fighting brigade (six full-time, eighteen part-time). Total cost: £300 p.a. By the middle of the Century, a widely applauded full-time force was operating; and after the water supply had been greatly improved, in the early 1850's, so did the efficiency of the new force. Not that the benefits it brought impinged very markedly on the collective consciousness of the citizenry, the average rate-payer being then far more concerned with cost than with cost-benefit.

*   *   *   *   *   *

Looking overall at the changes in local Government administration during the first half of the Nineteenth Century, it is easy to believe that the quality of life in many cities was radically improved (even if not transformed) in these years. Even so, the continuing rapid increase in population presented many problems both to the Central and to the Local Governments. Leading figures in the national and local scenes became increasingly aware of some of these—of the need for an entirely new water supply system, of the need for regulations to improve public health and finally of some form of provision of housing for the poor. Many of these aspects of progress, though, were realised only well into the future for the gestation period between the recognition of social problems and their remedies was long indeed. Such efforts, and their whole or partial success, have therefore to be the subject of the second section.

*   *   *   *   *   *

1850-1900: Local Government Organization

In the first half of the Century, a beginning had been made in the task of creating a greater degree of democracy in central and local government elections, in ameliorating some of the worst excesses of free enterprise operating in a totally unregulated housing market, and in providing councils with greater revenues in order to meet their enlarged functions. Nevertheless, by 1850 more than a slight degree of administrative untidiness still existed and the elimination of this together with the expansion of the 'social services' already introduced ensured that reformers would be kept busy. The Central Government had, understandably, a clearer awareness of the problems involved and in the second half of the Nineteenth Century it had to persuade, coerce and compel the local authorities to act, which they did although frequently unwillingly and tardily. Eventually, by about 1900, local government administration, finance and services assumed the forms, more or less, that we are familiar with today.

What applied to city councils throughout the country naturally applied to Norwich Council. Here again, what might be called a lack of willingness was in evidence at times although the familiar demon, economic depressions and the resultant lack of finance, was in evidence until the mid-1870's. After that, though, with conditions improving strongly, local provision of services escaped from the economic constraint and one may note a big step forward in local provision.

The legislation passed by Central Government in the period 1850-1900 forms at the same time not only an impressive tangle but also a tribute to the statesmen of the period. Local conditions varied so much that to make any real headway in improvement the government had to impose standardized conditions—on the police, markets, town improvements and so on—and this it did, with the Local Governments Act, 1858. At the same time, it required that all matters of public health were to be regulated by the Home Office, this again ensuring far greater standardization of conditions. This was the beginning of the transforming process. But there is little point in recapitulating all the legislation of the period. Suffice it is to say that the Local Government Act of 1888 was at the apex of this legislative structure and it compelled Norwich City Council, which had been rather laggard in accepting some of its responsibilities, to take stock of its position.

What the Council saw, it did not much like. To begin with, a confused mass of past legislation had either to be repealed or codified and incorporated into a new coherent whole. Additionally, and perhaps most worryingly, massive alterations and improvements to the quite recently constructed sewerage system (incorporating, alas, much substandard building) were urgently required, at a cost of £80,000. The Castle had to be purchased from the Prison Commissioners, a public library instituted, and a number of bridges had to be bought in order to free them of tolls. Finally, all the loans raised in the past under the Improvement Acts of 1806 and 1825 were still outstanding, no repayment having taken place, to the tune of £233,370. From all of which one can gather that since 1850 local government provision had been transformed, to become very big business indeed.

What the newly realised situation meant, in fact, was that another Improvement Act had become essential. It came in August 1889, a massive and comprehensive piece of legislation—the Norwich Corporation Act—regulating every aspect of public administration: sewerage, drainage, control of infectious diseases, the police and fire services, street work, employment of children and finally, and perhaps most importantly, new powers of borrowing together with the power to issue Corporation stock. An impressive catalogue indeed. In future, too, all

Council revenues were to pass into the hands of one body—the Board of the Guardians of the Poor—a strange choice it would seem today although there were doubtless good reasons for it then.

One can see, therefore, that the Local Government Act of 1888 finally provided local authorities for the first time in the Nineteenth Century with the regulatory powers needed to improve the physical environment and to better the quality of living. For Norwich, it permitted the gaining of the 1889 Act: and as one looks at the powers that this conferred on the Council one can only be struck by the enormous advance it represented.

The period 1850-1900, therefore, was a great one in local government history and truly represented enormous extensions and profound improvements. To use a gardening metaphor: if the year 1850 had witnessed the sowing of the seed of modern local government, some very sturdy shrubs indeed had developed in Norwich by the end of the Century.

*　　*　　*　　*　　*　　*

One last aspect of our study requires to be mentioned: the ever-widening range of knowledge and skill that had to be deployed and hence the increasing numbers of professional people who entered into public service in consequence. In the 1860's the Council relied on the efforts of twelve Committees (Watch, Gaol, Market, River, Tonnage, Finance, Pauper, etc.), much the same as thirty years earlier. After the Norwich Corporation Act of 1889, the number increased to twenty-one, two of which concentrated entirely on finance and borrowing.

Similarly, the numbers of professional employees increased. In 1851, there had been a Clerk, a Surveyor, an Inspector of Nuisances, a Collector of Rates and a Treasurer, all of them new positions. An Inspector of Gas (for the street lighting) and a City Architect appeared in 1865, to be followed seven years later by a City Engineer, a Medical Officer of Health, a Road Inspector, and in 1879 by a Public Analyst. By 1890, a Veterinary Surgeon and a Head Gardener (remarkable indicators, these) had been added, so bringing the complement of Council officers and the range of their responsibilities to a state recognisably modern.

From the contrast between the skill and knowledge drawn on by Councils all over the country with that of, say, before 1845, one can gain some idea of the scope, energy and (it should be said) genius in the central governments of the day. If events and conditions in Norwich could be judged typical of these in many of the towns and cities in the rest of the country, then, change for the better was profound indeed. For all the deficiencies, and these were manifold, urban living by 1900 paid a silent tribute to the legislators and administrators of mid-Victorian Britain who, faced in the 1840's with immensely complex social problems generated by industrialisation, rapid population growth and intensive urbanisation, had made so many provincial towns infinitely better for life and work.

1850-1900: Services

a) *Public Health*

As has been stated already, Norwich was a very different place in which to live, in 1850, than it had been fifty years earlier. Its streets, at least 'within the walls' were paved, gas lit, named and numbered, the bridges had been re-built or renovated, law was maintained by day and by night, and soon there was to be a modernised water supply system in operation. But all these changes were really only the forerunners of others, even more radical and equally beneficial.

These had their source in the setting up of the Paving, Cleansing, Sewerage and Lighting Committee in 1853, whose first job was to reduce and eventually eliminate 'nuisances' from the city streets in the interests of improved public health. In essence, 'a nuisance' was any act that had, or might have, a deleterious influence upon the welfare of the population of the city, and in particular upon public health, and nuisances of the day ranged from permitting the river bank to collapse and so block free river passage, to the use of the many 'dead' wells in the city as sewage pits, the extensive use of 'urinal corners' scattered about the city (there were, of course, no public lavatories), and the emitting of 'noxious vapours' by factories processing chemicals, tallow or manure.

For a Council to seek to control these and similar activities was then looked upon by many public figures as being outrageous interference with individual liberty and in consequence progress to cleaner, less squalid conditions was initially slow. Nevertheless, there does appear to have been a quite considerable amelioration of the dirtiness and pollution in the city by 1870; and even more encouraging to the council officers involved, it would seem that the generality of citizens had by then come to consider that the £15,000 expended annually in these ways was well spent.

It is also true, unfortunately, that so much required to be done and that, since financial resources in those years were so limited, much needing to be done was left undone.

The scope of the improvements required—road widening, adequate provision for the poor, sick and insane, and also for prisoners (for the first stirrings of a new urban social conscience were beginning to make themselves felt)—was so enormous as to make any city council, let alone a Norwich City Council strapped for cash, to think and plan in terms of decades rather than years. So it can with truth be held that more could have been done to relieve the mass of intense poverty and social deprivation that was centred around the unwholesome yards, alleys and courts that were then, and for decades into the Twentieth Century, such obvious blots on the housing scene in Norwich.

Under the Public Health Act of 1872, a Medical Officer of Health had to be appointed. In his first Annual Report, Thomas Crosse the M.O.H. recorded a birth-rate of 32 per thousand (very high indeed; some 10% were illegitimate); also, an infant mortality, similarly very high, that was not the product of insanitary living conditions but rather of parents' ignorance of how best to rear and feed their offspring and of their wilful neglect.

These were not conditions that could be changed quickly. Even so, social improvement there was until by the end of the Century a considerable decline in the death-rate had taken place. But, abnormally high infant mortality persisted despite all that the truly conscientious M.O.H. and his staff were able to do and for this the blame was laid fairly and squarely on the highly imperfect water supply, 'that abettor of filth and a powerful generator of debilitating and fatal disease'. Not until the new water supply and sewerage systems were in operation, from the mid-1890's onwards, in the courts and yards was the scourge of infant and child mortality diminished and alas, not until the 1920's was the problem finally resolved.

b) *Building Controls, Slum Clearance etc.*

A further group of Council activities, radical innovations in the 19th Century, had to be undertaken in order to meet the requirements of Public Health Acts in these years.

These were the regulation of all new building in the city—an enormous step forward in municipal controls—the demolition of some of the worst areas of slum housing, and finally the construction, at rate-payers' expense, of small areas of new housing, not erected as a council investment but rather as a social service. When one thinks back to mid-Century, on the need for ratepayers to contribute towards any urban improvement from which they might benefit and then consider the situation in 1900 in which all ratepayers had to pay to provide housing for impoverished and destitute citizens, then clearly the public conscience had been remarkably strengthened in these decades.

The Council had one great advantage: it owned much of the land 'within the walls'; and when leases came up for re-negotiation it was able not only to veto undesirable developments but also enforce statutory requirements. In this way, as is discussed in the next chapter, some very good housing was early laid down in the city—Victoria Street, the Town Close Estate, the Crescent (Chapel Field Road) being some of the surviving examples—the Council regulating the quality of the building work by stipulating the minimum annual rental as well as minimum sanitary requirements. Granted, such a method was slow; but in the long-term it was highly effective and reinforced the influence of other Council prohibitions.

The gradual involvement of the Council in 'slum clearance' (it had no such name then) derived from the provisions of the Public Health Act of 1872. The difficulties were enormous for the Council could only act through compulsory purchase and many of the old houses and tenements needing replacement were complex legal as well as physical tangles. To take one example only. Two-and-a-half acres in the parish of St Paul's, one of the worst housing areas in Norwich, held 144 dwellings with 38 owners and were occupied by 505 people. Of these, some were willing to sell but most preferred to await arbitration, a long drawn-out process. Finally, the Council had to pay some £11,000 for the buildings before it could even begin to demolish, a sum which could not but fail to displease ratepayers already less than enamoured with the new field of municipal enterprise.

Improvement did come, however; and what is perhaps more impressive is that this type of Council provision stimulated the desire of socially conscious private individuals, prospering in the years after 1875, to participate in this beneficence. In this way, some of the profits from the city's industries were siphoned into charitable housing estates and cottages let at low and subsidised rents. Once again, industrial enterprise, religion and practical philanthropy came together to the advantage of the less fortunate people.

c) *Other Activities*

In the first half of the 19th Century, the principal improvements effected to the roads and streets of the city had been the transforming of dirt thoroughfares without side-walks into wider, straighter streets having cobbled or granite-sett surfaces. Even by 1850, though, it is likely that dirt surfaces were still widely in evidence, particularly in the newly-built 'estates' thrown up, outside the walls, without any of the then-considered essential amenities. In consequence, cobbling, flagging and kerbing continued as a major (and expensive) aspect of improvement for decades after 1850, it being only in 1863 that Gentleman's Walk, London Street and Davey Place were first laid with '3 inch blue York flags, complete with new kerbstones'.

However, the weight of traffic, the cost of road maintenance, and the endless difficulty and expense of clearing the streets of the enormous depositions of horse-dung, bore increasingly heavily on the rates. It was a national problem, of course, and eventually science and invention were able to help reduce the burden, permitting the introduction in the 1870's of wood paving and of macadamised road surfaces to replace the cobbles and setts. London Street was once again in the van, being experimentally wood paved in 1874 and not long afterwards the Haymarket, Rampant Horse Street, Brigg Street and the Market Place had all been re-covered. So successful was the introduction (and so much cheaper was it to clean the new surface) that by 1883 most of the main streets of the city centre had been re-surfaced, at the then enormous cost of £24,000. Great though the outlay was, much had been recovered within ten years as a result of economies in street cleaning.

Apart from this, the widening of thoroughfares was the principal aim of improvers in the last decades of the Century, many of the main roads, such as St George's, Colegate, being given a new and lavish width of 36 feet. In consequence, most of the streets in the central city area of an age-old narrowness, had been widened and straightened by 1900 to become roughly as we know them today.

* * * * * *

Little of consequence remains to be told before the saga of municipal development has been fully recounted. The changeover from oil to gas lighting during the early 1850's brought its benefits for thirty years, after which scientific innovation permitted the substitution of electric lighting, more effective and cheaper, for the gas early in the 1880's. The police force, so revolutionary an introduction in the 1840's, was subsequently subject to six decades of improvement and expansion. More importantly it shed the semi-amateurism of its early years and, under the pressures and guidance exerted by the Central Government, came to full professionalism, with greatly improved standards of pay and conditions of employment. The same things can be said of the fire service whose activities were greatly facilitated and made more effectual by the installation of scores of rising mains.

These were not revolutionary changes: rather were they the product of the process of consolidation. But they did bring a recognizable modernity to the face of the city (and into the lives of the citizens) which the succeeding eight decades have not entirely obscured.

* * * * * *

Epilogue

In 1850, Norwich was a relatively small city whose eonomic past may have been glorious but whose future was highly uncertain. It was a city burdened with large numbers of poor, with extensive areas of dilapidated and congested housing, and one in which unemployment, dirt and disease were rife. Its local government, although reformed very much for the better in 1835, continued nevertheless to be dominated by the bitter antagonisms of 'party spirit' by which it was open to accusations of ineffectualness and even at times to the recrudescence of corruption.

And the entire expenditure of the Council upon the administration of the city, on physical renewal and improvement, and on the support of the poor, was equal only to a little over £1 per head of population.

As an employer of paid labour and as a provider of social services, the Council in 1850 was negligible; in which, of course, it differed little from provincial towns and cities in the rest of the country. The city still had a relative plenty of open spaces (relative that is to most of the industrialised towns, located in the Midlands or in the North West) and might still have been described, as it had been in the 17th century, as 'either a City in an orchard or an orchard in a city'; but for many of its poorer inhabitants it would seem to have offered only intermittent employment at minimum wages, little of that, and not much of anything else.

By 1900, after the passage of little more than a single generation, it had evolved into a city and into a society that were very different indeed. Disease and mortality rates had fallen steadily and appreciably; the entire urban area was healthier; the population had expanded; the proportion of poor to the total population had diminished and the general living standards of the majority had risen. The economy of Norwich had developed a new and intimate contact with the rural hinterland of the city and had benefited from the introduction and growth of many new activities and industries. Its local government, far more democratically elected than it had been in 1850, had left much of the party spirit behind and seen the last of corruption some thirty years earlier; and it had come to employ specialist professional workers able to give its amateur, part-time decision-takers knowledgeable advice over a wide spectrum of interests and activities.

Granted, some things were far from perfect. Slums existed extensively as John Pound has shown in Chapter I and slum clearance and council house building on any significant scale were decades in the future. Yet an initial small scale project had been completed, an earnest of more to come and in itself this represented quite revolutionary changes in the attitudes and philosophies of the past.

On the credit side, the city had adequate (as then considered) police and fire services; many of the streets and thoroughfares in the central area were macadamised, paved and drained and had footways on either side; and they were lit, dimly perhaps to the eyes of today but brightly to those of contemporaries reared on illumination by oil or gas. Many professional officers were at work in safeguarding the interests of citizens even though the inadequacy of their staffs permitted the continuation of abuses for many years to come. Finally, a free library, the Museum, and the several parks and gardens all bore witness to local government provision for the less worldly aspects of communal living and of individual development.

All these things made Norwich in 1900 a city and society vastly different in its actualities and, perhaps more important, in its potentialities than it had been fifty years earlier; and as Norwich was in no way unique or remarkably different from many other towns and cities in Britain, the national aggregate of all these processes of improvement at work during the latter part of the Nineteenth Century must have been enormous.

Although great credit must go to the central governments over the period, part must also go to the private sector whose individuals, by their initiative and wealth-seeking in industry and commerce, generated the prosperity which paid, by way of rates and taxes, for urban improvement and for social provision. Some of the credit must also be allowed to the spirit of the times, the philosophy of the Victorian middle-classs who embraced ideals both of hard work and of social obligation.

As in the Eighteenth Century, the possession of wealth brought its owners (at least, some of them) its responsibilities and the development of local government administration and services in these years provided a channel by which the ethic could be translated into practice.

One further point needs to be made. By 1900, Norwich City Council (supported by central government grants and subsidies) had developed into an socio-economic organisation operating on what was then a very large scale, using massive funds and directly and indirectly therefore employing large numbers of people. There were scores of such local Authorities in Britain in these years, all taxing, borrowing, spending and employing in the same way and in some cases to a much greater degree. Clearly, by the later decades of the Nineteenth Century the public sector—even if one considered only that embracing local governments—must have constituted a highly significant and dynamic part of the total national economy. It formed in fact a most socially useful complement to the private sector, extracting a portion of its profits and with this supplying services that the private sector could not or would not provide for those elements of society which it—the private sector—itself employed and benefited from. Herein perhaps lies a not very widely noted significance of much governmental legislation and of much local government initiative in these years. It is one which may well help to account for the high level of economic activity and of prosperity that the country enjoyed from the 1850's onwards.

*   *   *   *   *   *

Development of Local Government

Electoral Reform

Webb, S. & B. History of Local Government, (Manor & Borough), II; Commissioners' Report on Municipal Corporations 1835.
Assistant Commissioner's Report on the Conditions of Hand-loom Weavers, II, 1839.
Bye-Laws, Norwich Board of Health, under the Local Govt. Act, 1858.

Norfolk Chronicle, 8 April, 1871. Proposals for Local Government Reform.
Preamble, Norwich Corporation Act, 1889.

City Improvements

Mackie, C. Norfolk Annals, 2 Vols.
Evidence, House of Commons Committee on the Norwich Improvement Bill, 1839.
Proceedings, Norwich Board of Health, 1858-1872.
Recommendations of the Watch Committee, July, 1890.
Report, Watch Committee, 'Rules, Regulations & Instructions for Norwich Police', 1840.

For a complete account, see Edwards, J. K. unpublished typescript, 'Developments in Local Government Organization & Services in Norwich, 1800-1900'. Norfolk Local Studies Library.

CHAPTER FOUR

Nineteenth Century Norwich Houses
Stefan Muthesius

Norwich likes to stand aloof from the rest of the country. Is this also true for the history of its houses? By the nineteenth Century regional differences in housing were subtle ones. Perhaps the most important characteristic of Norwich was to take the English characteristic of low-density housing to the extreme: in no other major English town can flats and multi-occupation have been so unusual before 1930.[1]

The second remarkable feature in the history of Norwich housing is that there are few exuberant Georgian and Regency terraces or crescents. This not only applies when we compare the city with towns which were about to overtake Norwich in size, or with the famous watering places which drew residents from further afield, but even in comparison with smaller provincial centres, like Exeter, Shrewsbury, or even Lewes. East Anglia was behind generally as regards urban development during that period, and so was its coast; yet, when its seaside towns such as Lowestoft did begin to grow rapidly in the 1840's and 50's, terraces were built which immediately outdid anything that could be seen in Norwich. From 1800 to 1830 Norwich grew by a rate which was very respectable by national standards, 37,000 to 61,000 and we hear of a great 'building boom' between 1819 and 1826 and of the shift of capital from foreign investment into that of local bricks and mortar[2]—but it still did not result in much that could be called spectacular in architectural terms. It seemed that outsiders did not tend to invest in or reside in Norwich; business was entirely local.

Early Suburban Residences

Suburbanisation was a slow process.[3] It is difficult to define it properly. Obviously we cannot deal here with the old hamlets around Norwich,[4] nor with the self-sufficient country house and estate in the proximity of the city, such as Mousehold House built for the Harveys, an old landed family in Thorpe.[5] Another subject which would merit a separate study is the history of gardens and gardening: Norwich was known for the lavish provision of greenery for all classes. This essay is concerned with the houses built for those who worked in or near the city centre, but lived at some distance from their work and commuted at least once a day; those who had previously lived above the shop or workshop, or close to the factory. Probably the most important part of the definition of suburban life is increased communication, which included movement between the suburbs themselves. Roadmaking was, in low density conditions, almost as important an activity as building the houses.

What makes a small country house just outside the city a 'suburban' home? Perhaps Eaton Grove in Newmarket road, built c.1820 was a case in point:[6] it was owned early on by Horatio Bolingbroke, Norwich wine merchant, and occupied by Edward Willett, a manufacturer in Pottergate. Clusters of medium and smaller suburban houses usually grew along pre-existing major roads. Probably the first of these groups, just outside the wall, were those in Bracondale, singled out for praise by Stacy in 1819. More significant is the group of varied and comfortably sized houses at the corner of Newmarket Road and Mile End Road: for instance the corner house was planned in 1828 and is well preserved; it contains a first floor drawing room, servants' stairs, a room for a butler, two stables and a piggery, but, in all, its size is well below that of the houses previously mentioned.[7]

One of the chief reasons for suburbanisation was social segregation. Certain parts of the suburban land became reserved for the best classes of inhabitants. For reasons hard to pinpoint, the southern and western sides generally became the preferred ones. In the 1820's and 30's the north western side of Newmarket Road gradually filled up. On the other side lies Norwich's most exclusive residential area, the Town Close Estate. For centuries the land belonged— and partly still does—to a City charity, serving the Freemen of Norwich and their dependents. It is bordered on the other side by Ipswich and Eaton Roads.[8]

Norwich from the southwest between Unthank and Newmarket Roads. The Town Close Estate is to the right with small villas at the top and larger villas nearer the camera in the Albemarle Road area. In the background is the Unthank development and some remaining areas of the earlier small houses between Rupert Street and Union Street. (With permission of the University of Cambridge Air Photograph Collections.)

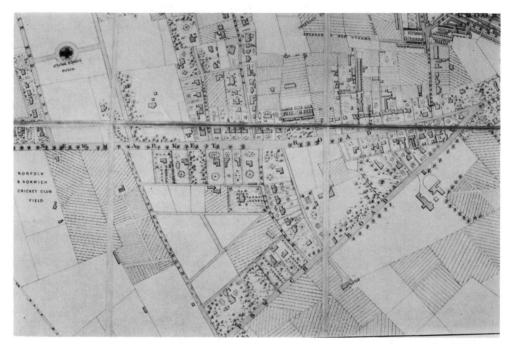

Town Close Estate. The early half of the Town Close Estate (1873) between Ipswich Road and Newmarket Road. "New Road" is now known as Limetree Road. From Morant's Map.

The first major development seems to have started in 1840 with the leasing of numerous plots on the south side of Newmarket Road, stipulating that houses should be of an annual rental of at least £20. This procedure was usual practice (see below); it is a convenient shorthand for the sizes of houses and, in this case, indicates a comfortable house at the medium to lower end of the middle class range, with one servant, this was only a fraction, for instance of the £120 value of Eaton Grove. In 1842 the road was turned into the tree lined avenue it still is and most subsequent houses were built of a size well above the initial £20 stipulation; later £50 houses were demanded. Gardens were, and are huge, an acre or more. Although progress was slow—there are still empty plots today, the area must be considered a success in terms of the initial aspirations, something that cannot very often be said about the planning of high class areas in the nineteenth century. It is probably fair to say that Norwich's most continuous area of middle-class housing between the wars in this century, east of Ipswich Road, still owed its success to the Town Close Estate nearby.

Next to Newmarket Road the somewhat smaller houses in Mount Pleasant developed, mostly in the 1840's and 50's. Albemarle Road came later, in the 1860's when things were also beginning to stir in Christchurch Road. By that time numerous other similar, but smaller, suburban groups of houses had been built, such as Heigham Grove and Thorpe Road; the latter an area for which we have a detailed investigation by Geoffrey Goreham.[9] Some of the architectural elements of the houses will be returned to later on.

It has already been said that Norwich lacks large terraces. Thomas Ivory's speculation of four huge, still surviving, terraced houses in Surrey Street of c.1760-69 was an oddity, in architectural and practical terms.[10] The same accommodation could be had in a much more convenient way, plus a large garden, in a suburban villa. In one of the two major examples of terraces in the 1820's, the Crescent, the builder John Bunn was given twenty years to complete 18 houses (which indicates how slowly growth in Norwich was expected in those years). In the event he did build them rather more quickly, from 1821-1826.[11] The houses, of a rental value of £30 and above were inhabited by accountants, solicitors, and merchants. They have three reception rooms on the ground floor, four bedrooms on the upper floor, plus attic, kitchen and ample service rooms and some also had a stable. The rather smaller houses in Newmarket Terrace Nos. 49-69 of the same period (£24-£30) have the same type of accommodation, though rooms are generally rather smaller. That splendour is relative is indicated by the fact that such a rental in London indicated the average lower middle class house. Below comes the somewhat earlier terrace on the north side of Sussex Street (£16-£18), still large enough to be singled out for praise by Stacy. With Richmond

Earlham Road: a pair of semidetached houses, c.1830. Note the fine Regency ironwork.

Place at the top end of Bracondale dating from 1817 (at £12), we reach the infinitely more frequent type of the lower middle class/better artisan type of dwelling.

The Small House: Earlier Period—before 1860

Norwich far outstripped other Eastern towns in the provision of small houses for its workers. Here speculative building reigned supreme. Virtually all of the houses of this period have been demolished by now and it is difficult to imagine what life was like in and around those tiny dwellings.[12] Furthermore, the pattern of finance still needs to be reconstructed. Only their general shape is clear from the maps and from some illustrations. Because Norwich is one of the oldest industrial towns the first groups of small houses were built, as in Nottingham or Wakefield, behind the older houses in the main streets. Hochstetter's map of 1789 already shows a great number of the so-called courts or yards, in reality narrow passages, containing strings of 10, 15 or more houses. By 1900 over 700 such courts of all sizes existed in Norwich. They contained single room dwellings of £2-£3 annual rental value, but mainly 'one up, one down' houses renting at £3-£5 per annum. When this sort of housing spilt outside the walls, as in Pockthorpe ('uninteresting . . . thickly inhabited by the poorer classes'[13] according to Stacy) this did not cause the arrangement to be any different. Many houses in these yards were accidentally 'back to back', that is, one row backing on to the next. There were also a substantial number of 'purpose built' back to backs. Only the remains of one row—hardly recognizable—has survived, at the north end of City Road (Nos. 27-33). No other town outside the North and the Midlands had such a number of back to backs and such a variety of court arrangements.

Next came houses renting at £5-£7, with 3 and a half or 4 small rooms and giving out to mostly communal yard or gardens. These tended to be outside the old city walls, sometimes quite a way beyond the built-up area, such as Mill Road and Mill Hill to the North of the city and built about 1820 and long since disappeared. A few much later examples of this type of development and with larger houses have been preserved: Rose Valley, begun probably in the 1850's, Ice House Lane c.1830 onwards, Jubilee Terrace, City Road, of c.1872. Characteristic is the lack of proper street access for some of the houses, which provides a link with the old 'court' system; on the other hand almost all these houses have a front and a back access in the normal way, whereas most houses in courts—and, of course all back to backs, had only one 'front' and one entrance. Jubilee Terrace formed part of the large holdings of small houses by the Colman firm for their workforce. They included houses of very low rentals and it is improbable that they were actually built by the firm. Although Colman were well known for their paternalism and their

Oak Street: this section of the 1885 Ordnance Survey Town Plan (sheets LXIII 11 7; LXIII 11 12, scale 1 cm approx. 68 ft. or 23 m) shows the 18th and early 19th century development of small houses in yards behind the older houses along the street, contrasting with the more regular larger houses in Sussex Street and the regular later, smaller houses in that area.

philanthropy, their housing cannot be compared to the well known nineteenth century industrialists' model colonies like Saltaire which also helped to proclaim the identity of the firm.[14]

By about 1820 speculators began to create larger and more ordered estates of houses in the £4 to £8 range. Crook's Place, west of St Stephen's Road, probably built by the Quaker doctor J. Crook, comprised about 250 houses along three wide streets with long front gardens, but rather narrow shared yards. Union Place, adjoining to the North west, probably of a slightly later date contained about the same number of houses, but the layout was different: about 30 houses each were drawn around a rectangular inner court. The third major area of this kind was called Peafield, in New Lakenham, around Trafalgar Street, and Southwell Road, with rows of houses, some carrying rather mechanical names, like 'Twentyone Row'. A much more special case which still survives was that of Railway Cottages near Thorpe Station, built in the 1840's to a very unified and rather ornamental design, though they share with the contemporary small houses the wide open court.[15]

Above these categories came the houses of £6-£8 annual value: almost all of them were placed along proper streets, with separate rear access to, increasingly, individual yards; around West Pottergate and the numerous smaller streets between Ber Street and King Street. The old non-street access was rare after the middle of the century. In 1879 a builder in Lakenham was told by the City that approval of his plan for a row of cottages depended on constructing a roadway along the front, instead of a path.[16] By contrast, Great Yarmouth carried on with garden-path access to most of its new smaller houses until the end of the century.

The Small House and Speculative Building: 1860-1910

Norwich's houses for its workers of the 1820's to 50's can be parallelled with the textile settlements of South Lancashire in the same period. Later on, most of the Northern and West Midlands towns carried on with the earlier types of houses. Norwich houses, became, on average, larger and corresponded more to the patterns of Northampton and Leicester, towns with a similar industrial structure. There is, of course, far more information about these houses, and many of them are still in use. The increase of over 10,000 houses in Norwich over that period is nothing spectacular given a population increase from 75,000 in 1861 to 122,000 in 1910. More significant is the proportion of small houses: about 7,000, Norwich was still a working class town, but there was now a far greater differentiation within that class. Housing was closely linked to this. According to Hawkins (1910) and a Board of Trade Report of 1908 into Working Class Rents etc. about 10% of the population lived in the older 1, 2 and 3 roomed dwellings.[17] These were largely the casual and

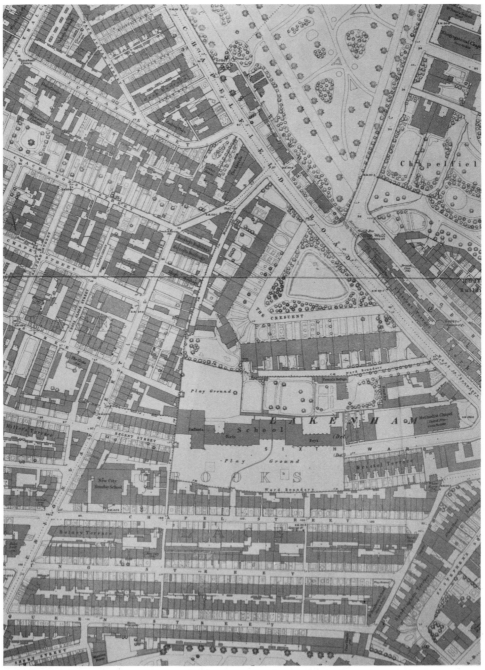

Lakenham, from the same map (Sheets LXIII 15 2; LXIII 15 7; scale 1 cm approx 80 ft. or 26 m). Crook's Place shows the first attempt at an ordered layout of small houses; Union Place presents a different solution. The later houses in Julian Place, off Chapelfield Road are examples of the garden-path access type.

Whitehouse Yard, Trafalgar Street: Typical of the higgledy-piggledy developments of the earlier 19th century. Note the primitive casement windows. Photo 1937 by City Engineers prior to demolition.

Jubilee Place, City Road, c. 1870—formerly part of Colman's housing for its workers: a late example of the garden-path access arrangment.

unskilled workers, the poorest courts still being extremely squalid, as is shown in Chapter II. A larger proportion of about 13% lived in the slightly more modern 4 room houses built in 1820's to 50's; the rest of Norwich inhabitants lived in houses with five rooms or more; this included the 6,000 houses with 3 bedrooms, 2 living rooms, plus kitchen/scullery built in the period under discussion. The majority would be of £8-£10 rental for skilled workers generally; the slightly better and mostly newer houses at £9-£11 for the 'better paid artisan', almost reaching the borderline of the lower middle class house. Rents in Norwich were generally low, lower than in the Northern Industrial cities, and houses had more space around them; rents were also much lower than those of London dwellings, although houses in the South East were larger, which resulted in much multi-occupation—something that was rare in Norwich.

There were also qualitative factors at work: Hawkins echoes a general nineteenth century opinion when he states '. . . factories with their constant work and enforced discipline have reacted favourably on the social habits of the work people'. One of the results was their greater willingness 'to pay for a better article' as regards the home, though this was a 'striking change of demand in all classes'.[18] In fact, the building industry supplied rather too many houses: by 1911 there were over 1,500 empty houses in Norwich, mostly, though, in the middle-class range. The economic and financial performance of the building of suburban houses has lately been studied in some English towns, though not sufficiently to pinpoint clear regional characteristics.[19] Like most provincial towns, Norwich showed largely freehold developments, in contrast to the London method of leasehold—though in the nineteenth century this did not seem to produce any significant difference in the housing pattern. In an East Anglian context Norwich is characterised by the very large and unified speculative developments, in contrast to the seemingly more hesitant performances in Ipswich and Peterborough. The main agents in any given development were always several; the original ground landlord, the owner of agricultural land who had to decide when to sell or develop. Next came the speculators in a narrower sense of the term, the builders or surveyors, now called the 'developers', who undertook the actual layout and saw to the streets and sewers. In some cases they also built most, or all of the houses, but usually the land was divided into smaller plots for the smaller firms of builders. There were also the solicitors who usually found the backers, those who lent money to the undercapitalized builders. Finally came the landlords who invested in a group of houses large or small; as in the case of the lenders, they were tradesmen, spinsters, sometimes banks and other institutions. The vast majority of dwellings in the nineteenth century were rented. Finally, estate agents began to play an important rôle, at first mainly in the administration of groups of houses owned by 'absentee' landlords.

Perhaps the development of the older part of what is now called the Sandringham General Improvement Area can be taken as a typical example (see opposite). Most of the land was owned by Robert Blake Humfrey, one of the more important gentlemen landowners around Norwich, himself a resident of Wroxham. Easily accessible between Earlham Road, and Dereham Road, as well as from Hangman's Lane, as Heigham Road was then called, the land occupied, in terms of status a middling position between the mostly small houses in West Pottergate and Dereham Road and the better houses in the Southern direction. Houses in these roads were developed first, like Earlham Road Terrace of 1858, (the bay windows were added by George Skipper in 1889). By 1859 the layout of Belvoir Street and Stafford Street had been determined. Various smaller builders put up the houses in Belvoir Street, and the south ends of Gladstone and Alexandra Roads in the following years.

In late 1861 Humfrey sold a larger tract to one builder-speculator, Stephen Howlett Meachen. Meachen came from a modest background, born 1817 as son of a husbandman in Yaxham near East Dereham; his name crops up in the 1850's in some speculations in Napier Street. He laid out the streets, constructed some fences and parcelled up the plots. Although he must have seemed a fairly influential figure at the time, he does not appear to have made a fortune for himself, as he lived in quite modest houses, for instance No. 32 Gladstone Street, a house somewhat larger than the surrounding ones and curiously rising above the roof line of its neighbours. He built about 60 houses himself in the area, i.e. much of Alexandra Road and Gladstone Street. The second most important builder was the young James Youngs, founder one of the most important Norwich building firms. However important Youngs and Meachen were, in Zipfel's Terrace in Alexandra Road they, in conjunction with more builders, came badly unstuck, they had to give up several times, defaulting, until the small houses were eventually built. Each time they had to go back to James Winter, a very influential solicitor, who finally also lent the purchase money for the five houses to Bernard Zipfel, a clockmaker. Nevertheless, within a few years Gladstone Street and Alexandra Road were filled with relatively neat houses, rented at £7-£9 a year by workers, craftsmen, salesmen and the like.

Another larger, slower development occurred east of Unthank Road, beginning with Essex and Trinity Streets in the 1850's and ending with Bury Street in the 1890's. Clement William Unthank dealt somewhat differently with the development in that he himself sold off parcel by parcel, large or small, to the Norwich builders. With the great building boom in the late 1890's came a greater concentration. A typical man of the large-scale, streamlined operation was G. Fitt, architect, surveyor, builder, estate agent . . . His 42 identical houses in Anchor Street between Pockthorpe Brewery and the Cavalry Barracks (now demolished) formed a single development. This new tendency is clearly visible in the generally more unified look of houses, e.g. in Portland Street or Marlborough Road. Another important new development was the trend towards pre-cut building components such as lintels, supplied by a more efficient building supply.

Rosemary O'Donoghue has shown that there were other factors which brought standardisation at the bottom range of new houses.[20] At first it was the original ground landlord who wanted to ensure standards as high as commercially possible on his land in order to secure his, or his successors' profits. This took the form of covenants inserted into the contracts for the sale of the land to builders but to which not only the

A map of what today is named the Sandringham General Improvement Area, showing the major areas of development and the smaller plots for individual builders. The large block, covering most of Gladstone Street, Belvoir Street and Alaxandra Road was sold by W. B. Humfrey to S. H. Meachen in 1861. Denmark Road, now Sandringham Road was built slowly from the 1860s into the 1880s. The large development of Connaught Road, St. Philip's Road, Stafford Street and part of Edinburgh Road was begun 1877 by the Winters (Jas. O. Winter, H. Burton Winter, M. Ann Winter). Helena Road followed around 1890. Curfew Terrace was planned 1897 by Arthur J. Chambers.

builders, but also the future inhabitants and buyers of the houses had to adhere. We still find them in our deeds sometimes. The covenant for the builder of the Crescent has already been mentioned: with a detailed list of materials it amounted to almost a building specification, doubtless shaped after metropolitan building agreements and building acts. In the 1820's this was a sign of modernity in the provinces, for the best kinds of houses; but after the middle of the century the practice of detailed covenants spread to the smaller new houses as well. These covenants are by far the best written source about the houses. The crucial stipulation is a simple one: the house must be a house and nothing else, not a workshop, no bone boiling etc. This is why shops and pubs are now usually found at street corners only, and it marks the beginning of modern town planning, that is, the planned separation of functions. Similarly, the country was kept at bay: no husbandry, no pigs. In most cases there is a stipulation about the size of the house expressed in the annual rental figure. There are further details concerning the facade of the house and the orderly treatment of the fence and garden gate. Even the kind of material could be specified for small houses: like white brick and slates for the front.

The second method of enforcing standards was created by central and local governments, the bye laws—today mostly called building regulations. Their concern was not with the beauty of the facade or the social status of the inhabitants, but with health and safety. Every builder had to obey, and the fact that they could be enacted and enforced was a result of the general concern for health after 1840 about which John Pound deals in Chapter II. The chief stipulations were a minimum room height of 8 feet, and 150 square feet of open space at the back of each house: this meant that new back to backs were forbidden. Norwich's first housing Byelaws followed the Local Government Act of 1858; the revised set of 1888 was very much longer and dealt especially with drainage (see Chapter III for more detail). Builders had to hand in plans to the municipal authority for approval—the beginnings of modern building control. Today, these plans, available from 1877 onwards, form a major source for the history of buildings. The basic shape of the 'bye-law house' was, of course, not new, but it was the small scale variations and developments that mattered, as even small variations in price and rent would make a difference as to the saleability and the prospective class of inhabitant. Saleability is an essential point in this context: not only were the new laws enforced, but people could also afford the new kinds of amenities—after all there were enough substandard older houses available for those who could not. It would thus be simplistic to say that the new features in the house were simply brought about by the bye-laws.

Inside these bye-law houses there was a major change in the positioning of the stairs, away from the cramped steps leading up from the back room, to the straight flight of stairs between the two main rooms of the house. Front and back room were now of the same size, which, among other factors encouraged the use of the front room as a parlour—a pattern that has remained in many houses until today. Even more sensitive and varied were the areas at the back of the house. The outdoor coalshed helped to keep the house clean. Almost all new houses had a scullery added to the kitchen/living room. Every house was now built with its own toilet—but Norwich was one of the more old-fashioned towns in adhering to the 'privy' or earth closet in many areas for a long time, even into the 1920's (see Chapter II). The water supply also varied, with pumps shared by several houses in the lower-class areas. Finally there was the problem of access from the rear: in contrast to the hall-entranced or basemented houses in London inaccessible from the back, Norwich provided back access for every new house. There were many variations of this arrangement: the principle being, the smaller the houses, the more people had to share the back access. Later on in the century many smaller houses, especially in North Norwich adopted the spacious back alley, something that had been the rule in Lancashire for some time.

Apart from the early part of the Sandringham Area and the Unthank developments already mentioned small houses sprang up in all parts of Norwich—even within the old walls, as in Esdelle Street (St Augustine's to Magpie Road). On the north side of Dereham Road much was built during the 1870's and early 80's: Orchard Street to Devonshire Street, which have now all disappeared and further out Livingstone Street, Connaught Road and much of Edinburgh Road and Stafford Street built around the 1880's. On the northern fringe Magpie Road and the Wingfield Estate were building, or just starting around 1880. In the south Harford and Cyprus Street were exceptional in that they have only very narrow front gardens and completely open shared yards. The later 1880's brought much activity again, e.g. around Swansea Road off the Avenues and Ella Road off St Leonard's Road. The boom around 1900 brought a vast increase of houses, of up to 800 in one year. By far the great estates were built on former Church land, around Spencer Street in the north—the largest unified district of small houses in Norwich, and Warwick Street to Glebe Road in the South West, engulfing the smarter College Road.

The Medium-sized House

Changes in law, structure and availability were less decisive in the houses for the middle classes than for those in the working classes (although there were more variations of plans). There had almost always been proper street access and a separate rear access. Houses always had hall entrances, though the smallest type meant a corridor only along the front room. Upstairs, 3 bedrooms were the minimum, all separately accessible,

107

A typical view of the streets north of the City, built around 1890.

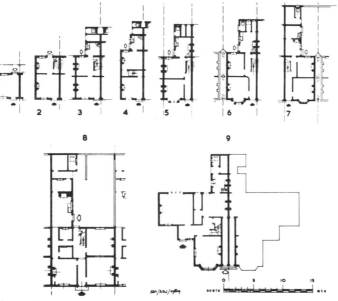

Ground floor plans of 19th Century houses in Norwich:
1   The smallest type of house, the "one up- one down"; hardly any examples are left today (Barrack Street, Lion & Castle Yard).
2   The smaller one of the two room deep-type with four, or rather 3½ rooms.
3   The same type is enlarged by an extension at the back.
4   The stairs are now placed in the centre, between the two main rooms. The house is now larger, but narrower.
5   A very important step up: a hall entrance, but in this case only along the front room.
6   The small version of the fully hall-entranced type.
7   A larger version with a larger back extension.
No 1 dates from the early 19th Century, Nos 2-3 from early to mid century; Nos 5-7 all date from the late 19th Century, but strict time brackets cannot be given for these types.
8   A house in the Crescent, Chapelfield Road, 1820s.
9   Half of a Semi-detached house, Newmarket Road, 1890s.

108

unlike the smaller houses, where the third, back bedroom could in most cases only be reached through the middle bedroom. Throughout the nineteenth century, there was an increase in bedrooms—in line with the greater desire for privacy generally. Most of those 3 to 4 bedroomed houses (sometimes the small box, or dressing room at the front also counted as a bedroom) had servants; very occasionally even families in the better working class houses had one servant (as in the case of Henry Salmon, Scripture Reader, 92 Alexandra Road). In Chester Place, with houses a little larger than the minimum middle class standard and built in the 1860's, the number of servants varied between one and three per house. Indoor bathrooms on the bedroom floor only became common in the 1890's, for instance in College Road, upstairs W.C.s can be found occasionally a little earlier: the best houses traditionally had portable baths prepared by the servants. Thus the majority of the lower middle classes at least had to use, like the working classes, the outdoor W.C. and only possessed the most primitive kinds of portable baths. But then their back extensions were far more generous than those of the smaller house; increasingly from mid-century there was a kitchen and a scullery, and the kitchen could be used as a breakfast room, so that the main room at the back of the house could be reserved as the exclusive dining room. There were very few larger terraces with basements and a third storey, so common in most Victorian towns: Norwich did not seem to need them; though many houses have attics. There simply was not the demand, as the large proportion of empty middle class houses afteer 1900 demonstrated.

As a rule the better class house in Norwich was built in the old fashioned way along the main suburban roads. Dereham Road, Earlham Road, Unthank Road and Thorpe Road, and to a lesser extent the northern main roads, were lined from about 1850 onwards, with small groups of terraced houses and semi-detached ones which at this early stage were not treated very differently in plan from terraced houses. The 'next best' houses are invariably found off these main roads, for a short stretch, before small houses take over again. We can observe this in Essex Street, Trinity Street, Cambridge Street, as well as in St Philip's Road and Connaught Road from about 1850 to 1880. Housing that was almost exclusively lower middle class and upwards was provided in what was initially called the 'Heigham Lodge Estate', laid out in 1877 by one of the best architects in the city Edward Boardman[21]—though it probably took very much longer to build than anticipated. The streets were at first called Grove Street East and Grove Street West, but as there were already so many Groves in Norwich, their names were changed into Clarendon and Grosvenor Roads. A near success was College Road, created from about 1890 onwards rather rapidly and in novel architectural dress—to which we shall come back—only a very small number of houses of the non-hall entranced type was built.

Middle-class houses, terraces and the narrower kind of detached and semi-detached ranged from about £12 to £30 rental. Houses above £40 were usually detached villas. Here servants could outnumber their masters; in many cases there was a coach house. Albemarle Road and the Town Close Estate have already been mentioned. Totally unsuccessful was the projected 'Park Town Estate' South of Earlham Road of 1860 by the already mentioned W. B. Humfrey.[22] Wellington and Havelock Roads later filled part of the land; but smaller villas did succeed in Park Lane during the 1860's and 70's. Later on it was characteristic for these houses to be situated not on the main roads, but on quiet side streets; Lime Tree Road, Town Close Road or Christchurch Road for example. The desire for privacy and separation developed into one for seclusion. By the end of the century a new possibility for the very desirable residence emerged, this was to live in the country, and commute to the city, and this marks the end of the story of suburban Norwich proper. From the late 1870's we find the first Norwich middle-class residents in Brundall with rail access to Norwich and no doubt other villages followed soon.

Building Crafts and Architecture

The Terrace, the Villa, the Cottage not only refer to types of practical living and building, but they also belong to the realm of architectural traditions and styles, and they carry meaning derived from general concepts of living or social status. So far, we have discussed houses in purely practical terms; what could be afforded by whom. Now we must turn to some considerations about the external form and decoration of the houses. Many would argue at this point that the design of ordinary houses could only come under 'building' not 'architecture'. But there is no doubt that many of their features are at least derived from 'High' architecture; it was their execution which was subjected strongly to the particular local conditions of materials and the building trade.

A very detailed hierarchy evolved in Britain during the seventeenth and eighteenth centuries regarding all aspects of architecture and building; in London one dealt with actual 'classes' of buildings. At the bottom were structures, built roughly of localized materials, in our district flint and thatch. By the middle of the century these 'primitive' methods had been completely phased out in Norwich. The forms and proportions of those buildings were usually low and squat. In 'better' buildings they had to be more vertical; the 'best' classically derived proportion of windows was 1 to 2. There was a whole range of 'classes' regarding the main features of houses, windows and doors. Most primitive was the small casement window, occasionally still to be found at the back. Then there was the sash window placed flush with the wall, and its smarter version, placed further inside the opening. By 1900 the two former kinds of windows were almost completely phased out, even in small houses. Doorways could carry anything from a simple, somewhat rickety hood to a full scale Classical portico with columns and entablature. Most important in the general appearance of the house was of course its size and height; most rooms were now considerably higher than they had been in the houses of equivalent status in previous centuries. We nowadays tend to admire the geometry and 'simplicity' of those square facades—which sufficed for villas and terraces of up to high middle class standard until the 1880's; but we must not forget that the very size and the evenness of brickwork did not come about 'automatically' as in much modern architecture, but required costly organisation and careful execution. After all only the facade was treated like this: 'Queen Anne front, Mary Ann back'.[23]

Norwich appears conservative particularly because of its strong brick tradition. No place in England was further away from good building stone. Stucco, so popular in the south from c.1820 to 1860, was very rarely seen in Norwich. (A notable, late, exception is St Phillip's Road—doubtless an attempt to strengthen the smart tone of the street adjacent to lesser houses—which by that time had acquired some sign of class by using grey brick on their fronts). Wooden decor was still belatedly fashionable for ornamental doorways in the 1820's (e.g. Newmarket Terrace), but by 1840 it had to be phased out in better houses and by 1860 even in smaller ones. Furthermore, Norwich lacks Regency ironwork. No doubt the brick trade thought there was no need for stucco or wood because the smooth, uniform and lightly coloured facade could be created with a new kind of brick, variously called Grey or Suffolk White, but normally produced locally. Holkham Hall and Shottesham Park, two major Norfolk houses of the eighteenth century had made it fashionable, but it was very rare in Norwich before the 1820's. Victoria Street, parallel to Queen's Road, of the 1830's is still mostly of red brick.[24] By 1840 the covenants of the first houses of the Town Close Estate in Newmarket Road specify it for the front. Other very fine examples are in Heigham Grove. The chief ornament of the larger facades is the 'reveal' by which is meant a projection, half a brick thick, around doorways and corners. For arches and window heads there was 'gaged' work, that is specially burnt bricks shaped in a concentric form with very thin joints. In general the joints between all the bricks of the grey fronts are narrower than in normal brickwork, which makes bonding with the rest of the walls a difficult matter. It must be stressed that this kind of brick facade, which found its way to the smallest houses, e.g. in Gladstone Street by the 1860's, seems unique to Norwich in its precision and its frequency. A related characteristic is the way front and back, grey and red bricks are always carefully juxtaposed, even when it comes to different parts of chimneys, where those are seen from the street or the back respectively.

However, from the 1850's a new method of brick ornamentation gained acceptance (at first in Lowestoft); bricks were now moulded individually into various ornamental shapes, which would run along cornices or as rustication around corners. Many of the earlier houses, of the 1860's belong to this style. A greater variety of this kind of decor can be found on Irstead House, Cotman Road of around 1870. Somewhat similar are the houses at the west end of Cambridge Street of the early 1880's, which are also reminiscent, with their high mansard roofs, of what in London was called the 'Second Empire Style'. Only very rarely indeed did styles other than Classical find their way into ordinary houses; Curfew Lodge in Earlham Road of c.1830 and the now destroyed 'Hatter's Castle' in Chapelfield Road of the 1850's were perhaps the major exceptions. There was a vast gap between the fashions practised within a select architectural world and common local building practice. One only needs to compare the latter with a house like the Canonry in the Close and its sophisticated High Victorian Gothic constructional poly-chromy, a house that was by no means extravagant in size or overall cost.[25] Occasionally we find builders taking up more carefully the ideas of constructional polychromy—that is colour variety achieved with the help of natural materials—in lesser houses, as for instance in Christchurch

Heigham Grove, a house of c.1840. The method of framing arches and panels is called "reveal"; all arches, whether square or round are constructed with "gaged" bricks. The precision of this work seems unmatched outside Norwich.

Cotman Road, Thorpe: a villa probably of the 1870s, typical of the more varied kind of brick decoration of the later 19th century.

Carlton Terrace, Surrey Street, early 1880s; the decor with thin stone bays, as well as the presence of a basement are untypical in Norwich, and reminiscent of London terraces of that period.

Road. By about 1880 came an important reversion for all better class houses: red brick had been rediscovered in Chelsea and Kensington by the Queen Anne Revival and Kensington Terrace in Unthank Road of 1880 must have seemed like a new stylistic programme in those years. Again, there are not many houses, that took up the other important elements of that Revival, its curious squat proportions and softly curved gables. No. 13 Ipswich Road of 1887 is perhaps the best example in Norwich. The decorative, moulded brickwork is now much finer and more individual in its motifs and usually coloured bright red and sometimes incorrectly called terracotta. The firm of Gunton's of Costessey was particularly known for this work, though its occurrence in medium and smaller houses is rare. The only major road sporting the Queen Anne Style, intermixed with cottagey elements, was College Road, dating mainly from the 1890's.[26] For the smallest houses stone decor

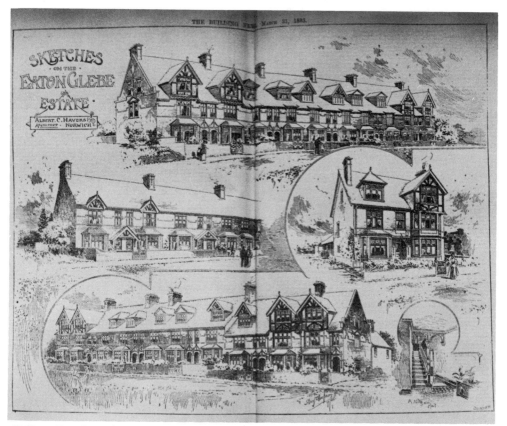

College Road, a view contemporary with the building (From *Building News*, March 31 1893). There is a much greater variety of treatment and use of "cottagy" features, like half-timbering.

seemed to have become cheaper, as it was probably brought in ready cut by rail. Finally brick on the facade lost out when half-timbering and pebble dash became more widespread after 1900; another cottagey technique was tile-hanging. A major example of this style is No. 13 Limetree Road of 1908-9 by the young London architect Morley Horder, a follower of Voysey and Lutyens.[27]

A house in Limetree Road, 1908 by Morley Horder (London): an asymmetrical plan with the most reticent treatment of the exterior.

The plan and style of the medium sized detached or semi-detached house had changed dramatically. Until the 1880's villas subscribed to the time honoured formula of a central doorway flanked by windows or a baywindow. Rooms at the front were as high as could be afforded. Now, after 1890-1900 houses—the term 'villa' is no longer liked—were low, irregular and often rambling. A steep roof became, once again, an important feature. There is no real 'facade' any more. Classical houses can be irregular and rambling at the back, but then one was not supposed to see that side. The desire for grandeur, the Classical tradition of vertical proportion and square outlines, had gone. Instead, motifs, the look of the house were taken from older, more primitive buildings, from cottages and manorhouses. With Classical styles, there was never a strong distinction between town and country or suburb; with the cottagy style suburbia had found its proper mode of expression. It was argued that this style should and does combine with modern living, the commuter's convenience. The argument has gone on ever since.

How to Research the History of a House:

It is rare to have all the major sources available: Deeds for some aspects of the history of the house, including finance; Directories for indentification and dating, Rate books ditto, plus the rental figure; Census enumerator books (1841, 1851, 1861, 1871, 1881) for details about the inhabitants, Advertisements for sales in the Newspaper often give detailed descriptions; Maps for dating and the basic shape of plot and houses; Building Control Plans (also called City Engineer's Plans) are available in Norwich for virtually all houses from 1877 onwards.

Notes

1. According to the Census, 168 people lived in flats in 1911.
2. Stacey, J. *A Topographical and Historical Account of the . . . City of Norwich*. London 1819, p. 65.
3. See recently F. M. L. Thompson (ed.) *The Rise of Suburbia*, Leicester 1982 and Arthur M. Edwards *The Design of Suburbia*, London 1981; Muthesius, S. *The English Terraced House*, London and New Haven 1982; Brunskill, R. *Houses*, London 1982.
4. See Rye, W., Short Monographs on Norwich Hamlets, 1917.
5. Built mainly in the 1820s, see Gorham, Mousehold House, 1969 (MS in Norwich City Library).
6. For some aspects of the history of the house, now part of Norwich High School, see Mottram, R. H., *A Speaking Likeness*, London 1967.
7. By Self, G. S., surveyor 1828; plans in Norfolk and Norwich Record Office.
8. Collection of Proceedings and Cuttings in Norwich City Library.
9. *The History of Thorpe Hamlet*, Ms. 1964 Norwich City Library.
10. See Wearing, S. *Georgian Norwich, its Builders*, Norwich 1926.
11. The Crescent History Group, *The Crescent*, Norwich 1978.
12. For some information about the houses and their then inhabitants see the Norwich Town Clerks' Slum Clearance Reports of the 1920's and 30's (Dr N. W. MacMaster drew my attention to this source).
13. Stacy, Op. cit., p. 16.
14. Further houses built by the Colman firm; the long terraces facing the Green at Trowse, and a model village at Corton, Lowestoft (Information David Butcher).
15. Day, M. 'Railway Cottages, Norwich', in *Transport History*, Vol 12, 1981 pp. 74-77.
16. Building Control Plans No. 195.
17. The 'Cost of Living Report' (*Working Class Rents, Housing, Retail Prices and Standard Rate of Wages in the United Kingdom;* Report of an Inquiry by the Board of Trade 1908; Command No. 3864 CVII. Hawkins, C. B. *Norwich, A Social Study*, London 1910.
18. Hawkins, pp. 25, 76.

19. See Thompson, Note 1, Dyos, H. J. *The Study of Urban History*, London 1968; Daunton, M. J. *House and Home in the Victorian City, Working Class Housing 1850-1914*, London 1983; O'Donoghue, R. 'A Victorian Suburb: Some Aspects of Town Planning in 19th Century Norwich', in *Norfolk Archeology*, Vol. *XXXVIII*, Part *III* 1983, pp. 321-328; see also C. W. Chalklin, The Provincial Towns of Georgian in England, A Study of the Building Access 1740-1820, London 1974.

20. See O'Donoghue, above.

21. Building Control Plan No. 27; this, of course, did not necessarily mean that Boardman designed the houses.

22. D.S. 255 Norfolk and Norwich Record Office.

23. For the Georgian style in housing see J. Summerson *Georgian London*, London 1945.

24. Lucas, R. (University of East Anglia), Norfolk Brick, 16th-19th Centuries (in progress); A. Clifton-Taylor, *The Pattern of English Building*, London 1972; see also in E. & W. Burgess, *Men Who Made Norwich*, Norwich 1904.

25. By J. H. Brown 1862. Today an old people's home, situated near the east end of the C.o.E. Cathedral; for aspects of Victorian architecture see Dixon, R. and Muthesius, S. *Victorian Architecture*, London 1978.

26. Other notable Norwich architects, active in housing, were Scott, A. F. and Skipper, G. (e.g. Nos. 55-61 College Road by the latter, 1891).

27. Phillips, R. & Weaver, L. *Small Country Houses of Today*, London Country Life, 1911; Richardson, M. *The Crafts Architects*, London (RIBA) 1983.

Acknowledgements

The author wishes to thank in particular the Norfolk and Norwich Record Office and the Norfolk Local Studies Library, as well as the City Rating authorities for allowing him access to rate books, and to A. D. Johnson for his drawing of the plans.

Special thanks are due to Robin Lucas, Barbara Miller and Rosemary O'Donoghue. But far more than to books and records the author is indebted to so many owners and occupiers of houses who willingly let him look at their houses and their deeds, who, I am sure, wish to remain anonymous.

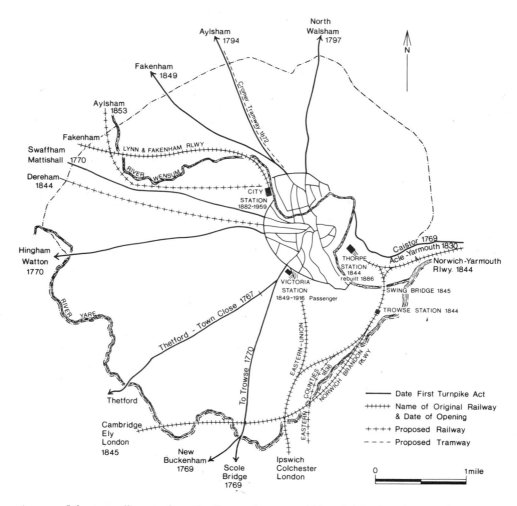

A map of the turnpikes roads and railways that served Norwich in the nineteenth century.

CHAPTER FIVE

Transport and Communications in the 19th Century

J. K. Edwards

Any account of the development of transport and communications of Norwich during the 19th Century is interesting in its own right for it demonstrates how a city with a quickly growing population—as so many English industrial cities had in the period—necessitated ever more effective links with its hinterland and markets. But more has to be considered than mere growth and speed or change of form. For the principal economic activity and that which supported the main bulk of the employed people—the manufacture of worsted fabrics—was in acute competition with the textile products of other areas, the cottons and silks of Lancashire and the woollens (and later worsteds) of the West Riding of Yorkshire. Communications must always provide the life-blood of urban aggregations of many scores of thousands of people; but if these economic links come to be relatively worse, by reason of inept or inadequate change, then the competitiveness of the city's economy must be threatened. Any account, then, of transport changes in Norwich and its hinterland must make some reference to those in competing industrial regions and in sum one can divide the 19th Century into two: pre-railway, when the forces of change operating on roads and canals, worsened the relative position of Norwich; and post-1850, when the building of the railway network, however tardily done and however sparsely operating, slowed the process of economic decline and even went some way to reversing it.

* * * * * *

At the beginning of the 19th Century, Norwich was a bustling city of 30,000-35,000 people, all needing to be fed, clothed, housed and provided with raw materials to work on. The feeding, clothing and housing needs were met without much difficulty, from local needs: from the easily accessible agricultural hinterland which supplied foodstuffs, animals for traction, wool, for coarse woollens, leather, timber, barley (for brewing), to name but a few. The several deposits of brick-earths around the city provided the bricks (pantiles had to be imported, though), and paper came from the several rural water mills within easy reach.

But many other essentials had to be imported—coal, iron, brass, glass, pottery, linens, and more besides. The list is a long one indeed. The most important of all were the supplies of fine, long staple wool used by the principal and almost the only large employer—the manufacture of worsted stuffs, and it is the modes of transport of these and of the equally essential movements to the various markets of the rolls of manufactured worsted cloth that 'transport and communications' most particularly applies.

Norwich in 1800, and for several previous decades, had depended heavily on three main lines of communication. The first was that which linked the city's main industry to the sources of the raw materials. For a century at least, the sheep farmers of Lincoln, Leicester and Northampton had supplied enormous quantities of fine, white, long-staple wool essential in the manufacture of worsted stuffs using the rivers and other waterways of the region. Down the Great Ouse, the Nene, the Welland and the Witham went thousands of packs of wool each year, going either to Lynn direct or else via Boston. Thence they went either overland to Norwich or by coaster to Yarmouth and so up the Yare. After they had been processed into manufactured stuffs, many of them travelled in the reverse direction so that a highly economic two-way trade developed on a considerable scale.

The second route was to London where large quantities were bought by the East India Company or else were exported to Rotterdam and thence throughout the length and breadth of Europe from Russia in the north to Iberia, Italy and Turkey in the south. But the miles to London, the first stage of their long travels, were often difficult, sometimes dangerous and always costly. Coastal traffic between Yarmouth and London was small by 1800 and remained so for several subsequent decades, probably because of the widespread off-shore shoaling allied to frequent strong easterly winds. As a result, the manufactured worsteds mainly went overland to the capital, a costly and arduous journey but one far shorter than some of their competitors—Exeter serges or the worsteds of the West Riding—had to bear. Then again, the Norwich worsteds were intricate and finely woven and an outstanding luxury product, so they could bear high transport costs.

All told, then, the worsted industry of Norwich during the early decades of the Nineteenth Century, was not greatly incommoded by the difficulties and dangers of transportation to London.

The third link was the 30-mile stretch of the River Yare that joined the manufacturing interests in Norwich to Yarmouth, one of the most important ports of the East coast of Britain at the time. Of the three routes, this was probably the most important and large numbers of Norwich worsteds were exported direct to Europe via Yarmouth. For Norwich, the River Yare had been a principal artery of trade for well over a hundred years. In fact, the manufacturing interests of Norwich, the shipping interests of Yarmouth, and the River Yare between them came together in 1682 and formed the Norwich & Yarmouth Navigation by which tonnage dues were imposed on all goods coming into Yarmouth, the proceeds being applied to the maintenance and improvement not only of Yarmouth Haven but also of the rivers Yare, Bure and Waveney. The original Act had to be reviewed every 20 years and Norwich interests were always keen supporters of renewal. So that, at the turn of the century, fleets of wherries carried innumerable cargoes of stuffs down from Norwich to Yarmouth and since there were no locks and the river was tidal almost up to Norwich, it is no wonder that the route was held to be 'of inestimable advantage' to the economy of that city.

It would seem, then, that the natural drainage pattern of the East Midlands facilitated the provision of adequate supplies of wool, while that of Norfolk helped greatly in the distribution of the product. The main road to London was probably the weakest link in the transport chain, but even this was comparatively advantageous. Good communications are the sinews of industry and one cannot doubt that by 1800 those focusing on Norwich must have exerted very great influence upon the profitability of the worsted trade. At this time, the products of the West Riding were not in active competition with those of Norwich, for they were more homely than luxurious: and in none of the main techniques—weaving, dyeing and finishing—were the West Riding makers equal to those of the East Anglian city. In consequence, Norwich worsteds dominated the country and continued to do so until the changes in freight transport and in production techniques effected their transformations.

But an economic society is always in a state of flux and never stands still. Lack of change, if fact, is synonymous with stagnation and there was, in the Britain of 1800-1850, nothing in the situation of the Norwich industries to fix them in a condition of unvarying prosperity. The Napoleonic Wars, as wars always do, stimulated demand enormously for some goods relating to the war effort but at the same time almost completely eliminated the markets for other goods. Inevitably, too, sea traffic—to Europe, the Mediterranean, the Far East—was badly disrupted. The consequence was that, over the period of the war and for 20 years subsequently, the entire structure of the Norwich worsted trade— its wool supply, its labour force, its entrepreneurs, and its markets—was gravely disrupted. Worse: the other regions in the country making competing textile products underwent technological revolution, in particular, mechanization and factory organization. Consequently, this was a time when deficiencies or relative weaknesses in the East Anglian city's lines of transport and communications had a gravely deleterious effect on its industry and economy.

During the first three decades of the 19th Century, a remarkable change took place in the transport system of England, less so in Wales and Scotland. Roads, bridges and harbours were all extensively im-

121

proved, re-built or extended and concurrently a network of canals was constructed which, criss-crossing the Midlands and the more favoured areas of the northern counties, linked the principal industrial regions to the main ports of Liverpool, Hull, Bristol and London and very greatly increased the efficiency and reduced the costs of freight transport. No-where were such beneficial changes more evident than in Lancashire and in the West Riding of Yorkshire, the very areas where mass-produced cottons and woollens were coming to be increasingly successful competitors of the Norwich products.

In the matter of roads, the industrial outworkers of Norwich were not greatly disadvantaged by the widespread improvements in the national system, for by 1810 most of the Turnpike Trusts that ever came to operate in Norfolk were formed and these provided improved transport from Norwich to Yarmouth, to Scole (for Ipswich), to Thetford (for London) and to Swaffham (for King's Lynn). In 1795, Nathaniel Kent, a man well-travelled in England, considered Norfolk roads to be better than most in the kingdom; and early in the nineteenth century that critical traveller Arthur Young thought them 'equal to those of most of the improved counties'. These judgments, however, applied only to the turnpike roads which, even by 1813, constituted only 7-8 per cent of the total in the county. Also, considerable gaps existed between turnpikes along the main roads; and since the length of trust-operated road increased only slowly over the next 25 years, it may be presumed that the gaps remained. Nevertheless, it seems probable that road improvements in East Anglia kept pace with the increases in the Norwich trade in these years. Evidence from a carefully drawn-up estimate of the traffic using the main road system focusing on Norwich, made in 1841 by the promoters of the East Anglian Railway, showed that freight totalling some 4,400 tons, together with some 22,000 passengers, went annually out of the city. Clearly, in the pre-railway age, there was a useful network of roads in this part of East Anglia and it was in fairly heavy use.

It was not the turnpikes but improved river navigations and the cutting of canals that radically altered the balance between the north and the east. By 1830, in fact, by which time the Leeds & Liverpool canal had been in full operation for more than ten years, not a single additional waterway had been cut for the benefit of the Norwich industry. This was not really to be wondered at, for the lands of eastern England contained no mineral wealth apart from brick earths; the prevalent agriculture produced no densities of population making canal-building worthwhile; and the agricultural produce of the region—wheat, barley, malt and flour—formed bulk freights best conveyed by coasting vessels, with coal from Northumberland and cordwood, oak bark and hops from Kent forming return cargoes. It was a lack that had very considerable force on the competitive ability of the Norwich textile products in the first half of the 19th Century and before the completion of a national railway grid.

The real problem was to move bulky freight more cheaply, regularly and safely by water both to Yarmouth and to London. It was all very well to be able to get goods to London within 24 hours but the cost of doing so, £11 a ton as compared with the 20s. a ton incurred in sending by water, made such movements economic only in the case of highly valuable goods (such as the Norwich silk shawls that retailed at between 15 and 20 guineas) or in cases of extreme urgency. For the pedestrian cloths that formed the greater part of the Norwich product, speed was very much a secondary consideration. At this time, even the Norwich & Yarmouth Navigation was perceived to have serious drawbacks, for the wherries used were open vessels with unsealed cargoes, and in consequence pilfering was easy and carried out on a large scale. Additionally, Breydon Water, almost at the conjunction of the Yare and the sea, was very shallow, and this restricted traffic to craft drawing less than 3ft. and carrying some 20-30 tons. The need for improved water-borne transport therefore, became imperative in these years.

To reduce the city's dependence on Yarmouth by enabling sea-going vessels to come direct to Norwich—in fact, to make Norwich a port—became the aim of city interests and produced the Norwich & Lowestoft Navigation Bill in 1827. Lowestoft was to be linked to the River Waveney by a short channel and a 'new cut', permitting the passage of vessels drawing up to 10ft., was to join the Waveney and Yare rivers, so avoiding Breydon Water. Pilfering would be prevented by cargoes being under hatches and this alone was expected to produce a fall in freight costs of 1s. a ton. Although the proposal provoked a deal of bitter antagonism from Yarmouth interests, it was acclaimed in both Norwich and Lowestoft, and Parliamentary sanction quickly obtained. Begun in 1827, it was completed in 1833 and opened with a tremendous display of public enthusiasm. Yet for some obscure reason, the new channel failed to attract sufficient traffic and during the 1830's annual net receipts totalled only some £2,000 thus yielding only a very moderate return on the capital invested. With the opening of the Norwich & Yarmouth Railway in 1844, the attraction of the Navigation was further reduced and finally, in 1850, the company was wound up and the assets sold for some £50,000.

Several other improvements were either projected or initiated experimentally in this period. The operation, in 1813, of a steam barge on the Yare that covered the 30 miles downstream in less than 3½ hours and apparently provided a useful and economic service, ended in 1817 when an explosion killed nine people aboard. Eight years after, a scheme for building a horse-drawn tramway, the Norfolk & Suffolk Rail Way, was prepared, with the purpose of carrying Norwich bombazines and crapes, 'a trade at once extensive and permanent', to London via Ipswich. Faced with the emptiness of eastern England, which could not have justified such a capital investment, this proposal was no more successful than many others had been in the past and failed to obtain an Act. On a smaller and more practical scale was the attempt, made in the same year, by a group of Norfolk and Suffolk traders to develop a road and sea route between Norwich and the metropolis, intending to avoid the hazards and obstacles of the Suffolk and Norfolk coast. A service of 14 fast sailing ships (later reinforced by a steamship of 20 h.p.) was organised to shuttle between London and Ipswich, integrating with 'a fleet of wains' bringing goods overland from Norwich. 'Norwich goods', it was claimed, 'will be delivered in London (on an average) within three days . . . the entire charge of transit (being) 3 shillings per cwt.' The low freight charge must have attracted many a Norwich manufacturer much concerned with his marginal costs; but by this time the weak link in the chain was the Norwich-Ipswich road, which became cut up increasingly by wain and van traffic and which, by 1846, was declared to be almost impassable at times. It is highly doubtful, therefore, if this particular commercial venture prospered for long. Finally, in 1828, direct steamship services were established between Norwich and London. The swell of these, however, caused much damage to the river banks and in general they were unpopular and provided little competition with the existing wherry traffic. Consequently, the transport of stuffs to London by coaster was never carried on to any serious extent.

By 1835 the disparity in the effectiveness of the regional transport systems in the Northern Counties and in Norfolk was considerable; subsequently, during the decade following the introduction of railways in the North of England, it became much greater. In 1830, the Liverpool & Manchester Railway came into operation; in 1834, the Leeds & Selby Railway had been built. In 1841 came the Manchester & Leeds Railway, linking the West Riding towns to Manchester and Liverpool; and finally, in 1847, the formation of the Lancashire & Yorkshire Railway provided a complex which brought the entire region into effective communication with its two great ports.

While it is true that freight traffic on several of these lines was secondary in importance to the carriage of passengers, railway building caused the canal companies to increase their operating efficiency. Direct competition between the two modes of transport became effective and general only after 1840, but when this finally occurred it led to some drastic cutting of canal rates, the Aire & Calder Navigation, for example reducing charges on general goods from 7s. to 2s. 3d. a ton. Greater efficiency, lower rates, and a wider network of through traffic could not have failed to exert a beneficial influence on the West Riding worsted manufactory. Overseas markets became increasingly important as the century advanced and of these the best customers for Yorkshire worsteds were still North America and Germany. Consequently, it is not surprising that, following railway-building developments in Lancashire and York-shire in the perid until 1847, 'a most astonishing extension of trade occurred in the stuff department of the West Riding'.

It is particularly noticeable that the period between the depression of 1831-2, which affected the entire country, and the introduction of the first railway in 1845 was a disturbed and unhappy one for the Norwich trade. Slackness of trade was intense and protracted during the entire period 1832-37; the subsequent five years, economically brisk for the country as whole, witnessed a great deal of distress among the city's unemployed; and, to complete the record of depression, unemployment again became widespread in 1845.

It is, of course, true that some of these troubles were directly inspired by the technical improvements effected in power-loom weaving, particularly after 1840; improvements which enabled the Yorkshire manufacturers to produce much more cheaply some of the lower qualities of the goods that had once been the prerogative of Norwich makers. Probably, however, this had less force than is commonly assumed, for the typical Norwich stuffs were of such intricate and delicate designs that very much later in the century it was still being declared that 'no fear need be entertained of competition with the manufacturers of other places'. Price and quality were the fundamentals. Handwork made the Norwich product expensive and any factor tending to increase the price differential between these and the lower-quality mass-produced Yorkshire stuffs would serve to affect marginal demand; the greater the price difference the greater the effect. During the period 1830-45, the transport revolution together with technological improvements both reduced prices and improved the quality of the Yorkshire products and in doing so created a crisis for the Norwich industry.

These conditions demonstrated clearly the urgent need for railways in eastern England. Here again, despite all the advantageous factors of low relief, slow shallow rivers little liable to flood, the slight call for tunnels, cuttings and embankments so costly to railway companies in other parts, East Anglia was unlucky in its first railway—the Eastern Counties. Parliament in granting the Act in 1836 'established the principle that Norwich ought to have a good railway to London' and the promoters, agreeing with this, saw the railway as giving 'a new impulse to every branch of industry in the city', creating employment and 'taking a large share of the burden of poor rates on itself, thus multiplying prodigiously the resources of the district while diminishing the demands made upon them'. Unfortunately for Norwich, it took seven years to totter as far as Colchester and then gave up. In consequence, very little benefit accrued to the textile manufacture of Norwich from this initial essay.

The next attempt, the Yarmouth & Norwich Railway, was a very different proposition. The prospectus was probably correct when it claimed that 'no two places in the kingdom had more prominent claims to a railway between them. The first . . . the metropolis of the Eastern District of the kingdom; the second, not only the port on which the

125

former is dependent but ... a watering place growing yearly in importance'. The returns, it was forecast, would be 14 per cent on outlay 'if 10 per cent is allowed for working expenses'.

Ten years earlier, when a railway from Norwich to Yarmouth had been planned as an extension of the Eastern Counties Railway, it had been claimed that this would bring an increase in the city's stuff trade by reason of the better links with Europe, increase her commercial importance, greatly stimulate trade in cattle, corn and fish, and provide a considerable increase in employment. The same ideas were clearly in the minds of the promoters in 1841. Nevertheless, so great was the opposition of the river and road interest that the local reception was lukewarm and the promoters had to do some hard selling. In 1842, however, the company received its Act and the Yarmouth & Norwich Railway was speedily constructed to open in May 1844. (To Robert Stephenson who planned it, the Yarmouth & Norwich Railway represented only the beginning of a grand trunk line from the east to the west of England, and a few years later Norwich was in fact linked to Peterborough and the Midlands.) The high returns anticipated were by no means realised at once, the first year's receipts approximating only £800 per mile on an outlay of some £10,000 per mile, or about 8 per cent. Despite this, the railway constituted a major improvement, for it enabled Norwich goods to be transported the 21 miles to Yarmouth quickly (in 50 minutes) cheaply and safely.

In 1840, the creation of a rail link between Norwich and London had been seen to be a matter of some urgency. 'The progress which railways are making in various parts of Great Britain, bringing the most distant counties in close connection with the Metropolis, loudly calls for the attention of the Agricultural, Commercial and Manufacturing interests of the Eastern Counties. Unless some means are taken to extend the benefits of speedy communication to the inhabitants of these counties, they will be left behind in the race of competition by counties at thrice the distance from the Metropolis.' To Norwich, such a railway was seen to offer 'a revival of their manufactures now suffering from the competition of the North of England'; to Yarmouth, the greatly facilitated carriage of fish; and to Norfolk and Suffolk generally, 'a greatly improved carriage of Coals, Lime, Chalk, etc., amounting to many thousand tons, now conveyed internally ... by land carriage'. The upshot was the East Anglian Railway, running from Bishop's Stortford to Ely, Brandon and Norwich, the first through trains from Norwich to London running in July 1845.

The construction of the rest of the main railway routes still existing in the mid-Twentieth Century was carried out during the next four years. The Eastern Union Railway linked Colchester and Ipswich by 1846 and the extension to Norwich was completed by November 1849, to give that city its second through route to London. The only other main-route gap remaining was between Norwich and East Dereham, the terminus of the East Anglian Railway which ran from Wisbech and through King's Lynn, and this was filled in February 1847 by a branch line which joined East Dereham to Wymondham and so to Norwich. Subsequently, several minor routes were added but essentially Norwich had by 1849 become the centre of an extensive and effective railway network.

Thorpe Station. The attractive iron-work reflecting the lavish use made of iron during the railway era in both its structural and ornamental forms.

Many of the troubles which confronted the industrialists of Norwich in these years originated in the lack of interest in railways so widely displayed in Norfolk and Suffolk, and it would seem that the very isolation of the area generated its own opposition to improvement. The writer of a letter to the *Norwich Mercury* described the attitude of the people of Norfolk to railways as one of 'apathy and inertness to their own salvation'. Of Lancashire investors he said, 'they hold 700,000 in shares and some hold 800 to 1,000 shares of £25 each'. And he asks, 'where shall we find a Norwich noodle to do that?'. Similarly, at the promotion of the Bungay & Halesworth (N. Suffolk) Railway in 1845, there were applications for shares from people in London, Manchester, Leeds, Dublin and Glasgow, but not a single one from Norwich or Norfolk. As late as 1845, it was still argued that there was no need for railways since 'the Yare . . . without any locks, with no dues on goods exported and only 4d. a ton on imports, is the cheapest in the Kingdom . . . constantly employed in carrying coals and heavy goods from the shipside at Yarmouth to Norwich at a charge of 1/6 per ton.'

Fortunately there were powerful interests on the side of improvement, including industrialists of the city and agriculturalists of the county. It was, they declared, 'of the greatest importance to maintain the present position of the city as a great entrepot for goods; otherwise the profits of the Norwich undertakings would go to Yorkshire, Lancashire and other places'. Without railways, it was recognised, trade must decline; and 'when once the trade of the town was gone, employment would be gone; and they had recently occasion to know something of the effects of depression of trade'. Given railways, 'the time was not far distant when they would see general prosperity in the city and its neighbourhood'.

The outcome was that railways, forming an effective system linking Norwich to her ports and to London, came much later than in the North of England. Nevertheless, although they seriously prejudiced road and shipping interests, they unquestionably promoted the public good by saving time, lowering costs of transport, reducing prices and extending markets, so greatly 'increasing commercial intercourse'. As a result, by 1846, the state of the manufactures of the city was declared 'the best for many years', and the entire period until at least the middle 1850's was consistently prosperous. It is impossible, however, to assign responsibility for this reanimation solely to local railway development, for at this time a similar upsurge in activity was experienced by the entire country as the economy worked itself out of the depression of the early 1840's. Whatever the precise causes of the city's new-found return to brisk trading conditions, it is clear that a spirit of improvement, a new attitude to the industrial problems of the city, was generated and a new optimism and confidence stimulated in the minds of Norwich industrialists. It is hard to believe that the railways were not in large part responsible for this.

Additionally, the coming of the railways greatly helped the agriculture of Norfolk and this in turn stimulated the introduction within the city of a number of light industries based on it. Industries, it was said, 'sprang into existence with the complex commercial relationships that arose out of the freer means of locomotion. Notwithstanding the flowery accounts given of the trade of Norwich a century ago, the present commercial position of the city must surpass it'. To the producer of the industries must be added the wealth deriving from its ancient function as market town; and the resulting affluence indicated clearly that the constrictions imposed by out-dated communications with the rest of the country and with the markets overseas had gone for good.

Thorpe Station. Built originally as the station for the Yarmouth and Norwich Railway in 1844 and rebuilt in 1886 for the Great Eastern Railway Company with the surviving station building.

Norwich, then, had by 1850 a network of good turnpike roads that linked it to the other major cities in East Anglia; it had its railways that carried its goods to London and Yarmouth and King's Lynn; and it still depended on the Norwich and Yarmouth Navigation.

Not all the transport improvements of 19th Century Norwich, however, were extra-mural. In common with much of the rest of the country, the East Anglian capital experienced considerable growth of population which roughly doubled in the period 1801-1861 partly through immigration and partly by national increase fostered by improved medical knowledge and the far greater effectiveness of local government administration and social provision. By mid-Century a situation began to manifest itself that was, in fact, rather akin to that in Britain during the early motor-way era when the motor-ways brought greatly increased traffic to some towns and necessitated in turn the building of other roads—the by-passes—in order to relieve choked high streets and to develop free flows of traffic once again. This, though perhaps a minor appendage to the revolution brought about by railways, toll-roads and canals, is worth a brief look.

A preliminary word about road and bridge maintenance in the city. At the beginning of the 19th Century, there was no such thing as the levying of a rate, the revenue from which to be used by the Corporation on city improvements. Instead, the upkeep of roads and bridges in the city was paid for out of revenues accruing from tolls on cargoes coming up-river and applied by the Tonnage Committee. These were sufficient to provide for the building improvement and/or re-building of such bridges as Coslany (in 1804), Carrow (1810), Foundry (1810), Hellesdon (1818) and Fye (1829). Very little was done for the roads though.

More general improvements came increasingly to be needed as trade and traffic grew, however, and following local Acts of Parliament in

Blackfriars or St. George's Bridge. This attractive bridge was designed by Sir John Soane and built in 1783 and was the only crossing of the Wensum between Fye Bridge and the New Mills until Dukes Palace Bridge was built in 1822 and St. Miles Bridge in 1804.

1805, 1825, and 1835, Improvement Commissions were instituted with widely ranging powers including road and street improvement as described in Chapter 4. By 1835, many of the main roads leading into the city, particularly Newmarket Road (as far as Cringleford), Ipswich Road, and St Stephen's had macadamised all-weather surfaces and were all drained and sewered.

Such improvements continued slowly but in the 1870's another major advance was made with the introduction of wooden paving blocks, first in London Street experimentally and subsequently, when the benefits had been widely demonstrated throughout the whole of the central area of the city, 17,688 square yards in all. The effects on the speed of transport and on street cleanliness were impressive, so much in contrast with the conditions in the years before 1850, when, if roads were surfaced at all they were paved with sea-shore flints.

But the real revolution of road transport within the city came in the years after the opening of the Norwich & Yarmouth Railway. The change—from horse-drawn or water-borne long distance transport to carriage by railway—was one that must have been experienced by many towns and cities newly served by railways. In the case of Norwich, the ancient road and street pattern had two foci: the river (for Yarmouth and thence to London or Boston and so to Hull and parts north); and the Market Place, St Stephen's Street and so to Newmarket or Ipswich Roads, with London as the long-distance objective.

This largely explains why St Stephen's Gate was one of the first to be demolished, why the street was always being widened, cleared and re-paved, and why its maintenance together with that of Newmarket Road as far as Cringleford always held a prominent place in the upkeep expenditures of the Corporation and the Council.

This ancient pattern of trade, by road and river, imposed a main road system upon the city, goods and passengers being drained to the west through St Stephen's and north to the river. The completion of the Yarmouth and Norwich Railway in 1844 and of the East Anglian Railway in 1845, two lines that were to provide a great commercial stimulus for the city, produced Thorpe Station on the east bank of the river and lying to the east of Norwich. The station was, however, badly linked to the centre of the city it was expected to serve, for Foundry Bridge, then old, wooden and narrow, led only to Rose Lane, itself tortuous and congested, and thence to the Castle Ditches (now Castle Meadow) and so to the Market Place via London Street, one of the narrowest streets in the city.

Thus in a very short space of time the railways, by the favourable cost and speed that they offered, drained much of the city's traffic eastwards which meant that a new main route was created along London Street, Castle Ditches and Rose Lane, a route which soon came to be choked with waggons, carts, omnibuses and carriages. Inevitably, therefore, the railway station at Thorpe forced an unwilling Council, and the equally unwilling Paving Commissioners, to face up to the need for a major programme of road widening and improvement.

The prospect offered considerable benefits to a city, the economy of which was at that time far from prosperous; yet it was a daunting one—to widen the whole of the equivalent of the present London Street so as to change its existing narrow, winding, almost medieval condition to a street thirty feet wide overall, having an 18ft. carriageway flanked by a 6ft. wide footway on each side; to create at least two new streets to link with the Castle Ditches and then to widen and extend Rose Lane together with a number of feeder streets, at a total cost of over £20,000. By these means, the Commissioners considered, 'they would entirely have removed the great nuisance that at present existed'.

However, the railway company was in a position to help the Council appreciably. Their original Act permitted them to extend the line from Thorpe Station and across the river to King Street; but the expense incurred in the bridge building would not, the Company considered, be worthwhile unless they could extend the line right up to Castle Ditches. This they were quite prepared to do, but of necessity needed a new bill for the purpose; and reasonably, it seems at a time distance of more than a century, they were prepared to pay the costs of all road widening, except that of London Street, providing that the Council merely agreed not to oppose the bill. Such a scheme would have left the Paving Commissioners with the expense of widening London Street only, estimated to be between £10,000 and £12,000, although one sceptical Commissioner, a realist perhaps before his time, 'recommended that the law of three should be applied'. On the face of it, the Paving Commissioners, the rate-payers, and most of all the textile manufacturers of the city, had a bargain offer, one that would greatly improve the city and yet convey freight to and from Yarmouth and London, the two major outlets for the city's products, more quickly, reliably and cheaply.

Even so, the Council refused the offer, on the grounds that it could not even afford the £10,000 or so for the reduced commitment. In one sense, it is easy to appreciate why. As one Council member described the situation: Norwich was 'an over-taxed town, which has arisen from a decline in trade and unless some new source of trade and occupation can be found for the poor Norwich will sink'. Consequently, it was hard for the Council to justify such an outlay.

But the expense involved was not the only problem. There was another difficulty. The traditional principle applied by the Improvement Commissioners was that the beneficiaries from any improvement should make a prior 'voluntary' contribution to the cost and in the case of the London Street scheme this was all the more necessary since road widening would produce higher property values. That the widening of London Street and other associated thoroughfares could bring general benefits to the city's inhabitants involved an abstract concept far too difficult for many rate-payers to accept. All would have to pay but a few only would reap the benefits, a proposition that was self-evidently unfair. As one Commissioner put the case: 'The people of Magdalen Street and other parts of the city are not in the least interested and yet they would be called upon to pay a portion of the expense . . . People of London Street should put their hands into their own pockets'. This was quite literally a parochial view; but Commissioner were, in the main, elected parochially for the express purpose of representing parish views. And the general view of the 'uninterested' parishes was strong enough to prevail.

So, in the event, the proposals were progressively diminished by amendments the end result being a relatively trifling modification at a cost of £4,000. And there this major matter of what was, in effect, early town planning rested for the next ten years or so. Inevitably, however, when revival of trade and the return of affluence to the city increased the revenues of the Commissioners and reduced the burdens of the poor-rate on ratepayers, the whole matter was brought up again.

Further widening was effected in 1856 when London Street, still little more than a passage way, was widened to 15ft. But this was an improvement that did little to solve the traffic problem of the city centre for sixteen years later, in 1872, the need to widen London Street so as to permit an increased flow of traffic 'resulting from the extension of our markets and the necessity for increased facilities for our trade and commerce' once again came to be regarded as pressing.

All the interminable arguments were again resumed. The principal argument against action being taken was the expense and the burden that would be placed on rate-payers at a time when the economy of the city had still not dragged itself out of its prolonged period of depression. Here it must be remembered that at this time the Council was facing the need for massive expenditures on its sewerage system, it was being compelled by the central government to spend £40,000 or so on the provision of a lunatic asylum, poor relief costs had soared from £27,000 tin 1850 to £37,000 in 1870, and that to all these expenditures education was soon to make a very considerable addition.

The setting up of the London Street Improvement Committee in 1876, however, eventually produced the strong recommendation that a large scheme of improvement including London Street, Castle Street and Davey Place (all of which had been the subject of the comprehensive plan of 1848) be carried out at a further cost of £27,000. By this time, the city was enjoying a markedly more favourable economic situation and the Council acted far more decisively than heretofore. It accepted the recommendation that the London Street roadway be 20ft. wide and be flanked with footways totalling 15ft. in width; accepted the estimate of £27,205; and empowered the Improvement Committee to negotiate all property purchases in London Street, Opie Street, Castle Street and in part of Red Lion Street. Subsequently, it was agreed that the widening of

Castle Street into a 44ft. thoroughfare be extended to Davey Place as was the further proposal that Red Lion Street be made 3ft. wider.

Here, then, was the termination of nearly thirty years of proposals, counter-proposals, procrastination and indecision, largely brought to an end because the economic climate had become much more favourable. Two years later, with the project completed, a major additional benefit to the trade of the city had been created. What is more, a pleasnt topographical form had been imposed upon the city centre, almost unchanged from that day to this.

The construction of Prince of Wales Road was rather a curious happening, again aimed at bettering the link between the railway station at Thorpe and the Market Place, then greatly impeded by the narrowness of Rose Lane. Right from the start the scheme had impressive proportions, the Norwich New Street Company being formed to acquire land to a width of 108ft. over a length of 500 yards from the station to Castle Meadow. This was a private enterprise and its outlook and direction contrasted markedly with that of the Corporation which, however, was involved since it owned a number of properties along the proposed route.

In the event, the Corporation's interest in the project intensified and came to the view that it was greatly to the public interest that the new street programme should be carried through. A New Street Committee, set up by the Council in 1860, reported that since the proposed new road was of such consequence to the entire population it ought to be provided by the Corporation. This, however, was too much for many Councilmen and eventually a compromise was effected by which the Corporation shared with the public company the actual construction of the street of which a small part only had been built by 1860.

In 1865, however, the Council took full control of Prince of Wales Road 'pursuant to the Norwich New Street Act,1859'. To the Council, this was something of a mixed blessing for the road, either very much used or very badly constructed, was two years later reported as being 'much cut up in trenches and greatly in need of repair', the implication being that this was no macadamised or wood-paved surface but simply a plain dirt road. Still, the Council made the best of a bad job and seeing the old city wall at Chapel Field as an obstacle in need of demolition it did two jobs at once, using the city wall debris as part of the new foundation for Prince of Wales Road.

The re-building of London Street and the construction of Prince of Wales Road were the principal improvements effected in these years but there were many others. Surrey Street and St George's, Colegate, were widened to 36ft; Lime Tree Road was made 47ft wide; and a new Foundry Bridge was built, the old one being dismantled, transported and re-erected at Heigham. Several similar schemes must have been carried out and in consequence, with many of the narrow streets in the city centre area having been widened and straightened, with large areas of roadway paved, kerbed and guttered and with flagged pavements, the city by 1890 had lost some of its 18th Century (and medieval) features and had acquired more than a few elements of its 20th Century look.

*   *   *   *   *   *

Note on Sources

There is a detailed list of sources for this chapter in
Edwards, J. K. Communications and the Economic Development of Norwich 1750-1850.
Journal of Transport History, November 1965.

For London Street improvements: Norfolk Chronicle, 15 Jan., 1848; 9 March, 1872; *Norwich Mercury,* 1 Jan., 1847; 12 Feb., 18 Mar., 1845.

Since Prince of Wales Road was a private enterprise easily accessible references are not available.

Detail of public right of way from Redwell Street down Church Alley.

CHAPTER SIX

Industrial Development—1800-1900
J. K. Edwards

Introduction

A city's people have to work in order to live. That is an unescapable fact. But they have to do more: unless they are self-sufficient and self-contained (which is highly unlikely) they have also to sell the products of their labour. Since all cities (and towns and agricultural and industrial regions) face the same problem, competition between them is inevitable, competition which may be keen and quite frequently is bitter and acute. Where there are winners, there must also be losers; and the social consequences of losing can be sad indeed.

The story of the way in which the people of Norwich 'earned a living' during the Nineteenth Century is interesting to historians (and may be, also, to many non-historians) for the manner in which the situation of affluence in Norwich at the beginning of the Century—when the city was 'a winner'—changed radically during a few decades of intense competitiveness to one in which, by 1850, she quite definitely became 'a loser'. Thenceforward, however, after a series of important and, at times, painful changes, the city's earners won through to a fair degree of prosperity by the decades prior to 1900, rather in the manner of a football team which, once threatened with relegation, ends the season halfway up the League.

Many people are familiar with the term 'The Industrial Revolution' and know it for a description of the process whereby the industry and commerce of Britain underwent transformation (and social disruption) during the period 1750-1850. The changes which occurred in Norwich in the 19th Century were part of the national 'Revolution' and the process that worked itself out in the East Anglian city formed one example of the hundreds which occurred throughout the kingdom, each with its tale of success or failure. Because, perhaps, the process can be described in detail (it is, in fact, part of the city's historical heritage) and because it is really, even now, on our historical doorstep, it is one that has quite considerable regional and national interest. It is a story, in fact, well worth the telling.

*   *   *   *   *   *

Space and time being limited, it is best, perhaps, to describe this process of change and adaptation by looking at conditions in the city at three contrasting periods: as they were at the beginning of the Century; then between 1800 and 1850; and finally by the 1890's.

I) **1800: Affluence**

A brief glimpse at the pattern of economic activities in the city today would reveal how closely they are linked to those of her rural hinterland. 'Norwich and her region' truly forms a single economic unit.

Even so, the links between the two were even greater at the beginning of the Nineteenth Century. The urban industries, then, depended very largely upon local products of the land, the population of a town growing in proportion as these were abundant. At the time, Norwich had an unusually large population and it follows that the region must have been a favoured one. And through the centre, like a main artery, flowed the Wensum-Yare system, providing more resources, transport and a highly effective channel of trade.

In essentials, agricultural activities were much the same then as now—barley and wheat growing on the sands or loams with cattle fattening on a grand scale being carried on throughout the river marshlands. There were some important differences however. Grassland for sheep rearing was far more extensive then; damp, clayey areas might be given over to the growing of flax or hemp and the hedgerows abounded in timber since, whenever enclosures occurred, a thorn hedge was immediately planted with an oak seedling every twenty paces or so. It is by no means an exaggeration to say that these agricultural activities and to a lesser extent the subsoil of the region dominated the work and lives of very many of the city people.

Sheep and cattle provided meat, of course, but quite as important were their by-products. The old Norfolk sheep, 'the native burglar of the heaths', had given way by 1800 to a Southdown cross with a thick rich fleece. Most of the wool went to the Yorkshire clothiers, but some remained for the local woollen (as distinct from worsted) industry to form coarse cloths with beguiling names, such as swansdown and everlastings. The skins then went to fellmongers, and eventually became coats and gloves.

Far more important were the hides, for the fattened cattle walked their way to London and their hides came back by wagon to form the basis of the Norwich leather industry. Nor were the products of cattle confined to the leather trade. Hooves and horns were boiled up by glue makers and the bones, shipped from London by the bargeload, were ground into fertiliser meal. Even the hair sloughed off by the tanners had its use for, with lime from the local chalk quarries it went to make builders' plaster.

But it was the oak which bore the bell for usefulness. Trunk wood was used in construction work or carried to Yarmouth for shipbuilding. The bark went to the tanners or else to the dyers for the black dyeing of cloth; and the small wood, apart from serving many carpentering needs, was readily taken by the charcoal burners. The city's maltsters depended on these, having need of a supply of fumeless fuel. The residue, with other woods, was probably burnt to produce potash which, applied to the abundant local supply of animal fats, made soap for washing the wool. Even sawdust had its uses and apart from covering the floors of shops and taverns it went to Yarmouth to be used in the smoking of fish. The flax and hemp grown locally were retted, the flax in water, the hemp in river mud, to provide the materials for a small linen industry and for sack-making.

In all these industries water was essential. The river at New Mills provided power to mill the wheat and to supply the central city area with piped water. Tanners, curriers and dyers needed large amounts, and so located their workshops along the banks. Sad to say, the water was fairly clear above but foul below. Brewers sited themselves similarly although some had their own wells bored into the chalk.

The building needs of the city's people were again met by the land. Brick-earths existed in half a dozen places in and around the city; clay for clay-lump was plentiful; flints, smoothed glacially or by the sea, were readily available; and although by 1800 almost all houses had come to be roofed with imported pantiles, reed thatch from the marshlands was still widely used a generation earlier.

All in all, then, occupations in the city in 1800 or so were very varied, and many of them, because they met fundamental needs, were both prosperous and stable. The principal activity, however, has yet to be mentioned, very prosperous indeed but, alas, highly unstable.

This was the manufacture of worsted fabrics of which Norwich was the sole producer in the British Isles and, in consequence, one of the most populous. It was, in fact, a monopoly which had developed out of the skills of local people and at the beginning of the 19th Century their efforts produced wealth on a grand scale, some £500,000 a year—a figure one would have to multiply by a factor of twenty, at least, to obtain a present day equivalent.

The position of Norwich was perhaps her greatest asset at that time. Worsted wool had to be long, fine and as white as possible and almost all came from Lincolnshire, Leicester and Northamptonshire, although some was grown locally on the Yare marshlands. Buyers from Norwich toured these counties, bought up the wool clip and sent it by pack-horse, wagon and river craft to Boston, where it was shipped to Lynn and Yarmouth.

The scale of these movements was immense, and one can picture a continuous procession of horses, wagons and river craft always on the move, extended throughout the whole of East England and by land, river, canal and sea converging on the Norfolk capital. For eight months of the year this went on, from the first shearings in March to the last in October, and seldom did the demands of the Norwich weavers slacken.

The first users of the wool were the woolcombers who pulled heated iron combs through it to smooth away the tangles—a hot, dirty but skilled job. The spinners come next. They received the combed wool from agents who, using heavy carts, toured the country within a radius of 20 and sometimes even 100 miles of Norwich.

At the village public-houses, they issued their parcels of wool, collecting in return the yarn spun since their previous visit. Worsted yarn was difficult to spin on a wheel and instead required the more primitive distaff and spindle. First, the wool was teased out, twisted loosely together by the fingers and then compacted tightly by rubbing the spindle between the palm of the hand and the thigh. In this way, a very fine hard thread was produced little thicker than the cotton thread of today.

Spinning was a part-time occupation and whenever a labourer's wife or a woman servant had time to spare she would take up her distaff. In small hamlets and villages, women would congregate in the sun and spin together, doubtless discussing local events at the same time. So telling a tale became spinning a yarn, for one went with the other.

Weaving was largely an urban occupation, most weavers working on their own account, buying the yarn, making the cloth and selling this to merchants. A weaver's house in those days needed three rooms: a living room, a bedroom and a weaving room, all very simply furnished; and in the last, the weaver spent most of his life.

Work had a simple repetitive rhythm. The weaver went to the city, bought his yarn from a comber or merchant and carried it home. There he wove his 30-yard piece in, possibly, ten days, working 12 or 14 hours daily, more in summer, less in winter. This he took to the city, sold to a merchant and bought his yarn, to begin all over again. It was a pattern of living that went on throughout the year unless broken by unemployment. Small wonder that he took frequent holidays or liked the bottle, or that occasionally he was prone to riot against this or for that.

From the merchants the cloth usually went to independent dyers who, operating on a large scale, needed considerable amounts of capital. Finally came the hot pressers who, using hot irons and probably starch, gave a stiff glaze to many fabrics, particularly those destined for Russia and for Central Asia.

The finished cloth was distributed by merchants who resided in Lynn, Yarmouth or London. They bought the cloth and then sold it at home or abroad. London merchants bought for the domestic market and dealt in fashionable clothes; but they also sent the Norwich pieces throughout the world, to Spain, Madeira, Turkey, America and the Far East.

Yarmouth supplied Scandinavia and the whole of Western Europe. Fifteen of her ships were continuously engaged in taking cargoes of cloth to the Continent to bring back the timber, rope, dyes, linen and iron that both Norwich and Yarmouth needed. It was a partnership by which both cities became greatly enriched.

These Norwich fabrics were beautifully coloured and patterned in a great variety of styles to suit the needs of the different markets. The British hung their rooms with cloths intricately patterned with flowers; Russia and Tartary took brightly coloured striped cloths that were stiff and shone with a high glaze; Southern Europe favoured vivid mixtures of reds, yellows and greens that showed to best advantage in a hot bright sun. Whether flowered, striped, spotted, tartan or plain, all were beautiful products of craft work. But it is useless to describe them. Far better, the interested should go to the Norwich museums and see some excellently preserved examples for themselves.

This then, was the industry that made Norwich the third city of the realm. A hundred thousand people—wool growers, buyers, carriers, combers, spinners, weavers, dyers and finishers—centred their lives on these fabrics and provided furnishings and clothing for half the known commercial world.

However, in addition to the manufacture of worsted stuffs, an important subordinate activity had appeared by 1800. Cotton thread had come to be spun mechanically and with steam power in Lancashire and it offered a much cheaper, if inferior, alternative to the hand-spun worsted. The same thing (but not the inferiority) applied to the machine spun silk of Macclesfield; and on an increasing scale these were imported from the north of England and incorporated, as weft, with the worsted warp, the result being a great extension of the types and qualities of fabrics produced and an even greater prosperity.

Some idea of what this meant may be gained from the fact that, in the period 1800-1815, the East India Company ordered between 16,000 and 24,000 worsted camlets annually, each 55 yards long and 30 inches wide. Again, in 1802, one manufacturer received an order for 60,000 silk-worsted shawls and another in 1804, one for 42,000. This was prosperity indeed, the time when weavers paraded the streets displaying £5 notes in their hat-bands. It wasn't always like that, even early in the Century, for much of the trade depended on distant markets—Russia, Tartary, China, India, South America—and interruptions to trade and the recessions in activity that they produced were by no means infrequent.

However, while it was entirely true that the making of worsted and mixed-fibre fabrics was far and away the dominant activity in the city, it was far from being the only one. Two other employments also stood out at the opening of the Century—leather manufacture and brewing—not so much for what they then were (they were then no more important in Norwich than they were in many another large town or city) than for their potentialities. Because local conditions, largely geographical, were so favourable, these industries persisted and grew throughout the entire hundred years of our survey. A few words on these become essential here.

For many decades before 1800, the marshes of the lower River Yare had provided some of the best lands for cattle fattening in the entire country and cattle came there from all over England. Whether cattle were slaughtered locally or whether they were driven down to the ever-voracious London market, their hides came to the tanners of Norwich and Norfolk on a large and growing scale.

The making of leather involved three processes: tanning, currying and dressing. In tanning, the hides were first scoured by being soaked in barley water after which they were laid away in bark for several months, the barks of oak, chestnut and willow (all grown widely in Norfolk) being preferred. Because of the time involved, the processes demanded much money and so tanners were often capitalists working on a large scale.

From tanning, the hides passed to the currier or dresser, according to the type of leather to be produced: greasy leather for farmers' boots and seamen's thigh-boots from currying and soft leather (as for shoe uppers) from dressing. But apart from footwear there was an enormous demand for leather goods of all descriptions: household equipment (such as buckets), coach harnesses, saddles and riding boots—a coach harness took 52 lbs. of rough leather and a pair of riding boots 5 lbs.—but the main use was for the boots and shoes of the city's population, demanded in all shapes, sizes and qualities.

In 1800, or thereabouts, at least nine tanners operated in the city together with some twenty curriers, a dozen saddlers and hundreds of shoemakers. Here, then, was a small but vital industry, as yet employing only some 500 people; but it was profitable and because it depended little on fashion and foreign markets, it fluctuated little. As has been said, it was as yet embryonic but had great potential.

Brewing was in many ways a similar activity within the city. The prime need for brewing good beer was (and probably is) good barley; and in Norfolk, the sunshine, the low rainfall and the warm dry autumns (harvests are much earlier today) helped to produce some of the best barley in the kingdom. First, it had to be malted, that is soaked in water until it germinated, after which it was heated and dried by fumeless charcoal in special ovens. Much barley and malt were sent to London brewers and keels and wherries brought back cargoes of hops from the Kentish fields, again tying Norwich to Yarmouth. The subsequent brewing needed clean hard water to give the beer the sparkle and more often than not the brewers got this from boreholes in the chalk underlying much of Norwich.

The malting of barley was really a small-scale activity natural to the rural environs of Norwich and by the beginning of the 19th Century almost every large village had its maltings. Brewing, though, was a large-scale urban industry needing, sometimes, surprisingly large amounts of capital. Inevitably individual brewers bought out several maltings (and even the farms that grew the barley) and then went on to buy or control scores of inns and public houses, so forming very large organisations indeed.

So, one reads in the local paper of 1792, 'Complete brewing house for sale. Includes two malting offices, 70 acres of good arable, with a river site by which an extensive coal-and-corn trade (corn to Newcastle and coal on the return trip) can be carried on'. Another, in 1794, included 53 inns and 'pubs', the whole valued at £53,000, probably £1 million at today's money values.

By 1801, six large breweries operated in Norwich one of which, the firm of Patterson, had an output as great as that of one of the larger London brewers; and this persisted throughout the 19th Century, as Steward and Patterson Ltd., and well into the Twentieth. It isn't possible to estimate how great an employer was the brewing industry—probably several hundred were employed directly and far more indirectly. But it had a stability and profitability that caused it to make an important contribution to the economic health of Norwich and in this it reinforced the beneficial effects of the leather trade.

These were the largest of the activities by which the people of Norwich 'earned their living'. There were many others, subordinate it is true, but most significant in aggregate. The first of these was linked to transport (see Chapter V). Norwich was the commercial centre and focus of a large part of Norfolk, North Suffolk and Cambridge. Then, as now, it was linked to London by two main road systems—via Ipswich and Thetford—and to much of Western Europe by the River Yare. To and from the centre came coaches, waggons and vans of every conceivable description, the whole forming with the coaching inns, the toll roads and the toll-bars, a highly developed transport complex, the motive power of which was the horse. Quite apart from all the coach and waggon building, and the forestry activities that lay behind these, horses were needed in their hundreds; and the breeding, rearing, training, stabling, feeding and replenishments of these truly represented large-scale industry for those times. The disruption of lives by the substitution of dead steel and steam for live-horse power, that came with the Industrial Revolution, was enormous.

Apart from all the above, the 36,000 people of Norwich had to be sheltered, clothed, shod, watered, fed and amused. Not surprisingly, house building and furnishing employed large numbers as did iron and brass founding, for in a prosperous city there was constant demand for household hardware. Soap making, paper making, sacking manufacture, brick making, mustard and starch manufacture were all there—all small but adding to the demand for labour. There were others—retailers of every description, lawyers, doctors, printers-cum-booksellers, wig makers, music masters: the list is almost endless, representing in total a society at one place, at one time, and during a period of prosperity. A not unattractive picture.

But the early decades of the 19th Century were years of great change. The prosperity and the economic stability of the city gave way to uncertainty and poverty for many. An element of decline became inevitable and it brought with it a great deal of social misery. But this really belongs to the next section.

II) 1800-1850: Turmoil

An observant visitor, returning in 1850 to Norwich after, say, an absence of 20 years, would have been struck with some force by the number of changes. The city itself would have had many more people for it had almost doubled in population (from 36,909 in 1801 to 68,195 in 1851) in fifty years, though it had not doubled in size. Most of the main streets had been paved and named and houses no longer shed rain from their gutterless roofs on patient pedestrians below; and the river, receiving tanners' and dyers' effluent, rubbish, dead dogs and cats, and, worst, raw sewage from thousands of houses, stank during rainy weather and was an abomination during drought. Additionally, though, 'the pleasant clack, clack' of looms in weavers' houses was far less frequently heard and the industrially aware visitor could not have missed a number of chimneys rearing into the heavens, chimneys of eight textile spinning and weaving mills powered by steam.

The chimneys and the absence of weavers' looms were connected, of course; and the story of the supplanting of one by the other is one of industrial and social distress such as must happen when revolutionary changes are speedily introduced. By no means the whole of the working people of Norwich were involved in the change or in the distress: just the weavers. But these formed such a large and vulnerable section of the city's work-force and the change was so inevitable and irresistible as to give the period all the starkness of a tragedy.

* * * * * *

In fact, the introduction of power looms into Norwich was the last of a long series of shocks. The Napoleonic Wars, ending only in 1815, had effectively cut off the worsted merchants from their markets, and that had been bad enough. But war not only blocks trade; it is also a spur to invention and it was in these years that steam power was successfully applied to the spinning of yarn suitable for worsted manufacture in the factories of the West Riding of Yorkshire. This had advantages over the hand-spun yarn: it was more homogeneous and it was cheaper. But using it made the manufacturers of Norwich dependent on the North, a situation which could be detrimental at times for the East Anglian manufacturers.

Far more serious, though, was the effect on the economy of the city and of twenty miles around. If one remembers the 20,000 or so people employed by the industry in preparing wool for the weavers, mostly

143

women and girl spinsters whose earnings supplemented those of weavers, of farm workers and of many servants; and then imagines the entire system being demolished within a period of five years or so by supplies of machine spun yarn, one can gain some impression of the social and economic disruption which then took place and the deprivation inflicted by this one innovation alone. Unfortunately it came at the same time as machinery was also being applied to agriculture, where it again displaced labour, and the result was a very considerable migration of workers into Norwich, all seeking work at almost any wage, while others made the journey to the factories of Lancashire and Yorkshire or else to that ancient absorber of the destitute, London.

Apart from the tribulations inflicted by mechanization there were others, for the twenty years or so after the war's end were very unsettled and witnessed a succession of economic boom-and-slump cycles. Orders would take up, profits increase, more labour be taken on, wages increase, the whole forming two or three years of frenzied prosperity in which workers could get almost anything they asked for. Then, quite suddenly activity would slow and finally almost cease. Competition for work became intense, weavers in their hundreds were forced 'to play', and wages fell catastrophically. Soon, weavers who during the boom years had paraded the streets advertising their prosperity, were forced to the degradation of applying for Poor Relief, until the whole process started all over again.

The period until the mid-1830's was bedevilled with such cycles, the result of free market forces and unbridled competition made worse by mechanization. And, as is usually the result in such cases, the poor became poorer, the rich richer and the economic position of the city's weavers underwent steady decline.

Steam power, having been successfully applied to spinning, then came to be applied to weaving, at first only of coarser and cheaper fabrics. The prizes of success were considerable. Improvements were introduced fairly rapidly and by the 1820's plain woven worsted fabrics, until then made only in Norwich, came increasingly to be manufactured elsewhere, whether made of silk, cotton or worsted. These were not quality products, though, and the new methods represented only a foretaste of what could come in the future. So the city's manufacturers were able to counter the threat posed by machinery by the constant innovation of finer products and patterns—fillover shawls, Norwich crapes, black silks and lunetta cloth—all of them very beautiful examples of the weaver's art.

The original Norwich shawl had been an early introduction, made of cotton and hand embroidered with worsted 'to form a very common kind of cloth' (common, that is, compared with the traditional fine worsteds). By 1820, shawls of silk-and-worsted were being produced, after which came the 'Fillover' (a technical weaving term) shawl, made entirely of silk,

The silk yarn mill built by the Norwich Yarn Company in 1834 in Cowgate, St. Edmund's. This was the first steam-powered mill in Norwich. It was a chocolate factory in 1914 before becoming part of Jarrold's printing works.

The complex of buildings now forming the Read Woodrow mills in King Street. The central building was Albion Mill, built in the 1830's as a worsted yarn mill. It was then used for silk and mohair spinning. By 1885 it had become a confectionary factory.

a most luxurious product on account of the fineness of the weave and one which sold for anything up to £20 a-piece. Incredibly, even at this price it had an enormous attraction for buyers at home and abroad and when it was first introduced weavers could earn up to £10 a week at a time when other craftsmen earned only 15/- or so.

The same was true, at least in part, of Norwich crapes. Made of a silk warp and worsted weft, they were also finely woven and then dyed black for mourning purposes. Quickly becoming highly fashionable, they too were very expensive and in the 1820's and 1830's, together with the rather similar black bombazines, they found great favour in Spanish America, Spain and other Mediterranean countries. There were many others, all high-class, fashionable and expensive—silk challis 'the neatest and most elegant silk-and-worsted ever manufactured', paramattas, silk camlets and others—all the products of hand weaving skills that the machine was not then able to emulate.

Invention, however, never stays still and the introduction, in the 1830's, into the West Riding factories of the Jacquard loom (by 1836, some 2,770 were at work), steam powered and able to produce intricately figured cloths, swiftly changed this situation and made the lives of Norwich hand weavers immeasurably more difficult and precarious. Not directly, for steam-powered spinning mills had been operating in Norwich since 1834 and powered weaving came by 1838. Indirectly, though, since the productivity of the powered loom was so much greater than the hand-loom, the introduction meant inevitably that the employment of weavers greatly diminished; and of course, those weaving by hand had their wages forced down so dramatically that, by the end of the 1830's and during the 1840's, many hand weavers were working 60 hours a week for as little as 5/6, being able to subsist simply by doles of Poor Relief. Today, it would be as if people were doing a full week's work in order to receive about one-third of what they would get in unemployment benefit, truly a hopeless condition.

All told, the period 1815-1845 was a scarifying one for the hand workers employed in the Norwich textile trade, although it has to be said that those who were able to get work in the eight mills in the city were able to enjoy very fair wages. But nearly all the spinning and much of the weaving employed women and girls rather than men and the 700 power looms at work produced more in aggregate than did all the 3,600 looms still at work in weavers' houses. Such a situation could only have one end.

By 1850, mechanization and factory production had gone as far, within the limits of current technology, as they could, although the finest textile products were still hand woven. The contrast in the city with conditions as they had existed in 1800 was dramatic. Gone was that complex of activity by which wool had been brought in by road, by river and by sea, from Northampton, Lincolnshire, Cambridge and southern Ireland. Gone were the wool factors and merchants, the cleaners, the spinners and the combers. And gone was all their purchasing power. The hand-weavers had been decimated and those who remained were forced for long periods into destitution.

Nevertheless, in 1851, over 5,000 persons—men, women and children—were still directly employed. It was still a big industry locally and it prospered. Of the total, 2,800 were employed in mills in the manufacture of silk-stuffs. One of these, Messrs. Grout, Martin & Co., was described as being 'a silk firm of the largest size in England' and was held to employ 800 in spinning, 200 in weaving together with many others at work in clerking, transporting and engineering, the whole 'working not full-time but 60 hours a week'.

Nationally, the years following 1848 enjoyed a long period of economic expansion. Railway building, and the impetus it gave to agriculture, industry and commerce, stimulated the home market and a simplified tariff system assisted in the expansion of overseas trade. In consequence, after all their travails, the Norwich textiles manufacturers entered the 1850's with their products 'eagerly sought by the London houses' (wholesalers), with variety and fashion, and hence constant change, being widely recognised as the keys to success.

So, in 1858, an authoritative Bradford commentator on the trade was able to declare, 'The annual value of the manufacturers (of Norwich) has been estimated at £2 million and this estimate is probably under the mark'. In such a way did the merchants, manufacturers, weavers and dyers (dyeing was always a stable and profitable part of the trade) of Norwich survive their traumas of the past fifty years, so to continue for much of the rest of the Century.

Interlude: Two Lives

The period 1830-1850 was one during which the economy of the city, particularly the making of textiles, experienced grave set-backs which brought much hardship and misery to many working people. Not everybody was impoverished, though, or faced with the possibility of having to depend on Poor Relief. For example, the house of John Jarrold, printer, flourished, as did Gurney's Bank (the forerunner of Barclay's Bank at Bank Plain) and Colman's the manufacturer of starch and mustard. And many shoemakers, brewers, wholesalers (such as Copemans) and retailers (the Robertson in Robertson & Colman) found little to criticize in the times.

It might be instructive, therefore, to look at the fortunes of two Norwich workmen living during these years, one a weaver the other a maker of stained glass, both skilled but treated by fortune in very different ways. History has preserved details of the first in the local newspapers (a forerunner of Eastern Counties Newspapers) and of the second in a miscellany of pencilled scraps of paper that euphemism only could term 'a diary'. The contrast is stark, indeed.

[handwritten note: Nationally 1848 → enjoys a long period of economic expansion]

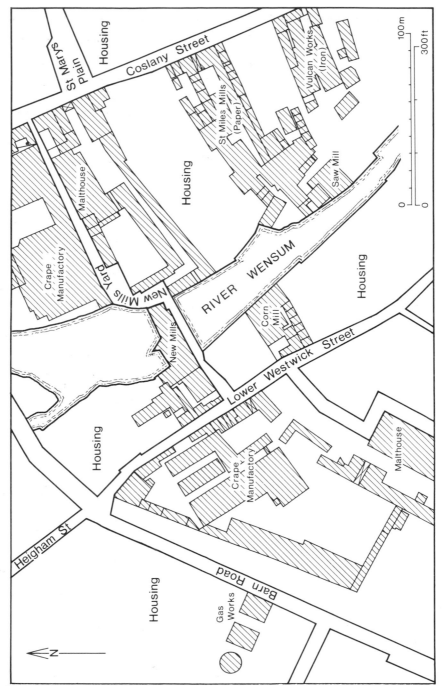

The New Mills area in 1885—based on the Ordnance Survey 1: 500 sheet LXIII.11.17. The New Mills, built originally as the City corn mills in 1401 became in part the pumping station for the City's water Supply in 1581 and finally the pumping station for the low level sewer in 1868. The declining textile industry was still in evidence in the premises of Grout and Co., silk crape makers as well as a wide range of 'new' industries.

John Love was a poor journeyman weaver living in Norwich during the first half of the Nineteenth Century and he comes to life in the newspapers of the 1830's and 1840's. Clearly a man of integrity, he was treasurer to the Norwich Weavers' Society and a Primitive Methodist lay-preacher, active both in the city and in South Norfolk. 'Few people', it was declared, 'remember him with any feelings but those of respect and attachment', and from all his action and sayings it is apparent that the prime interests of John Love were God and the condition of his fellow working people.

These were years of Chartist agitation, when the working-classes made vehement demands for universal adult suffrage and, amongst other things, for changes in the Poor Law of 1834 which forced people into workhouses before charity was provided. Locally, the movement began late in 1838, the early public meetings attracting enormous crowds. Some of the demands were for violent action: as, for example, for 'ten thousand Norwich men to rise and overthrow their oppressors'.

Involved in the movement from the time of its inception, John Love, however, was no advocate of violence. His view was that Almighty action would ensure the end of working-class oppression and that all he could do was to make the fact clear.

His arguments were sincere and, to him, logical. The Poor Law required that married couples forced into the workhouse should, as long as they remained there, be separated completely. This, Love declared, was 'inconsistent with the Scripture, for it separated those whom God had joined together', and so long as it was against the word of God, anyone who believed that word was not bound to obey that law. This was clearly mixing religion with politics. To Love, however, as to many thoughtful people of those times, there was no real divorce between the two, and it was on religious grounds that he and many other Nonconformists opposed State authority.

Throughout 1839, many Norwich Chartists worked whole-heartedly in the cause of revolution by armed violence. Yet, in the event, what violence occurred in the city was on a very small scale compared with outbreaks elsewhere and clearly a large number of people, despite the depths of their destitution and misery, were not prepared to resort to force.

Not that they were less hardy than the men of the industrial North and West. No one could accuse an angry Norwich crowd, quite accustomed to rip up the road cobbles for weapons, of being timorous. But behind the mass of disaffected working people there was the influence of Nonconformity. And there is no doubt that the message of John Love, to bring forward the revolution peacefully, was a great moderating influence.

An abortive rising in 1839 was followed by several years of peaceful agitation. These were bad times not only for the city weavers but also for the agricultural labourers, who voiced their discontent throughout the whole of the Eastern Counties. Love, after his 60-hour weaving week had ended, journeyed out to the towns and villages of the county taking a double message of hope, of Methodism and of Chartism, mixing prayer with economic reasoning.

Despite the many warnings they received from their employers, the labourers attended his meetings in hundreds: so much so that the Home Secretary came to interest himself in them. When not in the county, John Love held Sunday meetings on Mousehold Heath and on such occasions, it was not uncommon, the meeting over, for hundreds of people to descend into the city and go on to crowd the churches and chapels at divine service.

After 1845, Love left the city for a while to further the Chartist cause in the North. When the final petition was being organised in 1848, however, he returned to Norwich where his audiences were as large as ever. But by this time Norwich had entered upon a period of modest prosperity founded upon more varied activities, so the weavers were alone in their agitations. Failure was a foregone conclusion and by June, 1848, the Chartist movement in Norwich had died.

With its decease, John Love also disappeared. The last view we have of him and the few remaining Chartists attached to him, all rendered destitute by their activities, is the journey to the workhouse and to separation from their wives. He disappears in fact, suffering the very injustice against which he had agitated for the past ten years and more.

By his contemporaries John Love was variously regarded as a charlatan, a self-seeker, or a man inspired. It is to be doubted very much that he was a charlatan: and is it hard to believe self-seeking of a man who, at the outset of agitation, declared that 'he would only do that which was for the general good and that he would very likely sacrifice himself for that good'. Certainly he was a man before his time. The things he strove for—universal adult suffrage and humane provision for society's unfortunates—we now take for granted. He helped to sow and posterity reaps.

The case of James Zobel was very placid in comparison. He came to Norwich from London where he had served an apprenticeship to a glass-stainer. With the cathedral and many churches, the city doubtless held good prospects for a man carrying on such a trade and from what can be gathered from his 'diary' he seems to have enjoyed a good living. Like John Love, he was self-employed but unlike Love he would have had to possess sufficient capital to purchase a furnace, to obtain stocks of glass and to keep himself until his business was on a sound footing.

By the early 1840's, when he was about 40 years old, he lived in a rented house in Lady Lane (on the site of the modern Central Library) two rooms up and two down, one being the shop, for which he seems to have paid £10 a year. Bowling was then a popular pastime of working people, many public houses in the city having a green or two; and since Zobel enjoyed frequent sessions of bowling-cum-drinking he must have had quite a good income for a single man.

The Norwich inhabited by James Zobel, in fact, seems to have been a different city entirely from that in which John Love lived. Instead of the poverty and the misery so evident in the world of the weaver we see a city still invaded by the countryside, in which hawkers in great variety paraded the streets, crying fish, crabs, eels, cheese, flowers and fruits; a crowded, bustling, noisy (and probably noisome) city that we might not want to know today. But it was certainly, in Zobel's account, not a poor city.

Zobel married a widow of about his own age when he was nearly 40 years old, after a placid courtship; and with his marriage began a revolution in his life-style, his house being cleaned from top to bottom, whitewashed and disinfected. Reading his account, one feels that many houses must have been cleaner in the mid-19th Century than we are sometimes prepared to believe.

But Zobel not only took a wife; he also took his wife's father, a permanent invalid and this he seems to have done without regret. The weekly visits to the 'pubs' were maintained (no mention of economic hard-times in these pages), although as he got older the bowling was stopped for social drinking instead. Certainly, there seemed to have been sufficient money at this time—the late 1850's—to transform the Zobel trio into light-headedness and inebriation at times.

With increasing age and persistent illness, the father-in-law became progressively disabled and the burdens on Zobel and his wife increased. Eventually, the local Alderman was persuaded to bespeak a place for the invalid in the Great Hospital; and the last we see of him is his walking, with his bedding and personal effects loaded on a handcart, to the Great Hospital, to die there less than a year later.

Harder times also came to Zobel and his wife as they grew older and their income decreased. They moved into a smaller, cheaper house and, later, to one cheaper still. Finally, they occupied only two rooms in a 4½" wall, jerry-built house—a regular feature of life in those days. And there we leave him and his wife in their old age, the trials of which were so much harder then than now.

*   *   *   *   *   *

Zobel's diary holds no mention of hardship, misery, struggle. These were the lot of the oppressed and starving weavers. It does not mention political demands, for Zobel had the vote whereas John Love had lost his by the Municipal Reform Act of 1835. As a glass-stainer, Zobel was an upper working-class artisan and his life had an element of serenity noticeably absent from that of Love.

These, then, were two real people, living at the time when the textile industry was set in decline and when other industries were only partially taking its place. John Love typified the old; James Zobel the new. Their 'brief lives' help, perhaps, to bring personality and life to that rather dead term 'industrial change'.

III) **1900: Prosperity Regained**

The textiles manufacturing in Norwich was in reasonably good health at mid-Century and for perhaps two decades after. But when, eventually, the steam looms of the North of England had been so improved as to be capable of even the finest and most intricate work and when the coal they depended on was almost literally 'on the doorstep', competition became too much for many of the Norwich manufacturers. The result was a pronounced and progressive decline from 1870 onwards so that by 1900 some 2,000 people only, mainly women and girls, still earned their livings in the ancient trade. Thus, after a hundred years of difficulties and tribulations the industry which had entered the 19th Century with enormous zest, ability and capital, which in that time had produced hundreds of thousands of works of woven art and which had truly been the life-blood of generations of working-people in the city, passed quietly along the road to its ultimate extinction.

There was no tragedy attached to this for, in the second half of the Century, as one industrial door closed half-a-dozen or more opened, gently at first but uninhibitedly wide later. So, we read in *Directory of Norwich for 1900*, 'Notwithstanding the flowery accounts given of the trade of Norwich a century ago, the present commercial position of the city must surpass it . . . sending upwards its chimney shafts amongst the numerous steeples that adorn the area'. Clearly, capital and enterprise had turned away from textiles and entered the newer industries that changed economic circumstances now favoured. Of these, leather and brewing have already been mentioned as being long-established, even if still relatively small by 1850. But the latter part of the 19th Century witnessed the expansion of many others, some, like printing, already embryonic by 1850, and others, such as engineering almost entirely new.

The leather industry really divided into two: the processers—the tanners, curriers, finishers and cutters who, although they required much capital, were small users of labour; and the users—the saddlers, harness-makers and the boot-and-shoe makers—all of which were small-scale, self-employed and far more numerous. In fact, of the 8,000 or so 'leather workers' in Norwich at the end of Century, over 7,500 were boot-and-shoe-makers. So, in the words of one industrialist in 1900, 'Unable to compete with the North in the supply of covering for the back Norwich has gone in extensively for the manufacture of covering for the feet'—a fairly neat summary.

It isn't difficult to imagine the way in which shoe-making, whose employed workers would receive anything from 15/- to 35/- a week, replaced male workers in textiles earning 10/- a week, and often very much less. Adult workers didn't transfer from one to the other. They either lived their time out as weavers, or migrated, or emigrated. Their sons, who would normally have followed their fathers' trade, would make the transfer decision and swell the numbers seeking work in leather. Meantime, manufacturers (large or small) seeking employment for capital would go into leather as being the far more profitable. By roughly 1870, therefore, the leather industry, and in particular shoemaking, had become the natural 'inheritor' of the place once filled in Norwich by textiles manufacture.

Until about 1840, most shoe makers were self-employed craftsmen making to customer's order and operating in a very small way. Even so, standardization of sizes had for a long while been seen to offer immense advantages, for there is the record of a certain James Smith of Norwich who, in 1792, declared that the bespoke system 'made men dilatory' and that wholesale manufacture was the answer. By the 1860's, a number of such wholesalers had developed, one of which, the firm of Charles Winter, employed 800-900 shoemakers. Another such was James Howlett, founder of the long-lived Norwich firm of Howlett & White, Ltd., who, in 1850 or so, invested some £10,000 in a currying business and went forward into shoe making on a large scale.

This in fact set the pattern for the industry during the latter half of the Century. Leather was issued at a central office or factory and the 'self-employed shoe makers', working at home exactly as did weavers before 1850, collected the leather, made the shoes and took these back to the office in order to get their pay and further supplies of materials. It was skilled work and they appear to have been well paid; but it was wearisome and monotonous and, of course, there were no holidays as we know them, paid or unpaid. Heavy weekend drinking, in the nature of those times, became almost inevitable and the effects lasted from Saturday night till Monday, which thus became a regular holiday, or St Monday as the satirical then had it.

In the 1860's came the invention and introduction of leather-sewing machines which necessitated bringing the women and children, who closed (i.e. sewed together) the uppers and the linings, into factories while the heavy sole stitching continued to be done by men in their homes, the so-called garrett-masters. From this, it was only a short step to true mass-production in highly mechanised factories so that, of the 7,000-8,000 people who gained a livelihood from footwear making at or near the end of the Century, over 4,000 worked in factories.

By this time, too, the manufacturers had come to concentrate on high quality products, an echo of the policy of the silk manufacturers, and some 75,000 pairs of shoes were being made each week with an enormous annual value. The bulk of this production was effected by a few very large firms and some of these were famous for generations into the Twentieth Century.

Howlett & White of Colegate, for instance, operated 'one of the most extensive industrial establishments in the city and country'. Haldinstein & Sons in Queen Street not only employed two thousand boot and shoe workers but actually ran a large engineering works to make their own machinery. James Southall & Co., that had been founded in the 1770's by James Smith and controlled by the Charles Winter mentioned above, had a three storey factory in the Upper Market in which 'the lasting room alone measured 70 yards by 30 yards' and was packed with machinery. Lastly, there was Sexton & Sons in Fishergate which shipped its goods throughout the entire world. What an enormous faith in ability and enterprise each of these represented!

If one looks at the simple change (if there be such a thing) from the 100,000 or so people employed in the making of Norwich textiles in 1800 and see that by 1900 the major support of the city was in the hands of 8,000 or so workers one may indeed marvel. But there was no impoverishment as a result. It is true that change, the mechanism, brought a heavy burden of destitution and misery in its train. But the 8,000 workers of 1900 produced quite as much wealth as had the 100,000 of 1800 and, what is more, each workman enjoyed a higher standard of life. History does not really permit the reading of many lessons but maybe there is one here.

*   *   *   *   *   *

The brewing industry, so well established by 1850, was held (above) to be interesting, in that, like the textiles and leather industries, it linked the interests of the city and county—industry and agriculture—into prosperous inter-dependence. After 1850, the several brewers in the city gradually crystallised into about five large firms, famous in East Anglia until well into the Twentieth Century—Steward, Patterson & Finch, Bullard & Sons of the Anchor Brewery, John Youngs, Richard Crawshay (which became Young, Crawshay & Youngs, of Crown Brewery). All were highly organized and included the ownership of hop farms, malting and brewing establishments and hundreds of inns and 'pubs'. As an activity, they controlled immense amounts of capital and were stably profitable; but they employed comparatively few people, produced relatively few family incomes and so have little further interest for us.

Many other industries came to the fore instead, deriving simply out of the agglomeration of 50,000 or so people, all, as time went on, with increasing amounts of money to spend. At the same time, the city government progressively extended the range of its activities to give employment to many more workers than formerly, professional and manual. And the newer industries thrived under the stimulus. Paper-making, printing, newspaper production, advertising, represented a case in point and by 1900 these activities collectively brought well paid work to at least 1,600 people. The firm of Jarrold exemplifies the process. John Jarrold first came to Norwich in 1823 and took a print shop in London

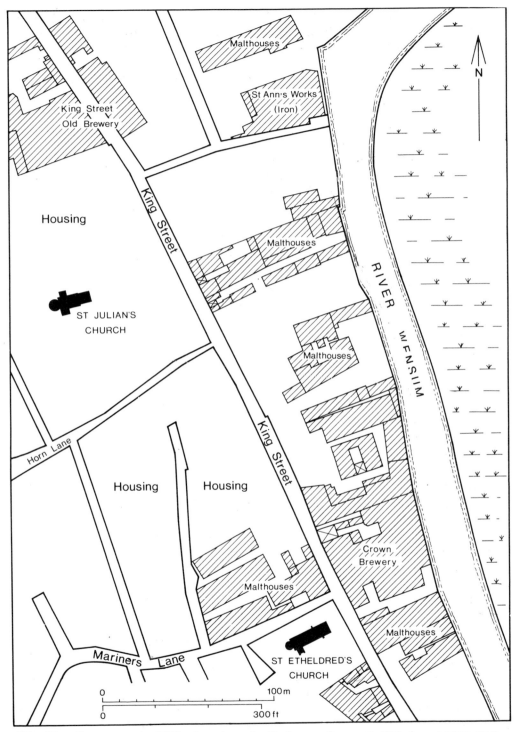

The King Street area in 1885—based on the Ordnance Survey 1: 500 sheet LXIII.15.9.
The importance of the malting and brewing industries and their dependence on river
trade is self-evident.

Street almost exactly where the store is now. After three Jarrold generations, this had come to be 'a very extensive, modern four-storey building in which all printing processes are carried on' (1895) plus 'two splendid shops'. It was more than, however, for John Jarrold was a firm in which 'the most cordial relations existed between employers and employed' and one which 'rendered invaluable assistance to the cause of education, the cause of temperance and the cause of religion'. It was a good example of the 'work ethic' so beloved of Victorians and of the operation of the 'social conscience' (see the first chapter also).

One of the less well-known income earners in Norwich by 1900 was iron-founding, not one that springs to mind quickly when considering the city's industries. Here, again, land ownership and agriculture were involved. Consider all the beautiful iron gates that kept out the hoi polloi from the country houses and the large—and not so large—estates for twenty miles around Norwich and all the tools and machines in use there; and consider also wire netting by the mile used to keep stock in and people out (Australia, too, used hundreds of miles of it) and some idea of the rural demand can be gained. Add all the fine grates, garden gates and domestic hardware for thousands of city households; and further add all the guttering, pipes, man-hole covers, etc. that were needed as the city council enforced improvements in drainage, roofing, water-supply and so on. Cumulatively, the demand for ironwork must have been immense and it was in reaction to this that a new large industry was generated.

But there was also a great variety of other industrial activities, the foundation of the wide economic base of the city. Perhaps the best example, certainly the most widely known was the firm of J. & J. Colman, the makers of starch (probably linked initially to the old textiles manufacture) and mustard, both of which tied city and hinterland yet again. The 100,000 people in Norwich not only provided the source of labour: they also consumed the products and J. & J. Colman thrived as Norwich thrived. Founded at Stoke Holy Cross, the firm transferred to Carrow in 1858 and by the end of the Century its single small factory had developed to cover twenty-six acres, with its stores, factories, workshops, wharves, timber and coal-yards, foundry, print shop, saw mills in one great agglomeration. Here again the Victorian 'work-ethic' was evidenced in Jeremiah James Colman, the senior partner (partner, note! None of the anonymity of Joint Stock organization there) 'in whose personality, unfaltering progress and untiring energy', it was said, 'went hand in hand'. But, as in the case of John Jarrold & Son, more was furnished than mere employment and educational (schools for the children of workpeople were provided, with 637 weekday and 570 Sunday pupils) and philanthropical needs were met and held to be just as essential.

In nothing though was the inter-dependence of city and country

The impressive ironwork facade of what was until 1984 Pank's on Cattle Market Street. The showrooms of what was then Holmes and Sons engineers were described as "new" by A. D. Bayne in his *History of Norwich* in 1869.

more greatly evidenced than in the produce which passed through the Agricultural Market. There was an abundant trade in wheat, moving from the country farmer to the city miller, and in barley which was collected in the city to be sent via Yarmouth to London or the North. The cattle market, the second largest in the kingdom, 'made an immense contribution to the prosperity of Norwich', the total value of cattle, sheep and lambs put up for sale during one period of six weeks amounting to £345,000, with a fair proportion trickling thence into the pockets of dealers, auctioneers, transporters, labourers, publicans and retailers. The old adage 'Where there's muck there's money' might have been coined originally in Yorkshire but it was certainly equally applicable to the Norwich market of the late 19th Century.

By 1900, in spite of all that has been written above of industrial variety in Norwich, such occupations accounted for less than 50% of the employment there. The Norwich Union Fire and Life Offices, founded late in the 18th Century, had enjoyed decades of prosperity and growth as, indeed, had the other if smaller insurance companies in the city. Additionally there were four major banks, meeting capital needs of both farmers and industrialists. Of the four, Gurney's Bank was by far the largest and it would appear that few significant developments took place in the area that were outside its purview. Clearly, such powerful organizations as the Norwich Union and Gurney's Bank must have greatly facilitated the expansion of commerce and trade in Norwich and brought wealth and influence to the leading citizens.

*   *   *   *   *   *

When all the activities noted above—textiles, footwear, iron founding, printing and commerce—have been taken into account, there still remain the occupations of the greatest part of the population mentioned. It is true that footwear manufacture and food processing employed some 4,000 of the city's women; yet domestic service, laundrywork and charring employed well over 5,500, a reflection, this, of the wealth of the rising middle classes in the city.

Similarly with male employment. The same two industries—footwear and food—employed some 9,000 males; but the total number of central and local government employees, members of the armed forces, professional people, gentlemen and students also totalled 9,000, while transportation and building work were almost as significant with 7,500 workers. It seems incredible to us, looking back from our highly industrialised 1980's, that there could have been 645 men tailors in the Norwich of 1900, and that women tailors, dressmakers and milliners should total 4,000. It was indeed the age of personal services from which, alas, it would seem that we have long since progressed. So, if one word could describe activities in the city at the end of a hundred years of development after 1800, it would be—variety.

So much for the economic activity of Norwich during the 19th Century. In 1800, the city was one of the wealthiest in the kingdom by reason of its worsted manufacture, founded as it was on two monopolies: skill in production and the East India Company's monopoly in marketing in the Far East. But monopolies always break down and those of Norwich did in the years before 1840, leaving an enormous gap in the earning pattern of the people—'The Years of Turmoil'. Gradually, other activities filled the gap and provided profitable uses for capital and labour, a process well in hand by 1870. After that, the economic base of the city was progressively extended, economically healthier and competitively efficient. This must have been the case for Norwich in 1900 was able to support a population almost three times as great as it did in 1800. 'Prosperity Regained' in fact.

It is really an interesting story; perhaps a salutory one. But certainly it is not one that can be lightly dismissed.

Industrial Development of Norwich 1800-1900

READING LIST

General

Directories of Norwich, 1801 (Peck), 1810 (Berry), 1830 (Pigot), 1835, 1845 (White).

Bayne, A. D. 'An account of the Industry & Trade of Norwich and Norfolk'. Norwich, 1852.

Beatniffe, R. 'Norfolk Tour', 1808.

Blakeley, E. 'History of the Manufacturers of Norwich'. No date but c.1850.

Hancock, R. 'Norwich Industries'. No date but post-1871.

Knights, M. 'Trades of Norwich, Past & Present'. Hicklings Almanac, 1889.

Robinson, Son & Pike. 'Descriptive Account of Norwich', 1895.

Textiles

Robberds J. W. 'Memoirs of W. Taylor', 1843.

Hudd, W. 'The Norwich and Norfolk Silk Industry'. Norfolk Archaeology, III, 1923.

Moreau, C. 'Rise & Progress of the Silk Trade', 1826.

Shoemaking

Sparkes, W. 'Shoemaking in Norwich', 1945.

Wheldon, F. 'A Norwich Century', 1946.

For more serious reading:

Edwards, J. K. 'The Decline of the Norwich Textile Industry'.
Yorkshire Bulletin of Economic and Social Research, Vol. 16, No. 1, May 1964.

CHAPTER SEVEN

The Church of England in Nineteenth Century Norwich
Richard Hale

On April 5th 1837 the Bishop of Norwich died. Henry Bathurst had been a friend of Parson Woodforde, who had collected his tithes for him when he was an absentee Norfolk rector. After long years at Oxford, and then at Durham, he had been at last promoted to a bishopric through the influences of Earl Bathurst with William Pitt. 'The more I hear of Norwich' he wrote to his wife 'the more I am convinced we shall like it.' As the Archbishop pointed out 'You will find it nearer £4,000 a year than £3,500.' Assuming the office of bishop at sixty, he early decided that reasons of health made it prudent to spend the winter at Bath, Cheltenham or Malvern. When in 1815, he was able to appoint his eldest son Henry, already installed in the wealthy living in South Creake, to the Archdeaconry of Norwich, he had a present help within the family circle. From one aspect he proved a surprise, for he soon showed himself an advocate of liberal causes. He voted for the emancipation of Roman Catholics: he showed an unusual tolerance and friendliness to dissenters: and finally he stood alone among the bishops as supporting parliamentary reform. As the years passed by he necessarily delegated episcopal functions to others. Helpful colleagues undertook the rare confirmations, and officiated at ordinations. There was growing criticism within the diocese: abuses were unchecked: in the church at large Norwich became known as 'the Dead See'.

When the Bishop died his son was hopeful. Had he not, in effect, run the diocese for some years? Had he not a claim on the see? Later he explained his feelings without restraint in a memoir of his father. Edward Stanley was made bishop, 'a *private* clergyman of no special note', wrote Archdeacon Bathurst, 'appointed over the head of the son who had been for twenty-three years Archdeacon in the diocese and most kindly treated by the clergy—a scholar and a gentleman.' With such statements the Archdeacon expressed his disgust, and soon after died at Cheltenham.

'A private clergyman' is, perhaps, an inadequate description of Edward Stanley.

His family was distinguished enough: he had been for thirty-two years rector of the family living of Alderley. He had been sixteenth wrangler at Cambridge, and had continued his interest in science and

Henry Bathurst. Bishop of Norwich 1805-1837. N.L.S.L.

Edward Stanley. Bishop of Norwich 1837-1849. N.L.S.L.

natural history: he had shown a concern about schools and education, and was liberally inclined in theology. He had refused the proposed new see of Manchester, and Melbourne's submission of his name for Norwich met with William IV's approval as one 'who added to exemplary duty as a parish priest the virtue of a good family, gentlemanly habits and literary and scientific pursuits'.

He at once met with obstacles. He asked that Thomas Arnold, of whom he was a friend and disciple, should preach his consecration sermon. The Archbishop of Canterbury refused on account of Arnold's heterodox reputation. Stanley declined to suggest an alternative, and the sermon was preached by the Archbishop's chaplain.

His arrival in Norwich was greeted with caution. He came with the reputation of a liberal and a reformer, neither calculated to commend him to his new see. His enthronement sermon defended conscientious dissent and non-religious education and as a result no request was made at the subsequent dinner to print what was stigmatised as 'the heretical sermon of a liberal bishop'—an omission that the Mayor and city fathers felt obliged in politeness to make good. The young Queen, however, read the sermon and six months later invited the Bishop to preach at Buckingham Palace.

161

The 'Dead See' soon began to feel winds of change. The most scandalous clergy were firmly dealt with: every effort was made to deal with the evil of pluralities and non-resident clergy, and ordination candidates were required to face searching examination—the rather frightening papers are still in the Cathedral Library. In Norwich itself the Bishop exercised an unusual personal ministry, unable to shed his long years as parish priest. He visited the poor and sick in yards and slums: he visited schools, delighting in children (he often took children of the Close for afternoon walks). He would attend the Cathedral service on Sunday morning, and in the afternoon would be found in the congregation of one of the city churches. No doubt it was a salutary stimulus! The vicar of St George Colegate never preached, but he preached an excellent sermon when Bishop Stanley arrived one Sunday. When the Bishop congratulated him he replied 'It should be good if it is like port—it has been in my pocket these many years.'

Stanley's coming to Norwich was at much about the same time as the Chartist agitation which reached its peak in 1839. He made no secret of his disapproval of 'Chartist Demagogues'. After a great meeting on Mousehold Heath the Chartists turned their attention to the churches: they would arrange to attend church in great numbers, sending the vicar some appropriate text for the sermon. 'Go to now, ye rich men: weep and wail for the miseries that are coming upon you' and 'If any will not work, neither shall he eat.' Some five thousand are alleged to have invaded St Stephen's, when the vicar instead preached on the Catechism duty of content with that state of life to which we are called. The congregation was not amused 'You get £200 a year' they shouted 'Come and weave bombazines'. The Bishop himself did not escape. Twice he had to expostulate with mobs who disrupted Cathedral services.

There was another occasion when, returning on foot from a meeting at St Andrew's Hall, Stanley found himself in the midst of a hostile crowd who 'saluted the active, spare little bishop with hoots and groans'. He went his way unperturbed only turning round every ten yards or so to fix the crowd with an 'eagle eye'. Harriet Martineau characterised him as 'timid as a hare'. It was a bad diagnosis. His courage was not only physical but moral, for he never shrank from exposing unpopular causes. In 1843 he took up the cause of Temperance, knowing the prevalence of drunkenness in Norwich. Father Matthew, the Irish Catholic Temperance pioneer had been asked to speak at St Andrew's Hall. The Bishop invited him to stay at the Palace, knowing that the unpopularity of Catholics and of the Temperance movement would draw criticism. In his own speech to the meeting of some two thousand people, Stanley was able to allude to his personal knowledge of Norwich men 'The day before yesterday I was passing through the streets when a rough and rude set of men, who knew me, spoke in tones loud enough to reach my ears. "What then—he would have us all Temperance men would he? And then he would want us to attend the sacrament." They were right. Unless you make drunken men sober you cannot sow the seed of religion in their hearts.'

When Jenny Lind came to sing in Norwich the bishop once more courted criticism by inviting her to the palace. It is difficult to understand the prejudice with which those concerned with public entertainment were regarded for much of the nineteenth century. Bishop Pelham, years later, would refuse to give his patronage to the Triennial Festival because he regarded the singers with suspicion. No such question troubled the more liberal Stanley, who was not averse to the theatre and concert. His generous welcome to Jenny Lind aroused her continuing interest in Norwich, and her subsequent benefactions are still commemorated by the Jenny Lind ward at the Norfolk and Norwich Hospital.

When Stanley died in 1849 he had overcome much of the opposition aroused by his liberal and reforming zeal. He was well known in the city not only among the wealthy and powerful, but among the poor in their crowded yards and the school children 'who would pull his coat tails to obtain his benignant smile'. Of his funeral his son, Dean Stanley, wrote 'Nothing like it has been seen in Norwich Cathedral since the Reformation—and I very much doubt, in any other Cathedral.' He was buried in the midst of the Nave, in the light of the west window, later glazed in accordance with his wishes. He was a good Bishop and a good

Zachariah Buck. Organist to Norwich Cathedral 1819-1877. N.L.S.L.

163

man, 'whose naturally unclerical tastes gave a double value to all he did, because it made people feel that what he said and did for them he said and did not merely as a clergyman and bishop, but as a friend, a man, and a Christian.'

In 1837 it had been suggested that the Palace, dreary, dilapidated and long neglected should be abandoned, and a suitably dignified house in the country bought for the Bishop. This Stanley refused. A residence in the city was essential not only for occasional visitors, but also as a place of meeting for such diocesan purposes as the conference of the newly revived Rural Deans. Furthermore the Bishop, some held, should not be divorced from his Cathedral. The Close should be his home.

Norwich Cathedral, like most others, was not at this time exactly a lively Christian centre: it had much in common with Barchester, and there were those who asked what justification there was for Cathedrals save 'Whatever is is right'. From 1822 to 1866 the Dean was the Hon. George Pellew: and from 1819 to 1877 the organist was Zachariah Buck. With such long tenure of two key positions it was inevitable that a certain somnolence should come to prevail, especially when the canonries were long occupied by pluralists—the Master of St Catharine's College, Cambridge; the Cambridge Professor of Geology and the Rector of St Giles in the Fields, London, while a fourth was mostly concerned with government military examinations.

Apart from official 'residential duties' for three months, the canons rarely lived in the Close.

The Cathedral services conformed to past tradition. Matins, Litany, Ante Communion on Sunday morning: Evensong, and on weekdays the two daily services. The Holy Communion was celebrated but once a month and Ascension Day and Saints' days utterly ignored. It was drearily respectable. Buck was an indifferent player and a still more indifferent composer. As organist his forte was the *Dead March in Saul* in which he obtained good effect by placing the whole of his forearm on the keyboard! He came to leave the organ to his assistants, himself concentrating on training the choir, where he had evidently something of genius. He invented a special wooden mouthpiece to help the boys to produce the tone he required, and was insistent on practice to produce the 'Runs and Shakes' which were in accordance with contemporary taste. The choir became renowned, and two of Dr Buck's boys were chosen for solos in the first church performance in England of Bach's *St Matthew Passion* at Westminster Abbey in 1871. Another of his pupils Dr Mann became organist of King's College, Cambridge, where he laid the foundations of the choir's present pre-eminence. The choristers were grossly overworked and little attention was paid to their welfare by the Cathedral dignitaries, with the honourable exception of Professor Sedgwick, who gave them strawberry and cream teas in the summer!

As the years passed by criticisms became vocal. In 1862 the *Norwich*

Spectator condemned the Cathedral roundly 'Nothing can be worse than the irreverent, careless and undevotional character of worship in the parish church of the diocese' and 'A more cold and miserable service I have seldom heard. Not a dignitary was present. The prayers were read with a most depressing effect, and as if to show how little was cared about the Christian Year—nay seemingly to run counter to it—the anthem was "Unto us a boy is born" thoroughly out of place at Ascensiontide'. Something of the same criticism was made by the vicar of Dereham at the enthronement of Bishop Pelham when the words of the anthem were 'I have exalted one chosen out of the people'. 'Hardly' said Armstrong, 'appropriate for the scion of a noble family'. In 1865 there were signs of progress. For the first time since the Revolution of 1688 there was a celebration of Holy Communion on Ascension Day—so largely attended as to astonish the Chapter. The Chapter also promised, after something of a storm to celebrate Communion every Sunday.

Behind this renewed activity in Cathedral circles lay the developments of the decade after Edward Stanley's death. His liberal sympathies had been followed by his successor, Samuel Hinds. A shy man, he had gained the reputation of a 'dry' bishop, very remote in comparison with

John Thomas Pelham. Bishop of Norwich 1857-1893. N.L.S.L.

Stanley. The death of his wife left him lonely and in ill health and he was little regretted when—to the delighted scandal of Norwich society he married his cook, and within a short time resigned to a long retirement. His successor, the Hon. John Pelham, was very much of the aristocracy: definitely of the 'Evangelical' school: puritanical and exceedingly energetic. He revived ruridecanal chapters with which he regularly met, and in his time the Diocesan Conference was to find its beginnings. Benjamin Armstrong, Vicar of Dereham comments in his diary that at Pelham's enthronement 'A vast number of clergy, "High" and "Low" assembled at the Palace to present an address'. Since 1849 new life, interest and energy was to be seen in the church. The influence of new ideas whether from Oxford theologians, Cambridge ritualists, or the broad church philosophies was making itself widely felt. The Victorian court with its strict morality and religious observance had wide social influence: men like Kingsley and Maurice were awaking the social conscience. One way and another the latter half of the century all over the county was a time of 'Boom in Religion'. The 1851 census was the only one in which investigation was made into church attendance. In Norwich the figures showed that the Church of England still held a preponderance: their total attendances on March 20th 1851 amounted to 15,087—far above their nearest rivals the Peculiar Baptists with 3,625. Such figures are not very meaningful, but the editor of the summary of the Census, H. Mann, provided a deal of food for thought on such matters as the churches and the working class: and how far there should or could be more co-operation between the churches.

One result of all the thought, writing and discussion about religion in the first half of the century had been a new sense of the nature of the Church, far different from the rationalist and Erastian concepts which had hitherto prevailed. The old accepted order was being questioned and challenged. New ideas of decency and order, of beauty in worship, demanded change. Revived ritualism entailed the rearrangement and renewal of church furnishings. Church music was coming to mean organs and surpliced choirs, not the parish orchestra in the gallery plodding away at the dull metrical psalms of Tate and Brady. The contrast between the comfortable cushioned pew for the rich and the hard bench for the poor was not tolerable to a church preaching of brotherhood. Alongside such considerations as these was the wide interest in church architecture and 'ecclesiology' which had its origins in Romanticism in general, and the work of the Cambridge *Camden Society* in particular. This is the background which explains the astonishing fact that in the latter half of the century every ancient church in Norwich except St Helen's and St Simon and St Jude's underwent some measure of restoration.

In the city one brief episode claims attention of necessity. In January 1864 the Reverend Joseph Leycester Lyne installed his monks in a tumbledown house on Elm Hill. He had become convinced that it was his vocation to restore to England the monastic life of earlier days. Imbued with ideas more romantic than scholarly, devout, eloquent and persuasive, he was throughout his life totally oblivious to the need for organisation and management and pursued his own way wilfully and without discretion. He and a few he had gathered round him had already for a few months experimented in the religious life at Claydon, where they had become a burden and embarrassment to Mr Drury, the vicar. By this time there were those in Norwich who were enthusiastically 'high' church, who knew something of the new 'ritualism' and were not averse to challenging the 'Evangelical' Bishop Pelham.

Lyne, who now took to himself the title of Father Ignatius, though still only a deacon, was immensely pleased with the offer of the Elm Hill house. Of late years it had been a rag merchant's warehouse, but to his romantic imagination the Elm Hill site gave him some sort of continuity with the Blackfriars of old. The little group of men huddled in the draughty cold house were even poorer than their neighbours, and, not unlike the friars of old, soon received generous help from those around. There was something heroic about it, as well as absurd—like the extraordinary gift of female nightdresses that they at first welcomed as popish vestments! A major difficulty was that there was no priest to celebrate Communion. Providence answered in the form of Mr Hillyard, vicar of St Lawrence.

A former curate of Dereham, where the church was accounted 'High', Mr Hillyard had an Evangelical background and found in Ignatius something to appeal to both sides of his personality. He offered a daily celebration of Holy Communion and each morning the monks processed from Elm Hill in their somewhat fanciful habits. Daily celebration was unheard of in a city where many churches still only had a quarterly communion. A procession of 'monks' was something of a rare show. Hillyard was persuaded to introduce vestments: to light candles: to place flowers on the altar. To some it was a public scandal. Mr Hibgame, remembering fifty years later, talks of the large congregations at Elm Hill, where a chapel was built (which still remains). 'There for the first time I heard hymns such as *Pilgrims of the night* and *Faith of our Fathers*, a great change from the still suriving Tate and Brady of some city churches'. He remembers, too, the services of St Lawrence with 'banners, vestments, incense'. But the great appeal was Mr Hillyard's preaching which attracted all young and old, rich and poor. Nowadays the decorations would be considered gaudy and unartistic, but the church was poor, the cheapest available got and this with sacrifices. At first there was rowdiness and the vicar needed a police escort home, but the fuss died down. It was Ignatius who caused trouble. Hearing that the vicar and some of his flock, together with some Elm Hill adherents intended going to a ball in St Andrew's Hall he forbade them on the grounds that this was a sacrilegious use of a consecrated building (this after three centuries of secularization). They refused to take this seriously, until Ignatius sent one of his monks to make a list of those going in, and next Sunday announced that they must perform absurd and degrading penances and 'excommunicated' Mr Hillyard.

The monks perforce departed from St Lawrence and endeavoured to find what they desired at St Saviour's, to the dismay of the vicar, who joyfully received Bishop Pelham's advice 'If these monks present themselves for Communion in this ridiculous dress, you have my authority to pass them over'. As had happened before and would happen again Ignatius in his egotism was alienating bishop and clergy. The financial state of the monks depended largely on what Ignatius could raise by preaching tours, which meant frequent absences during which the odd assortment of so called monks were left on their own. During one of these absences some of them rebelled, declared Ignatius deposed, and announced it all publicly. The 'Abbot' returned and restored peace by some conciliation and some expulsions, only to find a little later that a new scandal had become public concerning one of the monks which reflected most undesirably on the community. Added to this was the chaos of the finances. Ignatius retreated into a breakdown: the monastery was dissolved, and his local adherents left to pick up the pieces as best they could. A broadsheet expressed the feelings of many.

> 'We need no strange garb or close shaven skull
> Or unsightly mummery but a heart that is full
> Of thanks to the Almighty and pious regard
> For to lead a life godly and full of reward.'

Thus the affair ended, so far as Norwich was concerned, but it had its influence. Mr Hillyard was still at St Lawrence where the standard remained the same. At St Gregory there was something of a battle to retain the improvements made by a vicar when his successor endeavoured to undo them. St John Maddermarket was in an uproar when a curate of the notorious ritualistic church of St Barnabas Pimlico was appointed: but they found he was a deeply earnest man and soon his church became well attended. Later Mr Ram was in the course of a long ministry to make St John Timberhill a ritualist stronghold. This was all part of the church coming alive. On the other side St Giles was the great Evangelical stronghold, its clergy causing no small offence by preaching all over the city. The new Heigham churches, too, were in the whole of that direction: and the building of the new churches in the suburbs along these years was a witness to renewed zeal.

In the end much depended on the clergy, high, low or broad. Mr Hibgame in his *Norwich Recollections* emphasises the importance of selfless devotion 'I think it was about this time that a great epidemic of smallpox broke out over Norwich . . . Mr Nash, first rector of St Philip's especially signalised himself in the noble way he visited case after case utterly regardless of danger ... Mr Dixon of North Heigham was also indefatigable in his efforts to fight the disease in the low parts of his parish. These two men were splendid types of Evangelical clergymen and their names should not be forgotten. Mr Hillyard was equally brave and would go fearlessly into the worst courts and yards of his poor parish visiting all who wished to see him'. He had the assistance of the sisterhood he founded to help in the parish. That order still survives, for it followed him to Belper in Derbyshire and is still the Sisterhood of St Lawrence.

For most parishes the remaking of parish life is an unchronicled fact of history with no documentary evidence save the unrewarding figures of accounts and registers. For one parish however we have a well documented record of a decade of ministry. The Reverend John Durst was vicar of St Peter Permountergate in Conesford from 1862-1872. A scholar of Gonville Caius College, Cambridge and a Londoner by birth he was ordained at Norwich in 1859 and came to St Peter's after curacies at St Stephen's, Norwich and Mattishall. He left in the parish records a notebook entitled *Speculum Gregis* in which he lists communions over the years. In 1862 celebrations were infrequent and irregular. Hitherto the incumbent had usually been a minor canon and until 1859 the vicar had also charge of Eaton. In 1860 during the brief incumbency of Mr Day work had been done in the church. The gallery was removed, the pews done away with and the church reseated. To Durst fell the task of rebuilding the congregation. Within a year he had divided the parish between eleven district visitors, two of them men. With their assistance he completed a comprehensive survey, social and religious, of the parish, entering each family and recording children, earnings, rent, religious allegiance and other relevant details. Inevitably it is not complete nor the stuff that statistics are made of.

It shows, as one would expect, the nominal Church of England in the majority: next came those who professed no religious attachment: then 'Dissent'. Out of the inhabitants of sixteen yards and streets surveyed there was only one Roman Catholic and two 'Mormons or Infidels'. This compilation was one fruit of organised visiting. The other was to be seen in the Communion figures. In 1862 there were ten celebrations in the year: by 1869 a weekly communion had been established. Easter Communions had doubled and the total number of communicants risen from 832 to 2,283. A school was built in 1863 at a cost of over £1,200. Reporting to the Bishop for the 1865 visitation the vicar recorded that there were three services on Sunday. In the morning the average congregation was 350: in the afternoon 250: in the evening 350. Weekday services were held on Fridays and special days. The Sunday School numbered 220 average: the Adult Class attendance was 30 out of 35: the Bible Class 70 out of 93 in the books. There were 400 sittings in the church and all were free. Later there is record of a Sunday School

Shoe Club: a Charity and Coal Club and a weekday school Provident Club. Bodies as well as souls mattered.

Over the river Pockthorpe was even poorer than Conesford. The vicar of St James's in the 1850's had a hard task in his slum parish of courts and yards stinking with refuse, full of the unemployed and the unemployable. For 3,300 souls there were thirty-five public houses, places not only of drunkenness but of infidelity and vice. The vicar, Mr Ross, calculated that 2,490 out of a population of 3,300 never came into contact with the church. 'The soil is not naturally barren but lying fallow.' In his appeal for wider help he naturally urges his own need—one clergyman is not enough: but all must begin with material things. Housing must be improved: if someone would buy up or lease property and recondition it: purchase dilapidated and unhealthy tenements and rebuild: erect lodging houses for single people. This would not only be for official bodies to do, but private philanthropists could help. The streets should be cleaned—it was a disgrace to allow a district to be a nursery for pestilence: why not employ the unemployed? Help the pauper to feel he is a man! Why, too, should not the poor man have his club and reading room? A place for a pleasant and profitable evening. 'We appeal for the poor, the degraded, the dying . . .' It was an impassioned appeal which achieved little. It shows, however, the concern for people and education.

Another lasting memorial of this concern is the Church of England Young Men's Society (C.E.Y.M.S.) which started in 1847 'to foster personal religion and real improvement in members and to stir up interest in revisions. Not until it moved to Orford Hill in 1876 did the Society really flourish, achieving some 750 membership. It offered instruction in vocal music, Greek, Latin, French, Photography, Chemistry, Drawing, Mathematics, Building Construction, Architecture, Bookkeeping and Shorthand. In the end it was the recreational facilities that prevailed, Cricket, Tennis, Harriers and, of course, football. (Norwich City Football Club took its origins in a secession from C.E.Y.M.S.) This club would not, however, have met the needs of Pockthorpe. It attracted a middle class membership—young clerks and so forth: and indeed itself at one point endeavoured to establish a 'Settlement' in the Over-the-River slums, where by 1892 some things were happening. The Ditchingham sisters came to help at St James's and there was a 'Scripture Reader' to assist at the barracks. We gain little information from the vicar's visiting book, which in Pepys' fashion he wrote in French, here and there transliterated into Greek (perhaps he was fearful of losing it!) but the sisters published a pamphlet on their work. In forty years little had improved.

Pockthorpe was a place of 'Poverty, Wretchedness and Sin' where in some yards Satan ruled unchallenged, and the neighbourhood of the barracks fostered here the dishonourable side of a garrison town. Sunday was a day for drunkenness, quarrelling and open shops. Perhaps things had improved: there was more indifference than hostility. The church was now alone: 'Poverty appears to drive the Non Conformists out'. Certainly the church did what it could. Services were held twice on weekdays, and on all holy days besides Sundays. There were new buildings where the Sunday School met. A nursery had been set up where working mothers could leave their children for 2d. a day: there was a workroom where some occupation was found for the unemployed. The maternity club to help those expecting babies was usually known as the 'Eternity Club'. The sisters even ran a ward for the not too seriously sick, and provided meals for the sick at home, and a store of nursing requirements. All in all it amounted to a noble effort to alleviate the ills of Norwich's poorest slums. The Church was not idle in the parishes. No one could accuse it of unconcern.

Dean Goulburn. Dean of Norwich 1866-1889. N.L.S.L.

In 1866 a new era began at the Cathedral with the coming of Dean Goulburn. Eton, Balliol and a Fellowship at Merton had been followed by eight years as Headmaster of Rugby. He resigned in order to take up parish work in Paddington, and came to Norwich with good parish experience. A scholar and teacher, he now had time to preach widely and to write. He cared profoundly for the Cathedral and made improvements beyond necessary repairs, raising and extending the Presbytery, and providing an access stair to the 'Reliquary Chapel'. His large book on the Nave Bosses, made visible by the removal of layers of colourwash, remains authoritative and also contains the only available account of the

171

history of the Diocese. He was not in sympathy with those of his fellow deans who were making their cathedrals centres of diocesan life: rather he saw it as a centre of quiet scholarship and devotion. That, at least, was something to aim at, and he was anxious too, that the musical tradition should be maintained and improved, though his plans made with Dr Buck's successor for a new organ were frustrated by the Chapter.

It was with Dean Lefroy, who succeeded when Goulburn resigned in 1889 that the Cathedral really came to life. A Dubliner, he had become a reporter on the *Irish Times* on leaving school. By combining work at night and study by day he succeeded in gaining a degree in 1863, and then was accepted for ordination in the new diocese of Liverpool, becoming a canon, and then Archdeacon of Warrington. To come to Norwich in 1889, was to enter a strange world, unfamiliar to one who had risen from the people and served an industrial ministry. 'A beautiful somnolence rested over the Cathedral life of that day' wrote his biographer. 'Everyone was just doing the duties by statute and no more. The Dean needed to preach but few times a year . . . the canons were well paid and little worked. The masses in general knew the Cathedral by the prominence of its spire . . . Wealth and social rank had the Cathedral to themselves. The Sunday life of the Close was as charmingly exclusive as its life on the other six days of the week'. The new Dean at once decided to do at Norwich what had already been done with success elsewhere—to have a Nave mission service on Sunday evening. He was a good preacher and gathered a crowded congregation as he had done in special Lent services and recitals. For his purposes, however, it was the wrong congregation: regular members from the Close: visitors from other churches: not the poor, the unchurched, the seekers. His words in the first sermon were plain. He did not want them there—they should be in the streets, not in the Cathedral 'Go out into the slums and be missionaries in Norwich . . . another Sunday, be more self denying and watch the alleys, the slums and the doors of public houses'. He followed this with the announcement that henceforth there would be no appropriated pews in the Cathedral. 'This has led to the estrangement of many from the House of God, has fostered the notion that the Cathedral is for the privileged classes and has from the assertion of pecuniary considerations given to those who possess means undue advantage over those who do not'.

The repercussions in the Chapter and the Close can be imagined! Sacrifice of dignity; doing away with old traditions: inviting in the slums! In the end the Dean's view won sympathy, understanding and co-operation: the Nave service became a mission service, and Norwich acquired a reputation also for free musical services with such oratorios as Mendelssohn's *St Paul* and Gounod's *Redemption* offered for general edification.

The Cathedral fabric was in great need of attention. In Goulburn's time some work had been done: but much was still deplorable. Windows were blocked: the core of the tower piers was visible: flaking plaster and ochre covered wall surfaces and the transepts were still screened off. From 1892-4 the Choir was cleared for restoration. The Cathedral was to undergo the careful repair that had been given to the City churches. In 1899 a new organ was dedicated, replacing that which after sixty-five years was probably the poorest Cathedral organ in the country. By the end of the century the Cathedral would never be thought of, to use a seventeenth century description as a 'vast and altogether useless building'. Neglected chapels had been restored to use: the daily round of worship was carried out with dignity and beauty, and the 'parish church of the diocese' had become a centre of relevant activity for the city which it dominated.

Christ Church was built in 1873 (see Map III:i) one of the new suburban churches, it served the Town Close Estate and the wedge of development between Newmarket and Unthank roads.

The parishes of the city had been transformed. In 1900 the sort of service held for example at St Etheldreda's in 1850 sounded impossible. The rector then was a venerable looking old gentleman with an impediment in his speech. When the service was in the afternoon he would arrive just before 3 p.m. having driven over from his house at Heigham, and after waiting a little would say to the clerk . . . 'Well H, we might as well begin'. The church was full of massive pews with seats all round, and at the end of the nave was the three decker pulpit. The sexton in his green robe with yellow braid pulled the bell; the clerk in sombre black gown accompanied the vicar to the vestry. Despite the exhortation there were rarely any brethren to address: the regulars were six poor widows who enjoyed parish charity and a handful of children. The service was said: there were no hymns or music, and the sermon lasted a regular half an hour. Weddings were only solemnised on Sundays at 9.20 a.m. and Baptisms on Sunday afternoons. Little wonder that the congregation was minimal. St Etheldreda's was not untypical of what was happening in the lesser churches. The contrast of fifty years later is wonderful. All churches had acquired an organ—or at least an harmonium: surpliced choirs had won their way almost everywhere, and the hymn book had become an essential companion to the Book of Common Prayer. Flowers in church were no longer considered a sign of popish leanings, and the black gown was no longer thought a necessary costume for the preacher, and everywhere decency and order had come to prevail.

In the city and its life the Church had acquired a new energy and a new relevance. No longer was its concern shown only by traditional charity doles, which were now regarded as of little use and doubtful morality. Almost every church had its provident clubs, its social organisation which played a real part in helping the poorer folk and the unemployed, and were on occasion a missionary agency too. An introduction to the parish Penny Bank could lead on to contact with the clergy and an entirely new life in every way.

All in all the Church at the end of the Victorian age could look back with some satisfaction. Fortunately it did not always do so. Dean Lefroy for example, succumbed to no such temptation, and preaching in London at the Chapel Royal, gave something of a doom and gloom sermon. A critic wrote 'When he next comes . . . let him see if he can be more triumphantly eloquent by assuring us, as any man can see who doesn't go through life with his eyes shut, that the world is growing better'. Surveying the Victorian era one sees what the writer meant. But the cautious Dean had the better judgement.

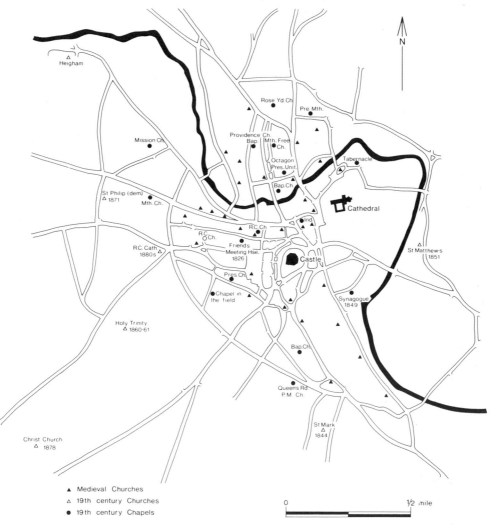

Heigham

Rose Yd. Ch.

Pre. Mth.

Mission Ch.

Providence Ch.
Bap. Mth. Free
Ch.

Octagon
Pres. Unit.

Tabernacle

St Philip (dem)
1871   Mth. Ch.

Bap. Ch.

Cathedral

R.C. Ch.

St Philip (dem)

Ind.

R.C.
Ch.

R.C. Cath
1880s

Friends
Meeting Hse.
1826

St Matthew's
1851

Castle

Pres. Ch.

Chapel in
the field

Synagogue
1849

Holy Trinity
1860-61

Bap. Ch.

Queen's Rd
P.M. Ch.

St Mark
1844

Christ Church
1878

▲ Medieval Churches
△ 19th century Churches
● 19th century Chapels

0   ½ mile

The Churches and Chapels in Norwich as shown on Morant's map 1873. The many new Non-Conformist chapels and the ring of new Anglican churches in the fast-growing suburbs show up clearly.

CHAPTER EIGHT

Nonconformity in Nineteenth Century Norwich
Richard Hale

On Monday, March 31st, 1851, there was a general census, by then an accepted feature of each decade. It had a unique accompaniment: an official, though voluntary, count of all attendance at places of worship on the previous day. Despite many objections and criticisms, the majority of returns were sent in, listing the number of churches in each denomination, the number of free and appropriated sittings available, and the number of those attending services morning, afternoon and evening. The results were published by Horace Mann, the Registrar's appointed officer in 1854. From the mass of statistics he produced an astonishing report, beginning with the religion of the Druids! Its final conclusions were disturbing. Five and a quarter million had attended Church of England services: five and a half million had attended those of other religious bodies: the largest part of the population had gone nowhere. Mann's figures were challenged. There were anomalies and discrepancies: returns were not complete: some were impossibly inaccurate. Nevertheless, by and large, his conclusions had to be accepted.

The figures for Norwich show that the Church of England was far stronger than any other single denomination: but the number of Nonconformists was greater. Church attendances on Sunday, March 30th, 1851 were 15,087 and Nonconformist attendances were 16,185 (a majority even discounting Roman Catholics, Latter Day Saints and Jews). The uncomfortably large number of 31,272 people had attended no church service. These conclusions gave Nonconformity something of a new status and underlined for all churches the need for missionary endeavour.

Norwich Nonconformity had a long history. The 'Lollards' Pit' down by the river kept green the memory of the martyrs of 1422. When Archbishop Parker was trying to suppress Puritan 'prophesyings', Queen Elizabeth I instructed him to 'begin with Norwich'. Trading contacts with the continent opened East Anglia to ideas of religious reform, and the arrival of the 'stranger' immigrants brought to Norwich more radical principles than those embodied in the Anglican Settlement. The Commonwealth regime, proscribing the Church of England, gave new freedom for the development of churches founded on different

Norwich table from H. Mann—Report on 1851 Census

Denomination	Number of Churches	Sittings			Attendance: March 30 1851		
		Free	Appropriated	Total	a.m.	aft.	p.m.
Church of England	41	3986	2533	15351	6520	6381	2186
Independent	3	380	1866	2246	1735	250	989
Peculiar Baptist	4	699	1748	2447	1639	817	1169
General Baptist	1	150	150	300	200	150	150
New Connection	3	206		236	116	198	132
Society of Friends	1	408		408	93	41	
Unitarians	1	130	380	500	491		136
Wesleyan Methodist	5	696	1495	2181	494	506	669
Primitive Methodist	4	196	838	1054	607	604	788
Wesleyan Reform	1	120	450	570	322	117	294
Countess of Huntingdon	1	250	700	950	100	115	80
New Church	1	12	120	132	90		106
Independent Congregations	11	1740		1740	497	974	1035
Roman Catholics	1				250		
Latter Day Saints	1	400		400		181	
Jews	1	59	30	89	26		24

Population of Norwich 68,195.
3 Church of England made no return on sittings: attended by c.300.
1 Church of England made no return on sittings or attendance.
1 Primitive Methodist made no return on sittings: attended by 13.
1 Roman Catholic made no return on sittings: attended by c.300.

doctrines and disciplines. They became firmly established and strong enough to survive the discouragement and persecution that followed the Restoration, and to take an accepted place in Society after the Toleration Act. The Repeal of the Test and Corporation Acts in 1828 and Catholic Emancipation in 1829 gave political freedom to those who were not members of the Church of England.

Nevertheless those outside the Established Church continued to suffer many disabilities which lasted into the nineteenth century. They were excluded from the older universities. John Joseph Gurney (1788-1847) was educated in Oxford—but not as a member of the university. Often they had to be buried in churchyards without their own service, a disability which the pioneer private 'Rosary Cemetery' in Norwich did something to meet. In the countryside tithes were a perennial source of grievance, and in the towns the compulsory church rates were regarded as an obnoxious burden. Such matters caused abiding dissension, and fostered a deal of anti-church feeling and agitation for disestablishment. Paradoxically, every Bishop of Norwich in this century showed friendliness to those of other persuasions.

The older 'Orthodox Dissenting' churches were the Presbyterian church, the Independents (later Congregationalists) and the Baptists. The Society of Friends, too, had a long history, but lay apart from Orthodoxy.

By the nineteenth century the Presbyterian line was represented by the Octagon Chapel. In 1688 the church had moved to the Colegate site and it flourished sufficiently to commission Thomas Ivory's masterpiece, the Octagon, in 1756. It raised doubts in the mind of John Wesley 'I was shown Dr Taylor's new Meeting House, perhaps the most elegant one in Europe . . . the Communion Table is fine mahogany, the very latches of the pew doors are polished brass. How can it be thought that the old coarse gospel should find admission here?' Wesley wrote ironically. He would have known that the Octagon sermons were of an intellectualised type in great contrast with his own.

In the second decade of the nineteenth century the Octagon, like the majority of Presbyterian churches, became Unitarian. Presbyterianism did not return to Norwich until 1866, when four Scottish linen drapers refounded the church, a chapel being built in Theatre Street in 1875. The last decades of the eighteenth century and the first of the nineteenth were the heyday of the Octagon. It was the religious centre for the Norwich intelligentsia—families such as the Taylors, the Aldersons and the Martineaus. Even William Taylor (see Chapter I) philologist and German scholar, free-thinker though he was, not only escorted his blind mother to service on the Sabbath, but also turned his poetical gifts to the writing of occasional hymns for the chapel. Successive ministers, while themselves keeping aloof from involvement, fostered the political as well as the intellectual activities of their flock in this age of Revolution. As the years passed so did the brilliant circle. The locality ceased to be fashionable. Rational religion lost its popular appeal. The Octagon survived, and if we read the description of a service in 1880, so did its traditions, for at the service there was 'a metaphysical disquisition on Tennyson's two voices' which overtaxed the hearer's understanding. It was however a 'concerned' congregation. They maintained the 'Presbyterian school' in the poor district of King Street, where 'Alcock's Yard' at the corner of Rose Lane commemorated Mr T. Alcock, headmaster for many years. Although a strict disciplinarian he left with his pupils pleasant memories of evening readings of the *Old Curiosity Shop* while being regaled with sausages cooked in a dustpan and potatoes roasted in the fire. Another memory was of the interview each school leaver had with members of the Octagon committee: evidently there was a real personal interest. This was shown, too, in the 'Brotherly Society' founded in 1824, to visit and help the sick. It was not just a 'Benefit Society', but was based on true fraternal principles. The offices of the Society circulated in democratic fashion: at one time the chairman might be a Martineau: at another the local bricklayer. They even developed a brass band as an expression of participation and harmony! It was said that the Octagon motto was 'Others' Need'—a far cry from barren intellectualism.

Almost next door to the Octagon is the Old Meeting House, which was built in 1698 and is typical of the best in dissenting architecture. By the nineteenth century it had become a quietist respectable church, preserving its orthodox principles if perhaps a little old fashioned. There were occasional dissensions. In 1808 a few members joined the French Church, and later joined the Octagon, and in 1823 the minister, Mr Hull seceded to the Church of England, becoming incumbent of St Gregory's. The church survived and in 1841 celebrated its bicentenary by the building of spacious new schoolrooms, evidence of renewal and activity. As the century passed the principle of absolutely independent churches yielded to the expediency of association, and a new spirit came into Congregationalism.

This was exemplified in the ministries of John Alexander (1797-1868) and George Barrett (1839-1916) which almost covered the century. Alexander was a student of the Hoxton Academy, one of those dissenting institutions which provided an excellent education for those excluded from the universities. He was invited to the Tabernacle to preach for a month 'with a view' as the phrase was. His beginnings were inauspicious. The London coach dropped him in Norwich in the early hours of Easter Eve 1817, when he found the city shocked by the fatal steam packet explosion at the Foundry. Proceeding to the minister's house, he knocked. He announced himself as a window opened. 'I don't know you, Sir'—the window slammed, and Alexander was stranded. Fortunately, next day introductions were amicably effected, and most encouraging

John Alexander. Minister of Princes Street United Reform Church 1818-1866. N.L.S.L.

179

The original Princes Street Chapel as built in 1818. Sillett 1828.

The surviving Princes Street Chapel showing the front which was added in 1869 by Boardman together with the adjoining building.

congregations came to the trial sermons. At once difficulties arose. The Tabernacle, built near the 'Adam and Eve' by James Wheatley, the pioneer Methodist, was now vested in the trustees of the Countess of Huntingdon's Connexion, a body owing something to Anglicanism, something to Independency, and most to Whitfield's legacy of Calvinism. To the trustees Alexander was not acceptable. For his final sermon he preached on 'Weeping may endure for a night, but joy cometh in the morning'. It was, he later said, 'the text which founded Princes Street'. Four hundred people asked him to stay and after an interval for reflection he agreed to do so, holding Sunday services in the Lancasterian school on Palace Plain, and weekday services in the 'French Church' in Queen Street. It proved to be a stable and enthusiastic congregation and in March 1819 the foundation stone of a new chapel was laid, opposite St Peter Hungate. Nine months later, on December 1st, the opening service was held.

There followed in the spring of 1820 the official constituting of the church and the ordination of Alexander, the beginning of a ministry that was to last until 1866. It was not all easy going. There was a debt on the building which was a constant anxiety. At one point the money for the minister's stipend had to be diverted to the building fund, and he offered to resign. It was only a temporary setback. The steady growth of the congregation brought financial security. By 1850 there were seven hundred members, and by 1866 eleven hundred, a telling testimony to the efficiency of Alexander's ministry. In 1869 the premises were expanded and rebuilt on a grander scale to Boardman's design.

The Baptist Church in St. Mary's parish. Sillett 1828.

This was no introverted church, nor one content to rest on its laurels. 'Churches' said Alexander 'exist not only for preserving and professing the truths of the Gospel, but for propagating them'. One early venture, as described in the next chapter, was a Sunday School, started in 1820 with eighty-one scholars, a work which was soon extended into the notorious slums of Pockthorpe. Similar work was done in Stepping Lane, off King Street, and Sunday services were held in a room nearby. As at the Octagon, there was a Society for the Sick and Poor, and a Provident Society which not only covered times of sickness but also in some cases provided meagre pensions. Such efforts as the Christian Instruction Society and a Vestry Library contributed to the building up of the Faith. It is apparent that here was a less rigidly traditional and more vigorously evangelical ministry than had hitherto been found in Independency.

The third of the churches of orthodox dissent was the Baptist Church, divided by early differences into General and Particular: Arminian and Calvinist. The General Baptists survived, but it was the Particular Baptists who flourished, with their four churches in Norwich by 1851. Pre-eminent was St Mary Baptist (to the stranger an odd title, but illustrating the custom of naming chapels from the parish in which they were situated). It was in 1743 that the congregation moved from a granary in St Miles, Coslany to the new building in St Mary's. A brief decline was followed by revival, and the arrival of Joseph Kinghorn as minister in 1789 began a new era. Kinghorn (1765-1832) had come from Fairford, and found Norwich strange 'an old comically built place'. His last charge had not been happy, and he was in bad health, so at first he lived in the salubrious air of Costessey. A scholarly and rather sedate

Joseph Kinghorn. Minister to St. Mary's Baptist Church 1789-1832. N.L.S.L.

bachelor, he complemented the popular minister of St Paul's Baptist church, Mark Wilks. Dismissed from the Tabernacle on his marriage, Wilks went over to the Baptists. His congregation being unable to support him, he farmed in Sprowston and Heigham, 'a remarkable man of great zeal and energy with considerable powers as a preacher', he was also a man of enterprise and humour. One of his financial ventures was a bath house at Heigham, which he advertised as being 'as respectable as Margate, Ramsgate, or even Brighthelmstone'. Shades of Regency!

Kinghorn was a man of deep and apparent piety, of the sort that attracts and not repels. He was a profound scholar and a painstaking Bible student. His circle of friends was wide. As a member of the Speculative Society he was familiar with the purpose of the Octagon group, and became an intimate friend of William Taylor despite radical theological differences. With John Gurney he had shown enthusiasm for Hebrew. A dutiful and affectionate son, he wrote home regularly, often engaging his minister father in argument about biblical exposition. In their old age he welcomed his parents into his own home on Pottergate, and when they died told his congregation that now they were his family.

His was a ministry 'calculated to make stalwart Bible Christians who knew what they believed and why'. In his later years he pioneered an important innovation. 'In early days the city was lighted at night by a few comparatively miserable gas lamps' wrote S. C. Colman 'and evening meetings were unheard of. Towards the close of his ministry he commenced a Sunday evening meeting, the first ever heard of in Norwich, and probably after gas lighting was introduced [in 1820]. As this was the only evening meeting many came from other churches.' These were soon to follow Kinghorn's lead. Colman goes on to say 'In his day there were sturdy Nonconformists in Norwich united in close fellowship amongst both Baptists and Independents, who held Mr Kinghorn in high esteem'. This fellowship was certainly assisted by John Joseph Gurney of the Society of Friends (see also Chapter I).

The Gurneys of Earlham had in Elizabeth Fry made a great contribution to Quaker renown and prison reform. John Joseph, her younger brother was twenty-four when he became a 'decided Friend' instead of being content with a less costing allegiance. It cost him the embarrassment of appearing at a social gathering 'in Friends attire, and with my hat on' and the adoption of the Quaker 'Thee' and 'Thou' in common speech. His religion was thus publicly proclaimed in the world of business and philanthropy. He was greatly occupied with con-temporary issues, especially the abolition of slavery, but his impact on Norwich was through Christian fellowship. Earlham Hall became, in the words of one who knew him 'the resort of the wise and good of all denominations and of all ranks. The nobleman, the Bishop, the Dissenting Minister might be seen at his table, and a gathering at the hospitable spot during the week of the Norwich Bible Meetings was the great religious festival of the county . . . We felt like the disciples on the Emmaus road'. The Bible Society was founded in 1811, and it afforded common ground not only to Dissenters, but also to the Church of England with them. At the inaugural meeting Bishop Bathurst was in the chair, and Gurney records that he 'harangued and admirably well, upon the excellence of the British and Foreign Bible Society. Kinghorn seconded with some excellent remarks on the Bishop's liberality, and the Bishop said some fine things of Kinghorn. It was really delightful to hear an old Puritan and a modern Bishop saying everything that was kind and Christianlike of each other.' Gurney was on friendly terms with Kinghorn and Alexander, as well as with the Cambridge evangelist Charles Simeon, and with Bishop Stanley. When he died, Stanley courageously made his Cathedral sermon a memorial tribute to one 'whose peaceful life was one unwearied comment on evangelical charity at its fullest and most expanded state'.

William Brock, who succeeded Kinghorn was a complete contrast, and somewhat less harmonious in his relations with the Establishment. After a white haired, scholarly, ascetic looking old man here was a young fellow 'tall, thin and pliant, with an easy and careless gait and flaxen hair lying in no particular direction.' 'Well' remarked one of the members 'we have a ploughboy for minister now!' He had none of Kinghorn's scholarship, but admitted it honestly, won over the critical scholars in his church, and humbly acceded to their offers to assist his continued education. There was that about him which induced the church officers to waive the usual probationary period. His sermons were full of eloquent and appealing common sense and soon there was rejoicing that so many young men were coming, attracted by Brock's personality as well as his sermons.

His first years were unclouded. He found, as he had been told, that 'social life among the Nonconformists was singularly agreeable and reputable'—and his church was alive and responsive. There was one issue, however, which was of general concern among Baptists. Was the Communion Service to be limited to baptised church members, or open to 'all who love the Lord'. Kinghorn had been strong for 'closed Communion', and the one condition of Brock's appointment had been that he should not preach against strict communion discipline as many younger ministers did. By his fifth year he found he could no longer keep this condition and resigned, withdrawing when an unsatisfactory compromise was reached which allowed occasional open Communions. This issue was to cause trouble to his successor.

Brock came into conflict with the Established Church on the matter of Church Rates, looked on with increasing resentment by Nonconformists who regarded compulsory contributions to the upkeep of the parish church as a crying injustice. In 1846 repairs were needed to St George's, Colegate. The churchwardens proposed to levy a rate. The vestry meeting, which consisted of dissenters, Brock among them as a parishioner, refused to grant a rate, while offering a voluntary contribution which was refused on principle. The Archdeacon intervened, threatening legal proceedings against Brock and other dissenters. He came to see Brock 'What will Norfolk and Norwich say to a minister in gaol?' he asked 'I cannot tell, but it will be to the detriment of your cause and the benefit of mine'. 'Yes—but a Christian minister shut up in prison!'—'Exactly—and the idea of you, a Christian minister shutting him up there!' In the event Brock was omitted from the citation and after appeal, the case was settled in the rebels' favour. It is understandable that Brock was a strong supporter of the 'Liberation Society' and the campaign for disestablishment, even to the extent of withdrawing support from Sir Morton Peto (M.P. for Norwich 1847-1855) a member of his church, in the 1847 election, when Peto refused to pledge himself to work in Parliament for the separation of Church and State. It is pleasant to know that fraternal feelings overcame political differences. In 1849 Peto secured Brock's invitation to the new Bloomsbury Chapel he had built, and which became the leading Baptist church in London.

So far we have considered 'Orthodox Dissent' of the old tradition, but as the 1851 figures remind us there was in the nineteenth century the growing contribution of the Methodists. They were in a different category from the older churches, and had been regarded by them with some suspicion. St Mary's Baptists ruled in 1753 that 'It is unlawful for any to attend upon the meetings of the Methodists'. The beginning had not been satisfactory. The pioneer preaching of James Wheatley had led to riots on the one hand, and on the other had received but qualified approval from Wesley. Wheatley became minister at the Tabernacle under the aegis of the Calvinist George Whitfield and the Countess of Huntingdon. After a time of difficulty and unstable membership during which services took place in several buildings—the Orford Hill 'Foundry': the 'Priory chapel' in St James: and the Old Swan playhouse, a chapel was built in Cherry Lane in 1769, with a membership of 160. Here John Wesley preached, and the congregation grew by 1810 to four or five hundred. A new chapel was built nearby in Calvert Street which provided the maximum of accommodation for the minimum of expense. The floor was of brick and there was no heating. One third of the seats were narrow backless forms, for the poor, the pews for subscribers being little better. There was no organ, but an 'orchestra' of cello, flute and clarinet. The church prospered. There was a large Sunday School, claimed as the first to be started outside the Church of England in the city (see Chapter IX). By 1824 there was a membership of seven hundred, and it was felt that a new chapel should be founded.

A meeting on January 1st decided definitely that in view of the inadequacy of Calvert Street and the increase of the city population to 60,000, many of whom had no access to religious instruction, a chapel as large as Calvert Street should be built in another district. Two hundred pounds was given at the meeting, and within a month the full cost of building was subscribed. The site chosen was that of the old theatre in Swan Yard used in earlier days. By October 24th the new church, St Peter's, Lady Lane (now City Library car park) was completed and opened by the President of Conference. Before long it was claimed that not less than two thousand heard Methodist preaching each Sabbath, and that many other churches had followed the example of Lady Lane in holding evening services.

At Calvert Street there was gloom. 'The Aristocracy of the congregation' had been removed, and pew rents slumped from £228 to £81. 4s. 6d. Soon worse difficulties were to come.

After Wesley's death the Methodists were haunted by constitutional problems of clericalism and centralisation. Divisions destroyed the unity of Methodism. In 1811 the Primitive Methodists seceded, advocates of open air revival campaigns, not ashamed to be called 'Ranters'. The constitutional conflicts of 1849 brought about the expulsion of some members and the formation of the Wesleyan Reform movement. The tragic effect is seen in the 1851 figures. The Methodists were the most numerous of the Nonconformists, but they were divided into four churches.

George Borrow on his way to his famous 'wind on the heath' conversation met some Primitive Methodists and tells touchingly of the

St. Peter's Chapel in Lady Lane: a Wesleyan Chapel built in 1824. Sillett 1828.

preachers on the horseless waggon up on Mousehold; the crowd of 'the lower classes, labourers and mechanics, their wives and childred, dusty people, unwashed people, people of no account whatsoever . . . There stood the preacher, one of those men—and thank God their number is not few—who animated by the spirit of Christ, amidst much poverty, and alas much contempt persist in carrying the light of the Gospel amidst the dark parishes of what, but for their instrumentality would scarcely be Christian England.' It was in the rural areas that Primitive Methodism made its greatest impact, later becoming closely connected with efforts to improve the labourers' lot. The lay-preacher John Love, for example, was a leading and energetic advocate of Chartist principles, though opposed to any sort of violent revolution. (See Chapter VI.) Such involvement was inevitable in a church existing mainly among the working class, though direct political action was not encouraged. In 1839 the Norwich Quarterly Methodist meeting expressed disapproval of 'Bro. Bowthorpe's new fashioned way of preaching' and declared that 'his conduct was unjustifiable on the 30th of June in walking from Ringland through Drayton to Norwich in the rain then stand up in the open air near our chapel to the ingery of our cause to make a speech for the Chartists'.

By 1851 the Primitive Methodists had four chapels and were the predominant section of Methodism. For the rest dissension was a disaster. A Directory of 1854 paints a gloomy picture 'St Peter's Chapel and a Schoolroom in Gildencroft are the only places held by the Conference, and are attended by a mere handful of the people who formerly attended. Four fifths of the members of the Society have been expelled by priestly despotism and these have formed themselves into a separate society. They worship at Calvert Street, Chapel Street, and a chapel in Philadelphia built in 1853.' The disruption was certainly a setback, but a temporary one. Divided though they were the different sections worked, increased and prospered. In 1850 a very biased critic, the *Daylight* reporter wrote 'Even in the byways of the city, Methodists are hard at work according to their lights.'

In the background of all Christian thought was the challenge so explicitly revealed in the 1851 Census, the vast number who professed no allegiance. Certainly all the churches were busy erecting new buildings, but what did that show? Mann in his report on the Census said new building was for the middle and upper class adherents. 'A regular attendance at church is now ranked among the recognised proprieties of life' . . . 'It is sadly certain that the vast, intelligent and growingly important section of our countrymen (the working class) is thoroughly estranged from our religious institutions' Mann proposed the invasion of artisan districts by 'aggressive Christian agencies': 'Ragged churches for those who would not mix with the well-to-do,' and 'street preaching would not be too energetic a measure for this terrible emergency.'

The United Methodist Free Church, Chapel Field Road.

The Census information was not new, but here were definite figures to confirm impressions. In many ways the churches were already reacting. Sunday schools, now springing up everywhere, as described in Chapter IX, had an evangelistic aim: so had organised benevolent and provident societies. Furthermore in Norwich the City Mission had been at work since 1837, chiefly sponsored by the Nonconformists, although with some Church of England co-operation. The Mission employed agents at a yearly stipend of £40.75; 'to visit the poor and persuade all to repent and believe in the Gospel. They read the Word of God and gave instruction to every family if permitted . . . distribute tracts . . . and draw attention to the duties of educating the young and attending regularly the worship of God'. Work began in Pockthorpe in the parishes of St James and St Paul, St Martin at Oak and Bull Close, areas of extreme poverty, deprivation and vice (see Chapter II).

The visitors gave a depressing view of life in this part of the city. In Pockthorpe itself there were '1275 persons and if infirm, aged and children are subtracted, 606 live in habitual neglect of public worship'. There were 14 Public Houses, and 17 of 19 shops opened on Sunday. 220 adults and 223 children over five were illiterate. 'Infidelity prevails to an awful extent and two shops are open for the sale of infidel works in a very cheap form'.

The mission was puritanical to a degree that would have been unacceptable in many circles. In 1839 the Report regrets that 'many persons professing religion were seen going to the races', and Tombland Fair was an annual target of disapprobation. In 1851 the Sunday opening of Kensington Gardens at Lakenham saw 'families seeking death in the error of their ways'. There was too a threat from 'increased Popish activity', somewhat offset by the diminution of the activity of the Mormons. A matter of difficulty was that 'Bathing has a demoralising effect upon the inhabitants near the river, especially the young. Scores of men and boys are found in a state of nudity on the meadows on Sunday afternoon . . .' The 1851 statistics showed 61 conversions: 42 'reformation and hopeful changes': 32 people joined churches: there were 35 'Happy deaths' and 25 'Hopeful' ones: 17 couples were married who had lived illicitly: 4 females were reclaimed from profligacy, as were 19 drunkards and 8 infidels.

These reports may read strangely in the twentieth century, but they show that a great deal was being done. It would be interesting to know how this activity fitted in with the more specific efforts of such parishes as St James and St Peter, Parmentergate. The annual distribution of tracts by the Mission was immense, ten thousand being given out at the races alone. It was an age of cheap printing and it was a force harnessed in evangelism. The Anglican Society for the Promotion of Christian Knowledge (S.P.C.K.) distributed 1,347 Bibles: 711 Testaments and 22,017 books and tracts through Norwich agents.

To such organised endeavour was added the earnest missionary activity of such people as Samuel Jarrold who, in addition to his participation in the family firm was an ardent evangelist and temperance worker. He had a religious assembly of his own founding, and in the advocacy of the cause he printed millions of tracts which he personally distributed on Sundays. It was a sincere work done in a Christian spirit which gained such respect that at his funeral all the public houses along the route closed their doors!

Jarrold's work is a reminder that in such a city as Norwich there were many small Protestant sects. The list of places licensed for worship is largely of odd rooms in houses, schoolrooms, warehouses, or even at a public house. An enthusiast would gather a small congregation which might have but a brief existence, leaving no record. Borrow's meeting with the *Antinomian* bookseller, for instance, evidences the survival of an odd and obscure seventeenth century sect. 'Did you never hear of Lodowick Muggleton?' he asked his young customer. 'Not I'. 'Strange. Know that he was the founder of the our poor society and after him we are frequently, though opprobriously, called Muggletonians, for we are Christians.' It would be interesting to know who the 'Rational Religionists' were, who met in the Bedding Lane Social Institute in 1841, and to gain light on other obscure sects. Some are better known. In 1801 a meeting place was registered in St Clement's for the 'New Jerusalem Church'. The applicant, John Bonsell had registered other venues as early as 1788. This was the Swedenborgian Church which at that time was attracting the attention of John Flaxman and William Blake. Later it rented the French Church in Queen Street, but adherents diminished and in the 1880's they were worshipping in a room on Elm Hill. They were succeeded at the French Church by the Irvingite 'Catholic Apostolic Church', a 'charismatic' body speaking with tongues, that developed a scholarly and exemplary liturgy of its own. A visitor recorded his impression of the 'gorgeous ritual' although objecting to the multiplicity of candles! Intimately bound up with millenial expectation this church befame defunct in the present century, having made no provision for the continuation of its ministry.

Outside Protestant Nonconformity, but included in the Census, were the Jews and the Roman Catholics. The Jewish community was small. In the early part of the century they met in St Stephen's Street, later at the Samson and Hercules. By 1838 there were twenty-nine members, mostly small shop keepers, and it was decided to build a synagogue. The Norwich congregation subscribed £155: the Mayor and Sheriffs and others £30: and Sir Morton Peto, M.P. £20. This enabled the congregation to acquire a site in St Faith's Lane and to build the Synagogue which remained until it was destroyed in air raids in 1942.

The Roman Catholic Church. Willow Lane 1828. Sillett 1828.

The Roman Catholic community was not large. The 1851 figures are useless since only one return was made, but by 1870 the numbers were around 1,200, with 215 in the schools. In 1791 a church was built in the garden of Strangers' Hall, which later became the presbytery. Refugees from revolutionary France did something to familiarise England with Roman Catholicism and to break down prejudice. It is interesting to find Joseph Kinghorn going to the Roman Catholic Church on Good Friday 1795 'to see whether I liked them better.' The Jesuits opened their church in Willow Lane in 1829, though they had been in the city longer. Mr Hibgame in his 'Recollections' recalled 'as a small boy looking in at the door and fearfully gazing at the painted windows and richly decorated altar . . . but I dare not linger, now knowing what would happen to me!' The Jesuits withdrew in 1850, handing over the church to the secular clergy. The sisters of Notre Dame settled in Surrey Street in 1864, Edward Trafford of Wroxham giving material assistance. The acceptance of the Convent and School is testimony to a more tolerant attitude to

St. John's Roman Catholic Cathedral. Built 1884-1910 to the design of George Gilbert Scott junior on the site of the former Norfolk County Gaol at the expense of the fifteenth Duke of Norfolk.

Catholicism. The long ministry of Dr Duckett also made a notable contribution to the prestige of the Roman Catholic Church. In 1878 he came into prominence in working to help those suffering after the floods, and came to take an active part in local affairs. He was on the Board of Guardians, served as chairman of the Relief Committee and was long a governor of the hospitals and 'a member of every society connected with the poor and suffering'. There were many who were attracted to Maddermarket sermons. Even a critical hearer like the medical student Shephard Taylor was often present at part of his Sunday round. By 1861 the congregation at Maddermarket was around 500, and by 1882 the numbers in the churches were sufficient to justify the great new church which the Duke of Norfolk proposed as a thank offering for his happy marriage. The site of the old city gaol provided a splendid situation and Dr Duckett showed admirable business acumen in putting the prison on show at sixpence a ticket. The nave of the new church was opened in 1894, and the Willow Lane and Maddermarket churches closed, the former being converted to a school.

Any survey of Nonconformity must take account of individuals as well as churches. George Gould who succeeded Brock at St Mary Baptist in 1848 was a stimulating leader, conscious of the need to fight social evils, whether it be slavery in the wider world or corruption in local politics, life in the city yards and rookeries or burial disabilities. Near his church was the growing shoe-making business of Tillyard and Howlett, both of whom were church members. When in 1856 George White joined the firm, he, too, became a member, being baptised in 1857. In the course of twenty years the firm was reorganised from traditional outwork to the better conditions of the factory system. In 1876 the 'Norvic' factory was built in Colegate, and took the name of Howlett and White. The shoe trade was precarious, low wages inevitable, and unrest to be expected. A large proportion of the workers lived locally and attended St Mary's, and this forged a bond between employers and employees. This was illustrated in the 1897 strike. Mason, leader of the men striking for higher wages, went to George White one day to tell him of their difficulties: the union cheque for strike pay had not arrived from London, and the men would be in want. At once White made out a cheque to cover the deficiency, and when Mason was unemployed after the strike White found him a place in his own factory. He showed the same sort of generosity when Henry Sexton, one of his employees, set up his own shoe-making business: White gave him his first order. After an apprenticeship in local politics, where he became Liberal leader, George White entered Parliament, where he was a spokesman for Liberalism and Nonconformity—a good Christian in public life.

Parallel with Sir George White's career was that of Jeremiah James Colman, enlightened industrialist, Liberal politician and staunch Nonconformist. He was brought up in the traditions of the expanding family business, and also in those of the family religious allegiance. Jeremiah, founder of the firm had been baptised by Kinghorn. He drove in from Stoke Holy Cross each Sunday to worship at St Mary Baptist Church. James, his nephew, head of the firm from 1841 was deacon and choir leader. Jeremiah James, who inherited the family business in 1854, had been an earnest youth, rising early in the morning to prepare papers for the 'Mutual Improvement Society' or to study French and Greek. He gave equal application to religious education, and taught in Sunday School. He was baptised by Gould at the same service as Howlett. For Brock he had a great affection. He was, he said, 'an instrument through the grace of God of importing spiritual comfort to the drooping and despondent mind.' To Gould he gave loyal support when the question of Open Communion was once again raised. He became leader of the more liberally inclined, who eventually won legal decision in this favour, and made his first public speech on this issue.

A loyal Nonconformist, he was conscious of the history of their disabilities and exposed the cause of the 'Liberation Society'. On religious grounds he deplored Christian disunity 'May no sectarian pride ever obscure the vital truths of our common Christianity' he wrote: and thanked Dean Goulburn 'for the example you have given us, that whilst firmly and consistently holding your own views, you also do so with full and Christian charity to those who differ.' It was in this unifying spirit that he regretted that the YMCA, started in 1856, of which he was President, did not arrive at some amalgamation with the CEYMS (see the previous chapter). At the YMCA he showed less narrowness than some of its officers. 'We have minds to cultivate, souls to save, duties to perform, but why not billiards?'

After Colman's marriage, since his wife wished the children to be baptised as infants, the family attended Princes Street, although J.J. continued his connection with St Mary's and the growing Baptist Union. A faithful churchman, he saw nonetheless that the churches were not achieving the urgent task indicated by the 1851 Census Report. 'Churches and chapels' he said 'do not really touch the great mass of the working class', and to a request for help in building a new Baptist Church he wrote 'The Congregation will be composed of people from other places who would be wonderfully astonished if the masses from the hovels around about came to use their fine pews. Are the churches so crowded as to need another?'

He appreciated the value of 'non church' based activities such as the City Mission and the Adult School movement of Quaker origin, which, by the end of the century, could claim 3000 members meeting each Sunday in twenty-one schools. One of these was set up at Carrow. He also applauded the new Salvation Army. General Booth stayed at Carrow three times and was reckoned 'a good sensible fellow'.

It was in August 1882 that the Salvation Army appeared on Norwich streets. 'Get a drum and rouse Norwich from end to end' were the General's words: and soon there was also a band, cymbals, tambourines, and concertinas to attract to open air meetings. There were rowdies and hecklers, and even complaints to the magistrates, but the Army soon won acceptance and approval. The empty skating rink in St Giles provided a useful meeting hall, replaced in 1892 by the new Citadel in St Giles Street. Unusually for those days the leader was a woman, Captain Harkey. Things had progressed a long way since the 1820 minute of the General Baptists in Priory Yard recorded 'We the members and deacons of this Church, knowing by experience the evils that attend the women having a voice to vote in church matters, do hereby enter our Solemn Protest against it. And of this we think ourselves justified by the words of the Apostle in I Corinthians'. The developing social work of the Army won sympathetic support. When the General came to appeal for this work his enthusiasm even drew contributions from the reporters at the meeting. 'God bless the reporters' he prayed. His experience of Norwich differed from Wesley's. 'I have an affection for your city. It has been good for the Salvation Army.'

Much of the strength of the Nonconformist churches lay in their realisation of the 'gathered' church. All had a remarkable history of meetings in warehouses, maltings, rooms in houses here and there. For the church always meant people, not building. With this corporate sense went a consciousness of duty to participate: to spread the Gospel and to improve the world. Church meetings and Methodist classes were an introduction to a wider world of action and social responsibility shown not only in the careers of White and Colman but in the quiet endeavour of lesser men serving on unchronicled local committees.

Many churches, too, were blessed with a capable and zealous ministry and a succession of eloquent and effective preachers in an age where sermons told. Brock and Gould were followed by J. H. Shakespeare who shed lustre on the Baptist Church at large. Alexander was succeeded by George Barrett, eloquent preacher of wide sympathies, and editor of the *Congregational Hymnal*, described as 'a book eminent as an expression of what is best in Congregationalism'. There were many others whose ministry was edifying in the literal sense, to whose forgotten labours their churches are indebted today. They were zealous and expectant. The first year of the Lady Lane church reported that in consequence of the years preaching 'the moral condition of the city has been much improved'. It is of a piece with the definite statistics of the City Mission. We may react with some sceptisicm: but the 'goodness' at which the multifarious evangelical activities aimed must have found some fulfilment. Many were brought to be Christian people: and to be better people. There was some truth in J. J. Colman's words. 'If we had more home missions we would need fewer policeman!'

One legacy of missionary activity was that bequeathed by Sankey and

Moody, the American evangelist of the 1870's. *Sacred Songs and Solos*, their hymn book, obtained a wide and continuing circulation. Wesley had made his a 'singing church'. Hymns mattered, and his hymn book was planned as 'a little body of practical and experimental divinity'. Words and music mattered, a far cry from the dreary Anglican metrical psalms that survived in some Norwich churches till mid century. Other churches learned from Methodism the value of good words and good tunes, and Sankey and Moody's book certainly provided catchy melodies which had much in common with drawing room ballads and music hall choruses: but as the old evangelist Rowland Hill asked 'Why should the devil have the best tunes?' At the other extreme the new Anglican hymns of more sober *Ancient and Modern* cast were gaining ground. Both helped spread the Gospel. Not everyone was happy. Colman looked back regretfully. He had seen the old manuscript books replaced by a *Norwich* and then *Bristol* book: and the old tunes falling into disuse: no *Calcutta* or *Diaden*. He lamented 'When tunes were based on fugue it gave the choir something to do.' Certainly Princes Street cannot have been altogether to his taste. The *Daylight* reporter was surprised to find there in 1879 'churchy' tunes with words by the high Anglican J. M. Neale, and a psalm sung to the seventh Gregorian tone. Queen's Road chapel provided the Kyrie of Mozart's Twelfth Mass together with Sankey's *Weary gleam*. At Providence Chapel the singing was atrocious, and the words of the hymns too. Only Calvert Street passed muster: here he 'had a sincere pleasure in performing his duty'. The very fact that our jaundiced reporter took such note of hymns testifies to their importance. Song was a great weapon in the evangelist's armoury: and if a thing is worth doing, it is worth doing badly in some circumstances.

The Princes Street church can show us another essential characteristic of the Nonconformist churches: a social life which helped to foster congregational 'solidarity'. A report of the 1898 Annual Meeting described how the Lecture Hall in which it took place 'had been converted into an elegant drawing room, covered with oriental rugs, lounges and chairs ranged around, with ferns and palms, and the walls hung with artistic draperies.' There were refreshments, and an entertainment which included duologues, violin and piano duet *Polacca in Re* and a song *The Sailor's Grave*. The Annual Report showed that membership was 883: there were 1600 children in Sunday School and 11-1200 at Pleasant Sunday Afternoons. Of course this was a church which 'drew the cream of Nonconformity', in some ways not very characteristic of 'chapel' ethos. The story was told of a lady of the congregation who met a friend coming away from Lady Lane Chapel with bitter criticisms of the service. 'Well, dear, you must come to Princes Street with me'. 'Oh I couldn't do that—it's too high chapel!'

At humbler levels than that of the fashionable churches some gatherings played their part in expressing and creating fellowship. The children of Crooks Place chapel were in 1828 regaled at a rally with cakes and ale: but already a different form of refreshment was coming into fashion—the 'tea fight', first recorded in Warminster in 1829 where a diarist noted 'Christmas: drank tea at church with Christian friends. A holy unction attended and great was the joy!' The thirteenth anniversary of Alexander's ordination was celebrated with a tea party at St Andrew's Hall for some eight hundred 'persons of all ranks and various religious bodies.' It was 'an example of those occasions of public interest stimulating social sympathies'. Even this was exceeded by the tea party for more than a thousand at Calvert Street in 1851 to welcome back the minister. Roland Hill called tea 'scandal broth' but it came to be the essential lubricant for ecclesiastical occasions, and played a serious part in encouraging temperance. In 1848 St Clement's Baptist Church reduced the price of tea meetings from a shilling to twopence, to help the poor.

This slight social aside may seem of small importance, but it was part of that transforming change which the century brought. Despite conflicts and difficulties it was a century where men believed in progress. If there were achievements to be counted, there were always fresh tasks ahead. The fields were white for harvest—there, ever apparent, was the abiding multitude who needed the gospel, the continuing world of evil, misery and want. The task could never be other than daunting. Jeremiah James Colman could speak for his brethren when he said 'I see no cause for despair only for increased zeal'.

The Friends' Meeting House, Upper Goat Lane. Built 1826. Sillett 1828.

Reading List for Chapters VII and VIII

Alexander, W. *Memoir of the Rev. J. Alexander,* Norwich, 1856.
Armstrong, B. J. *A Norfolk Diary 1 and 2,* 1949-63.
Bathurst, H. *Memoir of the late Dr. Henry Bathurst,* 2 Vols., 1837.
Bayne, A. D. *History of Norwich,* Norwich, 1869.
Burrell, C. M. *Life of William Brock, D.D.,* 1878.
Browne, J. *History of Congregationalism in Norfolk and Suffolk,* 1877.
Calder-Marshall, A. *The Enthusiast . . . Father Ignatius . . .,* 1962.
Colman, H. C. *Jeremiah James Colman,* Norwich, 1905.
Compton, B. *Edward Meyrick Goulburn, Dean of Norwich: A Memoir,* 1899.
Hibgame, E. T. *Recollections of Norwich fifty years ago,* Norwich, 1919.
Jewson, C. B. *The Baptists in Norwich,* 1972.
Jolly, C. *The Spreading Flame: The Coming of Methodism into Norfolk,* 1973.
Kitton, F. G. *Zechariah Buck 1817-1877: A Centenary Memoir,* 1899.
Leeds, H. *Life of Dean Lefroy 1840-1960,* Norwich, 1909.
Levine, H. *The Norwich Hebrew Congregation 1840-1960: A Short History,* Norwich, 1961.
Mann, H. *Report on Religious Census of 1851,*
Oxbury, H. F. *From St. Paul's to Unthank Road,* Norwich, 1925.
Stanley, A. P. *Memoir to Bishop Stanley in addresses and Charges of Edward Stanley,* 1851.
Swift, D. E. *John Joseph Gurney Middletown, Conn.,* 1962.
Thistlethwayte, F. *Memoirs and Correspondence of Dr Henry Bathurst . . .,* 1853.
Wilkin, M. H. *Joseph Kinghorn of Norwich,* Norwich, 1853.
Men Who made Norwich, Norwich, 1903.
A Memoir of the Rev. George Gould, Norwich, 1882.
Glory in the Church: Calvert Street Methodist Church, Norwich 1811-1961, Norwich, 1961.
A Great Gothic Fane . . . With Historical Retrospect of Catholicity in Norwich, 1913.
Daylight, 1878-82.
The Norwich Spectator 1-4, 1862-5.
Norwich City Mission Annual Reports, 1843 . . .

There are newspaper cuttings in the Bolingbroke Collection (Norwich Castle Museum) and in the Norfolk Local Studies Library in the Norwich Central Library.

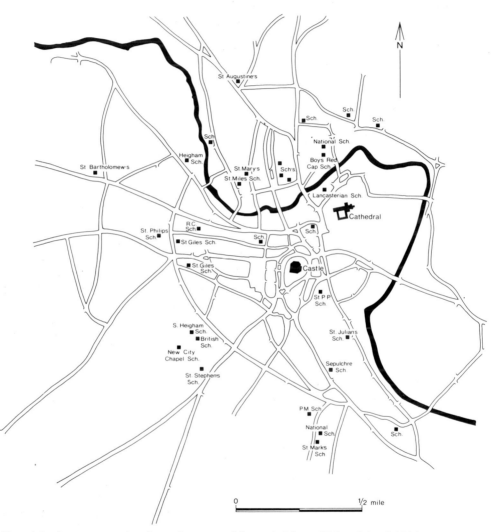

Norwich elementary schools as shown on Morant's Map of Norwich of 1873.

CHAPTER NINE

Politics, Religion and Education: The Provision of Elementary Schooling in Norwich 1800-1870[1]

W. David Smith

Introduction

The study of popular education in Norwich during this period indicates the way in which a local study illuminates the evolution of education on the national scale and may serve also to evaluate the significance of the local context. By and large, developments in Norwich reflect the national pattern, though local factors are of over-riding importance from time to time. The Norwich scene is one where political considerations impinge markedly upon education. Political acerbity is underlined by religious difference, so that for example, schemes for adult edcuation and for a ragged school are shortlived, in contrast with significant developments elsewhere by 1870. The fact that there is an actual decline in literacy in the early years of the century, even though Norwich is not part of a great industrial area, is also significant. Because of its reliance upon a staple industry, the city suffered unduly from fluctuations in the trade cycle and the pressures upon its population were more like those in the great industrial areas than was the case in other towns. It is clear too that particular circumstances determine the extent of the contribution made by educational institutions. Thus in Norwich the Sunday schools play a median role compared with their great importance in the northern industrial areas and their small significance in certain country towns.

However, developments in Norwich confirm the importance of national movements. As early as the 1780's the establishment of Sunday schools in the city is due to the force of the descriptions of such foundations elsewhere being propagated by the popular press. Robert Raikes used his newspaper *The Gloucester Journal* and later letters and articles in *The Gentleman's Magazine* to spread his ideas, with the result that Sunday schools sprang up all over the country. Individuals in Norwich were inspired to find out as much as possible about such initiatives and then to take action in their native city. Similarly, the initiative for the Lancasterian school in Norwich was taken by those in contact with the foundation of such schools elsewhere, and typically they used Joseph Lancaster himself to rally support locally.

The foundation of the local diocesan school society was the result of a national movement via the most prestigious local representatives of the Anglican Establishment to counteract Nonconformist influence. In the same way the Diocesan Infant School Society was the local version of a national movement. Again, in typical fashion, the leading propagandist, Samuel Wilderspin (1791-1866) was used to rally support for the foundation of Church infant schools as a counterbalance to the existing nondenominational parochial schools. The utilitarian influence resulting in a Penny Library and a Mechanics' Institute is also representative. Local initiatives depended upon the use of existing models, thus when the founders of the Norwich Ragged School began their enterprise, they asked the Rev. William Brock on one of his visits to London, to find out all he could about the London Ragged Schools, so that they might emulate what had been achieved in the capital. This illustrates the way in which many prominent local individuals were in constant touch with current national ideas; so that these in turn were disseminated back to provincial centres such as Norwich. The crucial determinants of the way in which local initiatives developed, however, were often those particular aspects of the economic, social, political and religious composition of the city.

Norwich society was disrupted by those violent transitions and upheavals which were commonplace features of the early decades of the century. The root causes were that the rapid growth of the population in combination with the city's continued over-dependence upon the textile industry led to insecurity and privation for its inhabitants. The principal cause of the increase of population during this period was the attraction of workers from the surrounding countryside to the city. The re-organisation of agriculture, the post-Napoleonic war depression and the introduction of threshing machines led to the seething discontent and periodic eruptions of rioting by the rural labourers. As the population expanded, depression and under-employment became endemic, with resulting acute distress and poverty. But the existence of charities for the relief of the destitute and of the large funds distributed as Poor Law relief seems to have made the city a more desirable haven than the countryside even at times when its industries were most depressed[2].

It is evident too that the main movement into the city was of families and therefore the need for educational provision was approximately proportionate to the total increase in population.

Depression, under-employment and the resulting acute distress and poverty brought changes in the character of the population. Violence becomes commonplace, food riots and attacks upon strike-breakers are the peaks upon the steady growth of crime amongst the impoverished and decaying section of society. The city accords with the national pattern of a low level of crime in the period 1800-1815, followed by an upsurge of violence and criminality after that date.[3] To keep the peace the magistrates had to rely upon the military, housed in barracks within the city, which could be supplemented by corps of volunteers.

The case for the provision of education for the poor as a means of the prevention of crime frequently was made. Again and again the connection between the criminal poor and their 'ignorance of true religion' was made. The moral and religious education of the children of the poor was a worthy endeavour, yet there was a hard-headed element of persuasion too, for, as R. A. Slaney argued in the House of Commons in 1837, the cost of education would be more than offset by a decrease in the cost of crime.[4] The official acceptance of this view is generally regarded as one of the main reasons for government grants for schools from 1833 onwards. It is evident that the development of a 'criminal class' could be observed mainly in relation to children, particularly because of the preponderance of youth in the expanding centres of population. At the lowest estimate, one obvious benefit of providing schools for the children of the poor was that it helped to remove them from the temptations of the streets.

Before the initiation of government aid in 1833 much had been accomplished by voluntary means, chiefly through the religious societies. The Established Church claimed exclusive rights over the provision of popular education. As a diocesan centre Norwich had a strong element supporting the Anglican Establishment: although as is pointed out in Chapter VII Bishops Bathurst and Stanley were liberal in outlook the Cathedral Close was traditionally conservative and because the city had a large number of parishes there were many parochial clergy to espouse the Anglican cause and to implement policies initiated by diocesan leaders.

Norwich was notable too for the strength of its Nonconformists and for the influence they wielded both politically and socially in its history and Richard Hale has discussed the Old Dissenting Sects and the New in the previous chapter. The New Dissent sprang from the eighteenth century evangelical revival. This evangelical influence was so pervasive that it led not only to the expansion of Methodism but also to the revival in the spiritual life of the entire nation, Old Dissent and the Established Church being influenced alike. Education was one of the evangelical movement's main reform agencies in its attack on 'the universal corruption and profligacy of the times', the Sunday school being seen as a particularly effective medium.

Sunday Schools

Sunday schools were in existence, scattered throughout the country, before 1780, but Robert Raikes through his letters and articles provided the impetus for their rapid spread. The first Sunday school in Norwich was established in the parish of St Stephen in October, 1785. The *Norwich*

Mercury supported the initiative and the Rev. Lancaster Adkin preached at St Peter's, Mancroft, stressing the value of the schools as agencies of moral reform.

> '. . . some steps are absolutely necessary for the reformation and comfort of the lower class of mankind with respect to their manners in society, and also their religious conduct'.[5]

The number of schools and the numbers in attendance rose rapidly, the schools being established on a parochial basis, but it was characteristic of the religious controversy of the period that they should develop along sectarian lines. The first Nonconformist Sunday school was opened by Methodists in 1808, but the foundation of the non-denominational day school, the Lancasterian school in 1811, initiated considerable local dissension and resulted in increased denominational activity. Such a separation seems to have occurred somewhat later in Norwich than elsewhere, indeed in some places Sunday schools established in the 1780's were denominational from the outset.[6]

The effect of the Evangelical Revival upon the city is to be seen in the raising of five new Nonconformist congregations in the period 1800-1820.[7] The Sunday school was a vital part of the thrusting missionary endeavour in the subsequent development of Nonconformity. The setting up of a Sunday school, initially for both children and adults created the basis for the subsequent establishment of an adult congregation. The pioneering Calvert Street Sunday school preceded the church by three years and the subsequent extension of Methodist influence into the newly developed parts of the city show the same pattern, for example, into Crooks Place or the 'New City' area. Here the Sunday school with 81 pupils was established in 1831 and the Chapel (later the Chapelfield Road Methodist Church) was opened eight years later.[8] The Baptists, also early to found and place a high evaluation upon such schools, show the same pattern of expansion, establishing the Pockthorpe Sunday school before the Silver Road Baptist Church and the Heigham Sunday school before the Dereham Road Church. The founding of new churches by secession intensified the process of development. A good example is provided by the Prince's Street Congregational Church, founded in 1819, the Sunday school following in the next year. Its missionary work resulted in the successive establishment of Sunday schools with subsequent chapels at Thorpe, Trowse and Thunder Lane.[9] The powerful Unitarian community was comparatively late in the field, their school for the teaching of reading, writing, arithmetic and passages of the Holy Scripture to poor boys, did not arrive until 1822, though the Presbyterians had a school there from 1709. Ellen Martineau indicates that this delay was due to the opposition of the deacons.[10] This opposition may have been due to the reaction of the elders against the consequences of the association of Unitarian leaders with radicalism in the 1790's.

The schools attached to Nonconformist chapels grew rapidly,

overtaking the Anglican schools within twenty years. By 1835 the number of children said to attend them was 5,861, of whom 3,327 were in Nonconformist institutions.[11] In the 1840's the resistance of Nonconformists, particularly Baptists and Congregationalists, to state provision of education, caused them to stress the value of their Sunday schools. The Educational Census of 1851 shows that the number of Sunday scholars had grown to nearly 7,000, well over 4,000 of whom were Nonconformists. Larger schoolrooms were built by many of the denominations and the foundation of new churches showed the marked emphasis upon the value of the schools in the evangelicalism of the various groups. A good illustration is the breaking away from the Church of England by the Rev. Robert Govett, who founded the large Surrey Street Chapel in 1854. Its congregation was undenominational and believed in open communion—it was essentially fundamentalist, devotional and missionary. The Sunday school was an essential part of its missionary endeavour and at its peak comprised over 600 scholars with some sixty teachers.[12] The overall numbers continued to increase in subsequent decades, thus by 1877 there were 7,293 'on the books' in the Nonconformist schools alone and the average attendance exceeded 5,000.[13]

The strength of the appeal of the Sunday schools from their initiation is illustrated in Norwich. The scale of support was such that they were popular institutions in the fullest sense. The Nonconformist strategy for conversion was so effective that it stimulated emulation. One of their spearheads was the 'rescue' of the children of the poor in the less favoured parts of the city and this provoked a response from the parish priests in the form of increased personal commitment and the consequent increase in the number of parochial Sunday schools.

The differences between the Anglican and Nonconformist schools became clearer as the decades passed. The chief aim of the former was to provide religious instruction, very often to supplement the instruction in religious education given in day schools, and the children it sought to influence were those of the 'poorer classes'.[14] This was an exceedingly limited role in comparison with the Nonconformist evaluation of the schools as the spearhead of conversion. The desire of the Anglican clergy to maintain close control over their schools had been reflected in their persistent employment of paid teachers. In addition, the role of Superintendent remained filled usually by the incumbent or else by some prominent middle class layman, such as H. S. Patterson: brewer, leader of the Conservatives, Sheriff and Mayor, who was Churchwarden and leading teacher at Cringleford Parish Church. The Rev. H. R. Neville revealed that by the 1860's Anglican clergy were aware of the deficiencies of their teachers when compared with their Nonconformist counterparts.[15] Every parent, whatever his position in society, attending chapel was expected to send his children to the Sunday school. Scholars progressed through the senior classes to become teachers. Their work evoked such tributes as that of John Alexander (see the previous chapter) who referred to the work of 120 members of his congregation so employed (and most of them were young men and women) as the 'joy and crown' of his ministry.[16]

The education provided in Sunday schools had strict limitations. Its first and main objective was the teaching of reading, the predominant text being the scriptures. These were supplemented by various texts and class books based upon biblical precept. In a number of places (though there is no evidence concerning Norwich), there was great controversy over the inclusion of writing. This was regarded by some as encouraging unreal aspiration among working class children and as a positive encouragement to overthrow the established social system. It was resisted by others, motivated by sabbatarian zeal, who regarded writing as a secular activity. The Anglican schools, with their more limited objectives, invariably eschewed writing instruction. The inclusion of writing in the school for girls in St John, Maddermarket was exceptional and a reflection of an unusually able priest, the Rev John Perowne.[17] In Anglican schools the customary curriculum was the reading of the Bible, the learning of the catechism and the reading and consideration of explanatory booklets provided by the Society for the Propagation of Christian Knowledge (SPCK). In certain Nonconformist chapels writing was taught at evening classes during the week, at others it was included as a Sunday subject. With such large numbers in attendance the teaching of subjects other than reading was reserved for the better scholars. The Sunday schools made an obvious contribution to the extension of literacy by providing a means of education for large numbers of children who were denied the opportunity of education in day schools. Clearly though, there was one stratum of society which was unable to take advantage even of this opportunity, for many children were unable to attend the schools because they lacked clean or decent clothes.

The Sunday schools are also important because they became centres providing a wide range of social and recreational amenities, bringing a means of mutual support for people who otherwise had little means of cushioning against adversity and bringing colour and enjoyment to relieve the drab monotony of their lives. The treats and excursions were long awaited and cherished events. The first excursion to the seaside at Yarmouth took place in 1846 when 1,600 children and 500 teachers processed from Castle Meadow to Thorpe station. Thereafter annual outings, either to the seaside or to the countryside for a programme of sports and games, were most popular features. Social services included sick benefit, self-help schemes, boot and clothing funds, benevolent funds and savings banks. Early accounts referred to the regaling of children with cakes and ale. The provision of the latter soon ceased, to be replaced by the founding of Temperance Societies among the young men and Bands of Hope among the children. In comparison with other English towns, the Sunday schools in Norwich occupy a median position. An analysis of the Reports of the National Society for Promoting the Education of the Poor in the Principles of the Established Church illustrates this graphically in the case of the Anglican Sunday schools, for in the City the main thrust of the church in its policy for the education of the children of the poor remained in its day schools. This was in remarkable contrast with the burgeoning textile areas of Manchester and Salford and Blackburn, where the Sunday schools were the life blood of education. On the other hand, in the old market towns of Worcester, Shrewsbury and Exeter attendance at Sunday schools was far less important than at Norwich. The inclusion of Nonconformist provision confirms the impression that overall their comparative importance is significantly less than in those of the rising industrial areas, but markedly greater than in other places.

Historians differ in their views of the social functioning of Sunday schools. Laqueur sees them as part of a 'uniquely working-class cultural constellation . . . effective in the transmission of certain values because these values were those of the working-class men and women who taught in and supported the schools'.[18] Dick, however, is sceptical of such a view, regarding them as predominantly middle-class dominated institutions, essentially conservative in outlook.[19] Because such numbers of teachers were involved it seems apparent that the majority of the teachers were of working class origin. Representatives of the entire class spectrum were involved in the foundation of schools ranging from the Misses Wodehouse, relatives of Baron Wodehouse of Kimberley, who patronised a day and Sunday school in the poor parish of St James, Pockthorpe to the members of the City Missions, small congregations such as the Independent Methodists and 'exceedingly poor' Primitive Methodists.

The pattern of support for Sunday schools by eminent citizens can be clearly illustrated. Professional men such as E. E. Blyth, solicitor, H. P. Gould, accountant; manufacturers and managers such as C. M. Thompson, J. Watling, W. B. Rutland; local business men such as J. A. Davy, J. W. Duncan, E. Morse, J. Parish and W. Parish, J. E. Read and M. E. Scarlett were all actively involved over a long period of years in the latter part of the century. Educationists varying from R. F. Betts, Secretary to the Education Committee and W. Stephenson of the High Grade School to a host of unnamed teachers were also prominent.[20] The tradition of family service and of service over long periods was characteristic and was a continuation from earlier decades. An example of long service is that of J. Clarke, tailor and woollen draper, born in 1837 who was successively scholar, teacher and superintendent of the Sun Lane school in New Catton over a period of sixty-five years. Another notable worker was Thomas Jarrold, printer and publisher, one of the original proprietors of the *Norfolk News* (see Chapter I). When he died in 1877 his obituary showed the significance of his work in a poor quarter of the city.

'The principal sphere of his activity was in connection with the day and Sunday schools in Silver Road, which have been for several years mainly sustained by his exertions'.[21]

From time to time the schools were overtly counter-revolutionary. Hence the concern of the superintendents of Prince's Street Sunday Schools in 1842, with infidelity associated with the 'new form of Socialism' and with its impact upon children.[22] Middle-class influence evidently permeates, indeed over the years there appears to have been remarkably little alteration in the motives and purposes of the schools. Again it is evident that many values were held in common by members of the middle and working classes, so that any attempted distinction between middle-class and working-class 'respectable' values seems totally false.

Charitable Schools

The concern of the churches with the salvation of souls and with social discipline is also made evident in the charitable and monitorial schools. As a result of bequests and endowments, Norwich possessed a number of day schools designed to cater for children belonging to specific categories. The lead in Norwich was taken by Nonconformists from 1700 onwards. Legacies from D. Maw and Joanna Scott were combined to provide the teaching of reading to children of the Presbyterian community. Later benefactions led to the provision of education for fifty children in 1833 at a school kept in premises given by William Harwin, the elder children being taught reading, writing and accounts, for an annual fee of £1 7s 4d. and the younger children being taught reading only for £1 a year. An additional attraction was an income of £45 per annum for apprenticeships, while the master was allowed the fees from twelve paying scholars. A second development was the result of a legacy from Bartholomew Balderstone who died in 1761. He left £1,000 for the teaching of boys, particularly from the congregation of the Independents. In 1833 £45 per annum was paid to a master to teach twenty-two boys and girls reading, writing and accounts.[23] A Presbyterian school continued in Norwich throughout the nineteenth century and the Presbyterian Boys' School was eventually amalgamated with other foundations to form the first City Municipal Grammar School (the City of Norwich School) in 1910.

Charitable schools known as the Boys' Hospital and Girls' Hospital had even longer pedigrees, originating in bequests from Thomas Anguish in 1617. Up to 1798 the boys were lodged and taught in a building in St Edmund's parish, but then the benefits were commuted to an annual payment and school fees. Additional bequests increased the income so that by 1833 sixty-one boys were educated, maintained, clothed and apprenticed. The clothing was so distinctive—red caps and blue jackets that the boys were known popularly as 'Blue bottles'.[24] the boys were required to attend the cathedral on Sundays accompanied by the Master. F. Gidney enjoyed this position from the 1830's until 1885 when the premises were sold and the school closed.

The girls were housed in a building in Golden Dog Lane (north of the Octagon Chapel) until 1802, until their benefits were also commuted. In 1833 forty-four girls were being taught needlework for three days a week and attended school with the boys on the other two. Girls could stay on until fifteen and were eligible for a leaving grant upon entering domestic service. In 1864 the trustees opened an Industrial School for forty girls, with a resident matron and schoolmistress, in Hospital Lane, Lakenham and the function of training girls for service continued until 1941.[25]

Norman's Endowed School was founded by benefactions from Alderman John Norman who died in 1724.[26] Norman made a most elaborate and detailed will, in which he stipulated that a school should be established for the relatives of himself and his first wife. He wished to give the school the status of a grammar school, to include the teaching of Latin and Greek so that pupils might proceed as exhibitioners to Cambridge. However, the school did not develop as envisaged and it became a mediocre elementary school. In addition to free education there were annual grants for maintenance, apprenticeship and for setting up in trade. To have been born as one of Norman's claimants was regarded as a much valued asset, even enhancing the marriage prospects of female descendants! After 1839 the pedigrees of entrants were vetted strictly by an association called the Claimants' Unity. In 1842 a new school was built in Cowgate Street and in the 1860's there were about sixty or seventy boys in the school of whom about thirty were 'on the Foundation' and therefore eligible for the benefits other than the free education. The Trustees, among whom there was a strong Anglican representation, exercised close control over the teaching and conduct of the school. In 1876 a plan for enlarging the school was drawn up, but this inaugurated a long period of warfare between the Charity Commissioners, who wished to close the school and the Trustees, who were bolstered by the resolve of the Claimants' Unity to oppose any attempts to alter the exclusive nature of the benefits. Under J. W. Howes, appointed head-master in 1899, the school enjoyed its most marked period of success, but by 1933 the numbers had fallen, so that the school was closed, the name Norman school being given to a new elementary school in the Mile Cross neighbourhood.

The Trustees continued to function, granting scholarships, maintenance and other allowances to the parents of eligible children. A new Scheme, drawn up in 1972 made girls eligible for benefits. The Claimants' Unity still flourishes in 1984.

Leading clergy and laymen of the Church of England were

responsible for the establishment of the group of charity schools known as the Norwich Charity Schools. The prime mover was Thomas Tanner, Chancellor of the Cathedral, who appears to have sponsored the first meeting to establish the schools in 1707. The schools were financed by donations in the form of annual subscriptions, by benefactions and from the collections taken from services when sermons for the benefit of the schools were preached. Trustees, both clerical and lay, managed the school exercising a close control of the teaching. Efforts to establish such schools had to counter arguments that schooling would render the poor unfit for menial labour. As a consequence, in the 1780's spinning was introduced on a half-time basis for boys and the girls were trained in the skills of domestic service.[27] Unpaid spinning was, however, unpopular with parents, the numbers fell and the practice was discontinued in 1803. The schools were known by the teachers' names and it appears that they were responsible for maintaining the premises used, often using their own houses. In 1785 there were nine boys' and one girls' school, though by 1804 the number of the former had declined to four. Another charity school, an Endowed English school had been established in the parish of St Peter, Mancroft, from the benefaction of John Risebrow in 1723. Two further charities provided an annual income to provide grants of £10 for each boy apprenticed from the charity schools.

Monitorial Schools

The main effort of the churches in the development of day schools came through the two voluntary societies, the British and Foreign School Society established in 1810 on the basis of the work of Joseph Lancaster, a Quaker schoolmaster and the Anglican 'National Society' founded in 1811 by the Rev. Andrew Bell. Both these men claimed to be the originators of the monitorial system, whereby the senior pupils were taught just by the master or mistress, then in turn they taught the lessons to groups of children. The monitors, aged from ten or eleven upwards, recited their lessons to their charges in sections of the one large school room.

This evidently economical method which enabled one adult to control large numbers of children—Lancaster claimed to be able to superintend up to a thousand at a cost of five or six shillings per head per annum—was a most appealing feature and the philanthropic gave their support.

The Lancasterian School in Norwich was established 2 April 1811 consequent to visits by Lancaster in March, 1810 when he lectured at the Theatre and at the *Maid's Head*. Prominent supporters included Joseph Gurney, Jeremiah Colman and Dr Henry Reeve. The school was opened in St Martin-at-Palace Street admitting 393 boys on the first day. However, the first year's statistics make melancholy reading, for though the total enrolled numbered 537, of these 160 quitted, 70 were discharged for non-attendance and seven died. Such a pattern continued, many children leaving after a week or two. Support declined in the 1820's but some revival came after 1834 when an Auxiliary Society and Corresponding Committees were set up. In 1838 there were 280 boys on the books and an average attendance of 240, but the period of stay remained exceedingly brief, for in 1839, 169 boys were admitted to the school and 170 left it.[28] The school was claimed to be non-denominational, supported by donations and subscriptions, the British and Foreign School Society supplying equipment. However, it had been clear from the start that it would not be supported by members of the established church.

At national level the Church of England founded its National School Society and at local level there was a conspicuous response from the county nobility, the city dignitaries and the Bishop, Dean and their clergy at the inaugural meeting of the Norfolk and Norwich National Society. The meeting held at the Shirehall in July, 1812, was instigated by an advertisement in the local press by Viscount Primrose, the Lord Lieutenant. Incentives for the comparatively early action may have been Norwich's reputation as a 'Jacobin city' at an earlier period and contemporary references to irreligion in the city. The existence of the Norwich Charity Schools provided a firm basis for the development of the work of the diocesan society. The trustees of the former body had decided to bring the boys together in one building in 1811, and when the link with the diocesan society was formalised in the following year it was decided to purchase land in Aldred's Court in the parish of St Peter, Hungate, nearly in the centre of the city for the erection of a school.

The diocesan society undertook to provide £300, towards the total cost of £850. However, the trustees forecast that the new arrangement would effect a saving of £49 a year. After the initial impetus there was slow growth in the provision of places within the city, partly because the diocesan society had concentrated upon the provision of schools in the country parishes and partly because the incumbents believed there were enough places for all the poor children whose parents wished to send them to school.[29] Another initiative came in 1824 which resulted in a number of new schools. However, in 1827 William Geary, a manufacturer and strong supporter of National schools criticised the scheme of provision and the apathy of the citizens.[30] The Trustees did not adopt Geary's proposals, but their attempt to cover the city on an area basis resulted in steady growth, so that by 1839, there were twenty-eight day schools with 2,632 children 'on the books'.[31]

The other chief thrust of the concern of the Established Church was infant education. Samuel Wilderspin claimed to be the first to develop a 'systematised' form of infant education in a school founded in Spitalfields in London in 1820.[32] Soon he was travelling all over the country lecturing and helping to establish new schools. Such work was supported by a powerful Evangelical 'rescue' lobby. Norwich showed early developments, schools being established at Lakenham, Crooks Place and St Giles from 1825. These were not sectarian schools and their committees included Dissenters and Anglicans. However, subsequent to a lecture and demonstration by Wilderspin before a large gathering in St Andrew's Hall in 1836 a diocesan Infant School Society was set up on an exclusive basis. The Rev. John Alexander (see Chapter VIII) protested vehemently but to no avail, for the Society represents another measure of Anglican determination to strengthen their control over education. The breach was widened in 1838 with the advent of a national movement to revive the zeal of the diocesan societies. Education became the focus of political disputation in Norwich as elsewhere. R. M. Bacon, the editor of the *Norwich Mercury* (see Chapter I) in a series of leading articles vehemently denounced the establishment and advocated the Whig policy of a genuinely national system of schooling.

The period from 1840-1870 sees Nonconformist groups seeking to mobilise their electoral power to secure redress of their grievances.

The principal development was the advent and growth of a distinctly Radical party, whose most important leader, J. H. Tillett, made the removal of the remaining political and religious inequalities, the central plank of his platform. Opposition to a 'dominant State Church' with its privileged hold over education was a key issue and education was the predominant focus of disputation in 1843 and 1847 and from 1867 to 1870. State aid for education, began in 1833 and channelled through the two voluntary societies, the major beneficiary being the National Society, was perceived as perpetuating the privileges of the established church. Another factor influencing education was that Norwich suffered from large scale endemic and periodic unemployment which placed a premium upon the recruitment of the cheapest form of labour, that of women and children. Hence the pattern of attendance at schools was intermittent, with very few children staying on after the age of eleven. Witnesses stated that a great many schools were provided 'if the children chose to attend them' but hardship prevented a high evaluation of education. At the national level attempts to regulate hours of work and to enforce attendance at schools had been made through the Factory Acts. The provision of the Act of 1833 concerning attendance proved unenforceable but the special feature of the employment of children in Norwich was that the greater proportion were employed in their homes or by out-workers on their own premises and thus they were outside the provisions of the Acts.

The concern of the Children's Employment Commission led to Sir James Graham's Factory Bill in 1843 which proposed the regulation of hours of employment and the establishment of schools financed by the poor rate. This proposal was defeated by the opposition of Nonconformists in Norwich as elsewhere, who demonstrated their adamant opposition to the benefits which would accrue to the Church of England.[33] To counteract state intervention they espoused 'voluntaryist' principles, providing their own schools. Thus seven new Nonconformist schools for 876 children were opened in the city between 1840 and 1846. The issue of state support for education split the Nonconformist vote in the 1847 general election and doubts about voluntaryism grew as the need for the extension of educational provision became more evident.

Dispute over the issue grew to a climax in the late 1860's. The national campaign for rate-aided and non-sectarian schools was led by the Birmingham based National Education League while the National Educational Union defended the existing denominational system. The rift in the city over the issue came to a head in December, 1870 when two public meetings, one chaired by the Mayor the other by J. H. Tillett, were held. On 28th February, 1871, the City Council after a 'stormy meeting' adopted the resolution to form a School Board. However, Nonconformist dissatisfaction with the 1870 Act which established the dual system, whereby the denominational schools were supplemented by board schools ensured the continuation of the argument at the newly elected School Board.[34]

Other Provisions

A number of other developments also occurred. For over two hundred years the penal laws against Roman Catholics forbade religious worship and the religious education of their children. The Relief Act of 1791 permitted open worship and the small community in Norwich opened a little chapel with a small school attached near the church of St John, Maddermarket. The Catholic community was unaffected by the mass Irish immigration that affected Lancashire and Glasgow so that it grew slowly, by 1870 amounting to about 1,200 people with 215 children at schools.[35] The Jesuit Mission expanded from the little chapel of St Swithin's hidden away in Ten Bell Lane to build a new chapel in Willow Lane in 1827. Here a flourishing day and Sunday school was held. By 1845 the Sunday school had been abandoned and the two day schools were housing 165 children. Both schools were dependent upon voluntary subscriptions, though two years later the Catholic Poor-School Committee was established as a medium for grant aid. Again it was the Jesuit Fathers, inspired by the strong missionary zeal of William Cobb, who built new schools in Ten Bell Lane in 1859. Five years later six sisters of the teaching order of Notre Dame arrived in the city to teach in the schools. However, in the following year they opened a boarding and day school for girls, who soon were being entered for the Oxford Local and other examinations. In the years immediately following the Education Act of 1870 the inadequacies of the accommodation in the two Catholic elementary schools caused them to be condemned. The Catholic community, however, refused to transfer their children to Board Schools and raised £3,000 to convert the chapel in Willow Lane, though this was not carried out until 1896.

The needs of children in employment have already been noted. William Geary who employed some 200 children in the manufacture of gloves, was not content merely to be a propagandist but supported financially a parochial school for a number of years. There was another manufacturing concern which was quick to see the need for education. In 1856 the Colmans moved their mustard milling business from the village of Stoke, where they had founded and ran a small Sunday and evening school, to Carrow within the city. At first a school was established in King Street, then in 1864 a 'spacious and elegant building' was erected on Carrow Hill.[36] By 1870 it was housing 324 children and was notable both for the quality of the work and its innovative curriculum, particularly in practical work and handicrafts. In 1900 the school was handed over to the School Board and it closed in 1919.

Interesting developments also took place in pauper education, the New Poor Law made schools compulsory in workhouses. The Norwich Incorporation was unusual in that it did not abandon the Old Poor Law system of apprenticeship after 1834, but continued to bind out boys to a variety of trades, but especially to shoemakers and cordwainers.[37] Norwich 'did different' in another respect too, for in 1847 at the suggestion of Isaac Bailey, master of the Workhouse School, a Boys' Home was established in St Faith's Lane. This was a model lodging house, to which the boys were transferred upon obtaining employment and it had considerable success in enabling them to make the transition to independence. Three years later a Girls' Home was established where in addition to their education, girls were given 'every requisite' for industrial training, principally with a view to domestic service.[38] The success of the homes aroused considerable interest and their example in the inculcation of social and work discipline was highly approved.

An attempt was made to meet the needs of the children of that submerged portion of the population not affected by the existing provision. A Ragged School Union had been formed in London in 1844, and in 1848 a Ragged School formed 'for the benefit of the lowest class of the city exclusively' was opened.[39]

Though the City Missions had established 'a working Evangelical Alliance' for the assault on the 'fearful aspect' of the moral and spiritual condition of the people, support for the Ragged School was confined to Nonconformists and radicals. Sundays and two evenings were used and within five years there were thirty teachers dealing with average attendances of ninety boys and sixty girls on the Sundays. By 1856 the need for better accommodation and for enlarged support was becoming imperative. The inadequacy of what was being provided for the immensity of the task was becoming all too apparent. In May of the following year attendance on Sunday rose to over 250, the boys were disorderly and fighting broke out. Subsequently the teachers failed to establish control and this brave effort to counter some of the evils of the neglect of youth petered out. It was in reality a replica of a Nonconformist Sunday school, the reading of the Bible being the staple ingredient of instruction and with small classes for writing, arithmetic and sewing.

The contribution of private schools must also be considered, though the traditional view has been to accord them of little importance to working-class education. Though essentially ephemeral these schools comprised a source where parents might purchase a cheap education untainted by charity or by the overtones of social control. There is evidence of parental resistance to the public supported schools and of the proliferation of small private ventures. A rough estimate would be that there were about thirty-six such schools catering for 960 children in the city in 1851.

The scale of provision of school places in Norwich can be compared with the national pattern. The School Board estimated in 1871 that accommodation was required for 13,880 children and that existing schools provided 8,674 places, a net deficiency of 5,206 or 37.5 per cent of the age group, a figure very close to the 39 per cent educed as the national deficiency.[40] The main weaknesses in the education being provided were the limited period of the children's schooling, their irregularity of attendance and limited attainments and lack of training of the monitors and of a proportion of the teachers.

To improve the quality and supply of teachers many dioceses established colleges after 1839.

Norwich was early in the field, for in the following year a house in the Lower Close was used for lodging a small number of women students. From this humble beginning developed the Diocesan Training College which moved into new quarters in St George's Plain in 1853. The vast majority of the students were Queen's Scholars admitted under the pupil teacher scheme initiated in 1846. Queen's Scholarships were awarded to senior scholars from the elementary schools upon their completion of five year apprenticeships and passing a qualifying examination. The maintenance grants awarded allowed them to become resident students at the Training Colleges. Within the Anglican schools in the city fewer than one-third of the pupil teachers proceeded to college. The schools continued to have a restricted curriculum—the basic skills of reading, writing and arithmetic with needlework for the girls and religious instruction remained the core of what was taught in the National and British schools.

However, all the elementary schools made a significant contribution to the growth of literacy. A picture of the literacy scores throughout the

213

period derived from analysis of the marriage registers reveals a steady advance from 1760 to 1812, to which the Sunday schools would have contributed from 1803 onwards. Then there is an apparent decline from 1813 which could be accounted for by the deterioration in working conditions and wages of the city's staple industry after 1798. (This allows for a gap of fifteen years between schooling and marriage). Similar conditions leading to the withdrawal of children from school were found in Lancashire.[41] The upward trend is renewed in the 1830's, reflecting the educational developments in the 1820's. In Norwich, as nationally, as education expanded after 1840 so literacy rates grew rapidly, the considerable achievement of the schools by 1870 being evident from the literacy rate of almost 87 per cent achieved in the mid-1880's. Literacy rates in Norwich are almost consistently higher than those for England as a whole, though the margin is a narrow one by 1870 and thereafter. Thus the impetus for mass elementary education had resulted in major achievements by 1870. The next stage was the advent of the School Boards to 'fill the gaps' in provision by building non-sectarian schools and for successive advances towards compulsory and full-time schooling, though attendance at school until the age of fourteen did not become compulsory until after the passing of the Education Act of 1918.

Notes

1. For the development of this theme and for a detailed consideration of many aspects of this essay see W. David Smith (1978) *Education and Society in Norwich 1800-1870* (Ph.D. Thesis, University of East Anglia).
2. *Reports to the Poor Law Board.* Parliamentary Papers 1850 CXVII, pp.27 ff.
3. Tobias, J. J. (1967) *Crime and Industrial Society in the Nineteenth Century*, pp. 37-9. For typical crimes and the punishment considered appropriate see *Quarter Sessions Minute Book—1843*, Norwich and Norfolk Record Office.
4. Slaney, R. A. (1837) *The State of Education of the Poorer Classes in Large Towns*, p. 23.
5. Adkin, L. (1785) *Proceedings for Sunday Schools . . .* p. 3.
6. Laqueur, T. W. (1976) *Religion and Respectability, Sunday Schools and Working Class Culture 1780-1850*, pp. 69-70.
7. Browne, J. (1877) *History of Congregationalism and Memorials of Churches in Norfolk and Suffolk*, p. 206.
8. Rye, G. (1931) *A Century of Methodism, Chapel Field Road United Methodist Church and New City Sunday School*, pp. 4-9.
9. Colman, H. C. (1919) *Prince's Street Congregational Church*, pp. 11 ff.
10. Quoted in R. V. Holt (1952) *The Unitarian Contribution to Social Progress in England*, pp. 252-3.
11. Calculated from reports in the *Sunday School Teachers' Magazine* (1835) No. 6, p. 178 and the *Report of the National Society* (1835) pp. 121 ff.
12. *The Christian* (31 December, 1954).
13. *Report of the Norwich Sunday Schools Union* 1877-78.
14. Nevill, H. R. and others (1862) *The Management of Sunday Schools*, pp. 5 and 17.
15. ibid. p. 6.
16. Alexander, J. (1847) *Prince's Street Chapel*, p. 32.
17. Bishops' Visitation Records 1820.
18. Laqueur op.cit., p. 239.

19. Dick, M. (1980) 'The Myth of the Working Class Sunday School' in *History of Education*, Vol. 9, No. 1.
20. Anon. (1910) *Citizens of No Mean City*.
21. *Norfolk News*, 1 December 1877.
22. *Sunday School Teachers' Magazine* (1842) No. 13, pp. 470-1.
23. *Report of the Charity Commissioners* 1833, (27) pp. 626 ff.
24. Hooper, J. (1898) *Norwich Charities*, p. 68.
25. *Girls' Hospital Admission Book 1849-1937*.
26. The main sources are the *Report of the Schools Inquiry Commission* 1869 XIII and the *Norman School Minute Books*.
27. *A Book of the Charity Schools in Norwich*, Vol 2, 1759-1815 and *Norwich Mercury*, 5 March, 1785.
28. *Annual Reports of the British and Foreign School Society* 1811-41.
29. Parliamentary Papers 1819 1XB pp. 607-10.
30. Geary, W. (1827) *A Letter to Edward Temple Booth Esq. Major of Norwich, on the State of Education among the Poor of that City*.
31. *Report of the National Society* 1840, p. 95.
32. See McCann, P. and Young, F. A. (1982) *Samuel Wilderspin and the Infant School Movement*.
33. Brock, W. (1843) *The position and duty of English Nonconformists in respect to National Education*.
34. The author deals in a forthcoming publication with education in the School Board period.
35. Anon. (1913) *Great Gothic Fane: A Retrospect of Catholicity in Norwich*, p. 95.
36. *Centenary Booklet Carrow Works School 1857-1957*.
37. Anne Digby (1971) *The Operation of the Poor Law in the Social and Economic Life of Nineteenth Century Norfolk* (Ph.D. Thesis, University of East Anglia) p. 217.
38. Parliamentary Papers 1852 XXXIX, p. 199.
39. Minute Book of the Norwich Ragged School 1848-58.
40. Minutes of the Norwich School Board, 8 April 1874 and W. P. McCann (1969) 'Elementary Education in England and Wales on the Eve of the 1870 Education Act' in *Journal of Educational Administration and History*, Vol. 2, No. 1, p. 20.
41. Sanderson, M. (1972) 'Literacy and Social Mobility in the Industrial Revolution in England' in *Past and Present*, No. 56, p. 78.

Index

216